PENGUIN BOOKS

GATES OF EDEN

Born in 1940, Morris Dickstein was educated at Columbia and Yale and was a Kellett Fellow at Clare College, Cambridge. He has taught at Columbia and is now Professor of English at Queens College. He is the author of *Keats and His Poetry* (1971) and his reviews and articles have appeared in many magazines including *The New York Times Book Review* and *Partisan Review*, of which he is a contributing editor.

Gates of Eden

American Culture in the Sixties

MORRIS DICKSTEIN

Penguin Books

PENGUIN BOOKS
Published by the Penguin Group
Viking Penguin, a division of Penguin Books USA Inc.,
375 Hudson Street, New York, New York 10014, U.S.A.
Penguin Books Ltd, 27 Wrights Lane,
London W8 5TZ, England
Penguin Books Australia Ltd, Ringwood,
Victoria, Australia
Penguin Books Canada Ltd, 2801 John Street,
Markham, Ontario, Canada L3R 1B4
Penguin Books (N.Z.) Ltd, 182–190 Wairau Road,
Auckland 10, New Zealand

Penguin Books Ltd, Registered Offices:
Harmondsworth, Middlesex, England

First published in the United States of America by Basic Books, Inc. 1977
This edition with a new introduction published in Penguin Books 1989
Published simultaneously in Canada

10 9 8 7 6 5 4 3 2

LIBRARY OF CONGRESS CATALOGING IN PUBLICATION DATA
Dickstein, Morris.
Gates of Eden: American culture in the sixties/Morris Dickstein.
p.   cm.
Reprint. Originally published: New York: Basic Books, c1977.
Bibliography: p.
Includes index.
ISBN 0 14 01.1617 6
1. United States—Civilization—1945–   I. Title.
[E169.12.D54   1989]
973.92—dc19   88-21787

Printed in the United States of America

Introduction to the Penguin Edition: The 1960s Today

ONE remarkable thing about the decade of the 1960s is how much it is still with us twenty years later. The activists of the era keep reliving their youth by writing books about it, while their conservative opponents, sour amid all their successes, never tire of invoking it as the root of all evil. Above all, though many of the events of the decade seem to belong to another world—to a raucous party that lasted long but ended badly—the sixties remain a tangible myth, a point of departure for every kind of social argument, as well as the source of values widely diffused throughout our culture. Some revolutions fail by succeeding; this one seemed to succeed by failing. How did this happen? *Why* did it happen? How do the 1960s continue to influence us today?

Nearly all the recently published books on the sixties deal primarily with the political side—with the Vietnam war, with student radicalism and the growth of SDS, with the civil rights movement and the antiwar movement, with bloody riots, assassinations, street demonstrations, and university uprisings. *Gates of Eden* is somewhat different. Without ignoring the politics—how could one do that?—this book deals more with changes in the texture of our lives as seen through cultural documents, including fiction, poetry, music, journalism, and social thought. Though these are not the only works I could have chosen ("What about Motown?" one reviewer asked), I hope they accurately reflect the shifting sensibility and moral climate of the era. This revolution in feelings and mores is also where the 1960s have proved to be most long-lasting. The sixties were not simply a time when the young grew long hair and took to the streets; it was also when many others dramatically reexamined their lives, with consequences that can still be felt.

This change in the landscape of feeling extended to politics as well. The political *forms* of the sixties have proved perishable; the *attitudes* that developed have cast a long shadow. As a national movement, the sixties Left came to an end when SDS destroyed itself in the streets of Chicago, when the McGovern campaign was swamped by a Nixon landslide, when the end of the war and the draft undercut the basis for large-scale protest. These tactics have been revived only when certain issues like nuclear arms, apartheid, or Central America evoke intense passion and moral outrage. The sixties left behind not a mass movement but rather a deep sense of skepticism and suspicion directed at our own leaders, especially on questions of war and peace, on environmental issues, on official lying and corruption, and on threats to individual rights. Still, as economic issues became more pressing in the early seventies, a conservative reaction set in, and Ronald Reagan sprang forth as its spokesman and beneficiary. More traditional values—religion, family, patriotism—came to the fore, and many Americans recoiled from the carnival-like instability of the preceding decade.

Culturally the sixties seemed to expire as well, for many leading figures scarcely survived the era. Writers as different as Allen Ginsberg and Kurt Vonnegut, Bob Dylan and Thomas Pynchon, Ken Kesey and John Barth did not thrive in the quieter, more "normal" atmosphere that followed. Beat poetry and black humor, which crystallized the sensibility of one era, were quite marginal to another. Some political art began to look dated and overheated, but the cooler culture of celebrity typified by Andy Warhol went on and on. That part of the sixties would always continue to sell.

For artists and performers in the sixties, drugs and booze were a major occupational hazard. Self-destructive figures like Jack Kerouac, Lenny Bruce, Jim Morrison, and Janis Joplin burned themselves out. For others, nature took its course: the pied-pipers from an earlier generation—Paul Goodman and Herbert Marcuse, for example—exhausted their message and passed from the scene. Radical comedians like Abbie Hoffman and firebrands like Mark Rudd were forced underground as others like Jerry Rubin and Tom Hayden navigated their celebrity and ambition toward the mainstream. Among writers, perhaps the strongest survivors were the realistic novelists formed in a slightly earlier time, such as Philip Roth and John Updike, who simply took the changing scene and the ebb and flow of their own lives as their fundamental subject. Higher journalists like Tom Wolfe and Norman Mailer, ever-watchful observers of cultural change, were also able to adapt to a climate in which radical was no longer chic, in which style and consumption were the motive forces, not political commitment. It was easier for those who had come of age in the fifties to adapt to the seventies and eighties.

As I mention these names, it comes to mind how few writers and filmmakers were able to make much of the topical concerns that agitated people in the 1960s. Despite the flood of long-delayed novels and films about Vietnam, including powerful if simplistic works like *Apocalypse Now* and *Platoon* that showed that the popular imagination could at last come to terms with the Vietnam trauma, only a few gifted journalists like Michael Herr (in *Dispatches*) and Hunter Thompson, as well as Mailer and Wolfe, were able to find a style that responded directly to the turmoil of the era.

But if these writers kept going creatively as the sixties disintegrated, it was only by turning to quite different subjects, Mailer to the frighteningly bleak and bland American heartland of *The Executioner's Song*, written in a documentary style far removed from his usual first-person baroque, and Wolfe in his heroic treatment of the space program (*The Right Stuff*) and in his pointedly satirical bulletins from the urban frontier (*The Bonfire of the Vanities*). Wolfe, with his conservative politics, his dandyish detachment from his subjects, and his glib fascination with money, class, and cultural style, was the only sixties writer who was able to make a seamless transition into the Reagan era—an achievement, like Andy Warhol's, that underlines his limitations rather than his strength.

The sixties were a period of wild and sometimes ephemeral experimentation in the arts, as in daily life as well, from Fluxus and Happenings to postmodern fiction and psychedelic rock lyrics. At first the aftereffect of this festival of sounds and images was to engender its opposite—the eerily effective low-key blue-collar realism of Raymond Carver, reminiscent of Hemingway, and the chic minimalism of

Carver's young admirers; the smooth pop sound of the disco era and other machine-tooled rock of the 1970s; the revival of figurative painting beginning with photo-realism, with its flattened picture-postcard abstractions of everyday life. This pendulum effect, marked by a seeming return to more conservative styles, managed to mask the real impact of the sixties in the arts, which was to open the floodgates to a wild eclecticism and cultural pluralism in which no single style could predominate. This was liberating to some artists, disquieting to many critics, but to the entrepreneurs of culture, especially art dealers, it became a good way to turn a dollar.

Thanks to an endless appetite for cultural novelty, the avant-garde became good business, at once commercial and prestigious, chic and austere. As culture and money grew more and more intertwined, as corporations became powerful and sometimes intrusive supporters of museums, arts festivals, and public television, as the booming art market became a virtual offshoot of the booming stock market and the real estate market, the avant-garde began to lose its meaning as an iconoclastic and oppositional force. In this as in many other ways, the seventies and eighties were a caricature of the sixties, whose experimental energy had made them possible.

But there's a positive side to this anarchic proliferation of styles, a new openness that took hold amid these wild swings of novelty and fashion. For twenty years now, in an atmosphere charged with the heady pursuit of the outrageous and the unconventional, abstract painting has coexisted with representational painting, experimental fiction with realistic fiction, free verse with formal verse, hard rock with soft rock, atonal with tonal music, modernism with postmodernism and antimodernism. Detached and difficult artists like Robert Wilson have become fashionable, but so have impassioned traditional storytellers like Cynthia Ozick and Robert Stone. The anger and machismo of black male writers, a keynote of the sixties, became shrill and repetitive just as the anger and tenderness of black women writers began to move people deeply. Feminism, the most legitimate heir to the sixties idea that the personal is political, came into its own just as the New Left, grown increasingly rigid and ideological, was expiring as an organizational force.

But the success of feminism as a *movement* was atypical of the post-1970 era, when movements had trouble finding adherents and gaining attention. Like much that had preceded it in the 1960s, especially the civil rights movement, feminism was an unstable mixture of politics and culture—legislative goals and economic goals along with deeply personal changes in self-image, in feelings of identity, in sexual as well as social relationships. Contemporary feminism began with concrete issues of inequality and discrimination but also with polemical works of social history (Friedan's *The Feminine Mystique*) and literary history (Millett's *Sexual Politics*) that had real impact on how individuals thought about their lives.

Feminism reached more women through media coverage and personal contact, such as small consciousness-raising groups, than through large organizations like NOW. Women sought and achieved better control over their own bodies and more freedom from demeaning roles and stereotypes. Abortion rights became a battleground between feminists and religious conservatives, and the accelerated entry of married women into the work force made day-care an urgent economic issue. Even when feminism stumbled politically, as in the campaign to ratify the Equal Rights Amendment, its cultural influence spread. Thanks to the mass media, feminism touched a nerve in many women who joined no organization, and who probably did not consider themselves feminists. This is typical of how many sixties values seeped into the mainstream.

By remaining loyal to the sixties ideal of self-development through political as well as personal effort, women were laying claim to a terrain that young men had virtually abandoned. In *Making History*, Richard Flacks, an SDS founder, describes the balance of values on the sixties Left between an "ethic of self-expression" and an "ethic of social responsibility." The seventies and eighties have proved far more congenial to the ideal of personal growth than to any form of altruism. The free-market faith of the Reagan administration made self-seeking legitimate, even socially desirable. Losing its political bearings in an era of economic strain, the counterculture of the sixties turned into the narcissistic Me Generation of the 1970s and the ambitious, self-involved young professionals of the 1980s. Despite their starting salaries and carefully planned lives, these young people remain the children of the sixties, the decade when they were born. Snorting coke instead of smoking joints, jogging and joining health clubs instead of communes, seeking utopia on Wall Street rather than in rural Vermont, they remained curiously bound up with the sixties values they seemed to caricature—above all, the search for self-fulfillment here and now.

The most faithful carrier of the values and attitudes of the 1960s has been the sixties generation itself. Near the end of this book I predicted that "we'll hear from it yet, for noisy and visible as it was, it hasn't fully had its say. The members of a generation which made its mark collectively at an abnormally young age have yet to make their mark separately and personally. . . . most have disappeared into families, guilds, and professions in every area of society." At the twenty-year reunion of student strikers who had taken over the Columbia campus in April 1968, it was remarkable how many had somehow remained true to their old ideals. Their hair was shorter, but none wore ties and jackets. They had had their children late—and brought them all along. Some who had seen themselves marching bravely towards a new society had probably never expected to join nuclear families at all.

Beneath the easy informality, they seemed touched by a feeling that they were *special*, for they had been cast, however briefly, in a historic role. There were no signs of the dramatic deconversions that had marked the middle-aging of the Old Left. Few of these radicals were still politically active, but many had become socially concerned writers, editors, teachers, filmmakers, or labor organizers, bringing old commitments into their professional lives. Others had gone in for local activism, serving on school boards or community boards, or organizing campaigns to stop a highway from being built or open land from being developed. Few, it seemed, had just gone for the money, despite the Gilded Age ethics of the Reagan years. It was clear that some sense of communal responsibility would continue to shape the remainder of their lives.

As members of this generation have moved into positions of authority, their ideals have transformed institutions as well as individual lives. To neoconservative polemicists, these sixties people are a.

hydra-headed monster popping up everywhere, distorting American values, warping our educational system with their political agendas, fraying the fabric of American capitalism, and sapping our will to police the world. In their view, the "death" of the New Left and counterculture merely camouflaged a subterranean triumph, an insidious integration into the American heartland. Like many exaggerations, this updated version of the Red Menace contains more than a grain of truth.

Anyone who remembers the quiet conformities of the 1950s will be quick to see how much the attitudes of the sixties and the arrival of a new generation have affected the press, the universities, advertising, the film industry, and even the Church and Congress. On issues like nuclear war, new weapons-systems, and armed intervention in Central America, issues which raise the spectre of Vietnam and the cold war, the press asks probing, disrespectful questions it would never have asked before. Meanwhile, the Church speaks out and organizes on matters of conscience, helping Congress find the will to resist the executive branch. At the same time, the universities, where many radicals of the sixties found a niche, remain centers of political dissent as well as of dissident scholarship.

Scandals like Watergate and the Iran-Contra affair, involving large-scale official deception and abuse of power, helped keep alive the spirit of skepticism that developed during the Vietnam war. Eight years of patriotic rhetoric about Central America, far from laying to rest the "Vietnam syndrome," showed that most Americans remained dubious about such adventures unless our vital interests were at stake. Even Reagan could not always play the anticommunist card, or restore an unquestioning faith in American virtue. The depth of Congressional resistance to arming the Nicaraguan rebels showed how much American liberalism had shifted since the days of the cold war.

But on domestic issues, liberalism was on the defensive throughout the 1980s. Here the Reagan presidency transformed the political arena beyond recognition as budget deficits and increased military spending made new social programs unthinkable. The big battles of liberals, on court appointments, for example, were fought to halt retreat, not to make fresh advances. While liberals were in disarray, conservative intellectuals, fostered by corporate largesse and a receptive political climate, developed a sweeping vision of "democratic capitalism" as a dynamic social and economic force. "Thus, ironically," writes Richard Flacks, "the left, previously the most explicitly ideological current in American political culture, now operates in pragmatic, piecemeal fashion according to the rules of pluralist interest group politics, while the right presents itself as the moral, visionary force."

Of course, "pluralist interest group politics" is really no novelty for the American Left. It was the staple of the New Deal, which first created the modern liberal coalition. But during the Depression this was combined with an acute sense of national crisis and an active pursuit of the public interest. The New Deal used public works not only to create jobs but also to improve our physical environment and, in its arts programs, to foster a unifying sense of the American heritage. Nor was the New Left as much an "ideological current" as it was an inchoate moral force, stronger in protest and resistance than in its own social initiatives. This helps account for how it went under, since protest movements inevitably wane when their immediate goals are achieved. As Barrington Moore has written, "moral passions without material interests rarely if ever suffice to move large bodies of men and women in a way that leaves a deep mark upon the historical record." The New Left could work to stop the war and end discrimination, but it was the old-line liberals who pushed through the social programs of the Kennedy-Johnson years while the Warren court was dramatically expanding the scope of individual rights. With its freedom rides, sit-ins, and voter registration in the South and its community organizing projects in the North, the New Left began as a movement with practical as well as visionary goals. But as the war and the Black Power movement transformed moral witness and local activism into protest and finally rage, they gradually severed the New Left from the political arena and insured its ultimate demise.

Despite this political failure, many of the fundamental rights we now accord to women, gay people, and blacks belong to the legacy of the sixties, which a conservative administration could impede but not reverse. The same could be said of the impact of the peace movement in the early 1980s and, even more markedly, of the environmental movement, which is now a permanent part of our political landscape. In spite of the fundamentalist backlash against the new freedoms of the 1960s, the Reagan administration made little headway in pushing its social agenda—as in its attacks on pornography, abortion, and the separation of church and state. Even in the age of a rampant AIDS epidemic, Americans seem unwilling to turn back the clock on the sexual freedoms they won in the 1960s, especially the freedom of expression.

The passage of time has made it easier to take a long view of the events of the sixties. The gradual acceptance of women's equality, the relaxation of sexual mores, the rise of the divorce rate, the changing relationships between parents and children, the growth of a separate youth culture with a great deal of disposable income, the vast expansion of higher education and its influence, the growing importance of technology and the mass media—all these developments can be documented in earlier periods such as the 1920s or 1940s. In the sixties these trends took a dramatic political and cultural turn, but they were part of larger social changes that lay hidden beneath the conservatism of the postwar years.

There was certainly a dark side to much that happened in the 1960s. No one will be nostalgic for the bloodshed and social conflict that resulted from the war—or for the violence in the ghetto, whether it was born of new hope or sheer hopelessness. No one should shed a tear for the inflammatory rhetoric of the era, or for the self-righteousness of the student radicals, which few as yet have seriously reexamined. At the Columbia reunion, Mark Rudd, describing the final descent into rage and violence, which had left friends dead or in jail, commented: "We were completely out of touch with reality. I now believe the Vietnam War drove us crazy." Yet aside from attributing some of his radicalism to his Jewish roots and to the Holocaust, he gave no sign of having reflected much on anything he had done. Understandably, he had too much invested in the drama of his own past.

The naivete of some of the millennial dreams of the period is breathtaking today, yet somehow this vision remains one of the most attractive features of the sixties. Though it sometimes led to drugs and violence, to sexual anomie and moral smugness, it also forged a gentler dream of community and equality that will always be ahead of its time. My daughter, now eighteen, a college freshman, wears a pin that reads, "Desperately Clinging to Utopian Illusions." This seems somehow to strike the right balance today, at least for her generation. *Credo quia absurdum est*. Utopians not only express a vision, a set of hopes, but they also sketch out distant goals for more practical people to achieve. Unlike the Old Left, with its tenacious illusions about a massmurderer like Uncle Joe Stalin, the New Left and the counterculture did few people any harm—except, at times, themselves. Yet even the drugs of the sixties, principally grass and LSD, seem relatively harmless compared with the coke, crack, heroin, and (again) alcohol that have become epidemic today. Here the yellow brick road leads not to paradise but to hell, a road not even paved with good intentions.

Morris Dickstein

Sag Harbor, New York, August 1988

CONTENTS

Contents

PREFACE

WHEN she first heard the title of this book my mother asked me, with a twinge of hope, whether it had anything to do with religion. I've asked myself the same question many times. Religion, after all, has many guises, and it's sometimes hard to recognize in modern dress. There's one great vein of religious feeling that expresses contempt for the world and pity for mortal man; it stresses the transience and tragedy of life and the constraints of the human condition. It counsels stoicism and otherworldliness and exhorts us to rise above the temptations of the flesh, hinting that we can attain spirituality and transcendence in a purely mental sphere. Even the most bleak and absurdist writers of the sixties had little in common with such a vision.

But there's another strain of religious thinking that is utopian rather than tragic. In line with a long heretical tradition, it tells us that we can achieve spiritual and moral victories even in the fleshpots of the world, through what Blake called ''an improvement of sensual enjoyment.'' It encourages us to make exorbitant, apocalyptic demands upon life and tells us that we can break through the joyless forms of everyday existence toward a radiant communality and wholeness. It insists that we and the world we live in are more malleable, more alive with possibility, less restricted by circumstance, than society or the notion of original sin would have us believe.

Many students of early American culture have shown how deeply rooted this latter tendency was in our nation's first conception of itself. Early preachers and writers saw Europe as a decadent and corrupt old order, a culture in its dotage. They portrayed America as a virgin land, a garden world, and the individual American as a redemptive new Adam, untainted by history, free of corruption and moral decay. The new land was a fulfillment of scriptural prophecy, whose mission was to give history a fresh start, if not to usher in the millennium. The persistence of this idea helps explain the peculiar moralism of America's vision of itself on the world stage. By the time of Henry James, the stereotypes of the innocent yet wily American and the corrupt, worldly European were already material for the most subtle social comedy. American writers, of course, were rarely as innocent or high-minded as the characters they loved to portray. Even the most visionary transcendentalist could not fail to notice at times how intractable the world could be, how little it might collaborate with his grandiose hopes. The beautiful enigma of Melville's white whale shows how fiercely reality can resist our compulsion to master it. Great aspirations may finally harden rather than dissolve our sense of tragic limit.

"We Shall Overcome" was a Baptist hymn which became the anthem of a social movement. The spirit of the sixties witnessed the transformation of utopian religion into the terms of secular humanism. Just as Hegel and Marx turned Christian eschatology—the faith in the progress of history toward a specific goal—into secular theories of social change, so the sixties translated the Edenic impulse once again into political terms. This is why my account of the sixties doesn't stress the blissed-out side: the fascination with the occult, the attraction to Eastern gurus and meditative practices, the short-lived Nirvanas that come by way of drugs, polymorphous sexuality, or quickie therapies. In the seventies, when avenues of political change were suddenly closed off, these shortcuts to heaven became much more popular. But in the sixties the religious impulse took a more political turn, starting with the civil rights movement, which was propelled by the millennial spirit of Southern black religion.

The cultural synthesis of the sixties doesn't fit our usual presuppositions about "the pursuit of the millennium." Millennial thinking was the special *bête noire* of fifties ideologues who celebrated the end of ideology. They taught us to see utopianism as inconsistent with the painstaking business of reform, just as we learned to believe that the pleasure principle, the cultivation of the self, ruled out altruism and social concern. These distinctions were articles of faith of the ascetic Old Left, and they continued to color the viewpoint of disaffected ex-Leftists. But the sixties gave impetus to both revolution and reform, and tried to combine the quest for social justice with the search for personal authenticity. The civil rights movement and the "human potential" movement were agreed on one thing: man's right to happiness in the here-and-now.

The culture of the fifties was European in its irony and sophistication. It put its faith in what it called "the tragic sense of life," a fateful determinism that affirmed the obduracy of man's nature and his surroundings. But for the culture of the sixties the watchword was *liberation:* the shackles of tradition and circumstance were to be thrown off, society was to be molded to the shape of human possibility.

Today, when the sixties have come to feel like a distant memory—was it that long ago? did all that really happen?—it's easy to see through the naive, youthful ardor that contributed to this vision. To grow up is to feel for the first time a sense of the irretrievable, the irremediable; we learn that for each road taken there must be many not taken, many that never will be taken. The bittersweet wisdom of maturity always differs from the impulsive ardor of youth; but the path of experience needn't end in futility and frustration, any more than the vision of youth is confined to innocence and hope. The cold war, the bomb, the draft, and the Vietnam war gave young people a premature look at the dark side of our national life, at the same time that it galvanized many older people already jaded in their pessimism. Both the self and the world proved more resistant than the activism of the sixties dared to hope, but the effects of a decade of struggle are still there to see. There's an agenda of unfinished business that won't be put off; much as the American people have recoiled from the instability of the sixties, they recently refused to reelect a president who campaigned solely on complacency and fear of change. If we have as yet little reason to rejoice, we have even less cause for bitterness and disillusionment.

Preface

What happened in the sixties was no one's deliberate choice, but one of those deep-seated shifts of sensibility that alters the whole moral terrain. Grasping these inward changes requires an experimental approach to cultural history. I've chosen to exploit the ambiguity of that slippery word *culture,* which we apply both to the narrower realm of art and thought and, in the anthropological sense, to the tissue of assumptions and mores of a whole society. My wager is that one can tell us a great deal about the other. I've operated on two premises, both of them loosely Hegelian—first, that each phase of culture is coherent and full of meaning, that it can be read like a text, and second, that it's precisely our texts—novels, poems, songs, polemics, autobiographies—that can shed light on the larger Text. In other words, the culture of the arts can illuminate the texture of feeling and opinion in the culture as a whole. This is hardly new, but historians rarely do it in more than a perfunctory way. Historians neglect mutations of form in the arts, which tell us everything about the artists' unconscious assumptions, while critics busily sort out the forms as if no assumptions were involved, merely the proliferation of artifacts, the more the merrier.

In making this hybrid of cultural history and criticism, my aim is not only to trace the curve of these recent changes in moral temper, but also to shed some light on individual developments in writing and the arts which have left many people feeling puzzled or confused. Unlike those historians who try to catalogue everything, I've slighted cultural phenomena for which I felt little affinity, as well as others that were more conservative than innovative, and therefore tell us little about cultural change. In each phase I've scrutinized a few tendencies that seem to offer a key, but the cultural upheaval was so pervasive that the story could have come out roughly the same with a quite different set of examples. Most of mine are from literature, or from para-literary forms of writing that aren't usually subjected to critical examination.

Because of my cultural theme I was drawn frequently to point up parallels between changes in the arts—shifts in consciousness—and changes in society. Art exists in a nexus of social meanings, but it's no use to document them extrinsically, for they're mediated by formal qualities that have their own logic and rigor. In method, I tried not only to respect these exigencies of form but to make them central to the subject, as historians and social scientists never do. My purpose was twofold: to show that cultural history can work from within the artistic and verbal imagination, and to ascertain whether criticism, which is often tempted to be hermetic, can tell us something about the real world.

MORRIS DICKSTEIN

New York, November 1976

For Lore, who lived through it all

I

BREAKING OUT:

NEW SHOOTS FROM

OLD ROOTS

It is no use merely trying to modify present forms. The whole great form of our era will have to go. And nothing will really send it down but the new shoots of life springing up and slowly bursting the foundations. And one can do nothing but fight tooth and nail to defend the new shoots of life from being crushed out, and let them grow. We can't make life. We can but fight for the life that grows in us.

D. H. Lawrence,
Note to "The Crown"

1

Prologue: Allen Ginsberg and the Sixties

A generation is fashion: but there is more to history than costume and jargon. The people of an era must either carry the burden of change assigned to their time or die under its weight in the wilderness.

HAROLD ROSENBERG,
"Death in the Wilderness"

1959. Once in a while a public event comes in retrospect to appear emblematic of a whole era. Such an occasion was the poetry reading that Allen Ginsberg, Gregory Corso, and Peter Orlovsky gave at Columbia University near the end of the fifties, which became quite widely known when Diana Trilling wrote it up, or put it down, in a celebrated essay in *Partisan Review*.* Mrs. Trilling seized on the reading as a cultural episode. She told the story of Ginsberg's turbulent relations with his Alma Mater, where he had been a student of Mark Van Doren and Lionel Trilling, where he had been expelled and readmitted after allegedly scrawling an anti-Semitic obscenity on a window pane, and to which he had now returned in some sort of triumph as the avatar of a new poetic and cultural movement.

* This and other significant allusions, quotations, and sources are identified in a bibliographical essay which begins on page 279.

Gates of Eden

What happened that night at McMillin Theater, what became the subject of Mrs. Trilling's essay, was the collision of two forces, the bohemian and the academic, whose origins and purpose were curiously intertwined. Ginsberg and Columbia, Ginsberg and the Trillings, seemed on the surface to belong to wholly different worlds: one to the "high" culture that was revealed to every freshman in Humanities and Contemporary Civilization, the other to what a different student of Trilling's, also writing in *Partisan Review*, called a rabble of "Know-Nothing Bohemians."

But what *was* high culture but the ordered record of previous insurgencies: the history of successful vanguards, a body of scandals that took, and lasted to become a pantheon? Yet nothing was more characteristic of the fifties than its weakness for hard-and-fast cultural distinctions, exclusions, hierarchies—between a poem and not-a-poem; between masscult and midcult, or highbrow, middlebrow, and lowbrow; between poetry and publicity; between culture and barbarism.

I was a sophomore at Columbia at the time of the Beat reading, and I unwittingly testified my assent to the prevailing hierarchy by going downtown that night to a Shakespeare production. This was less a deliberate conservative gesture than one might think. It's true that neither my background nor my fragment of a college education had given me much affinity for bohemianism, whether of the "know-nothing" or any other variety. But at the time I was still such a novice in the world of "official" culture that going to hear and see live Shakespeare remained a real breakthrough, even something of an adventure. I had to hear Beethoven before I could ask him to roll over.

But a few days later a friend at the campus radio station played me a tape of the Beat reading and I was moved, overwhelmed. I caught up with Ginsberg soon afterward as he read and wept through an unfinished poem called *Kaddish* in a crowded loft above the shabby offices of the *Catholic Worker*. For me the paradigm now became somewhat personal. It was a Friday night, already the Sabbath, and though I had come some distance from orthodox Judaism it was still

4

a wrenching for me to travel downtown—to the Lower East Side of all places!

Yet there was something appropriate about it, something exhilarating: alienated Jews and radical Catholics coming together on a Sabbath eve to hear a heretical kaddish for a Communist Jewish mother. The *Worker* was in a quite different section of the Lower East Side from where I had grown up, and Ginsberg had returned to a different corner of Judaism from the one I still essentially lived in. I too had a mother, who would have mightily disapproved of my being there—that much we had in common—but for the first time I knew that poetry meant more to me than faith or ritual. Like many before me I had passed through a gateway into secular society. Ginsberg's reading was not only powerful and moving but it became for me another avenue into that very culture from which Mrs. Trilling and *Partisan Review* had virtually ruled him out—a culture which, by the end of the sixties, would embrace both Shakespeare and Ginsberg, literature and movies, Beethoven and rock. How this change came about is one of the subjects of this book.

But at the end of the fifties Ginsberg was still very much an outsider, and wonderfully symbolic of the energies, traditions, and heresies for which the prevailing culture had no use. It was just at that time that Jacques Barzun published a book designating Art as one of the three chief enemies of Intellect in America. What he demonstrated instead was that the culture of the universities was growing thin and brittle, and was deeply in need of revitalization from without. Much of the sixties would prove to be a lesson in avoiding rigid and exclusionary definitions of the cultural tradition. No one knew it at the time, but what Ginsberg stood for was where a large part of American culture would soon be headed.

1968. It was almost a decade later when I next heard Allen Ginsberg read. He was back at Columbia in more muted and modest surroundings, but circumstances again conspired to make the occasion rich with symbolism. This time, however, the theme was not the collision but the reconciliation of two cultures. The reading took place in Earl Hall, on neutral, even sacred ground, where the university's religious ministries had managed to coexist over the years. Two old Columbia poets, Ginsberg and John Hollander, had come back after twenty years to do a benefit for a campus literary magazine. It was an intriguing combination. I knew from Hollander's fine poem "Helicon" that he and Ginsberg had been friends then, in a strange, intense, perhaps mistrusting way. I also knew how archetypally their lives had since diverged. There was almost a cultural parable here: could any two closely contemporary poets have come to public notice more differently? For Hollander there had been recognition from *Partisan Review,* of which he became poetry editor, a Yale Younger Poets award (carrying Auden's sponsorship, for a very Audenesque book), and a successful academic career. For Ginsberg there had been the literary bohemian scene of San Francisco and the notoriety of *Howl,* cheap exploitation in *Time,* and olympian putdown from *Partisan Review* (by Hollander among others).

Times had changed however. Instead of canzoni, sestinas (!), madrigals, songs, and sonnets, Hollander had published an impressive sequence of autobiographical poems, some almost as free and personal as anything Ginsberg had written. And Ginsberg, as far as I knew, might not have written any poems for years. None of his books contained anything from after 1960. Perhaps alone among the Beat poets he had survived, magnificently—that much was clear. But as I had followed his gentle, newly bearded eminence from week to week in the pages of the *Village Voice* he seemed to have become entirely a public figure, the guru to a new generation. It was not as a poet, it seemed, that he lent his magnetic spiritual presence to so many of the most obscene and solemn moments of the 1960s, from New York to Berkeley and London to Prague; rather, he was the elder statesman, the wise and worldly Lord of the Revels, a live link with the germinal protest culture of the fifties.

So it was the performer, the public Ginsberg, that many came to see, see even more than hear, that night in Earl Hall. Nor was anyone disappointed, not by either poet. The surprise was how close Hollander came to stealing the show. For all his change of style he

remained the complete university poet in the best sense: witty, liter-
ate, brilliant, breathlessly enthusiastic yet ironical. The crowd had
not come for *him* perhaps but they were his nonetheless; he knew
their stops, he could sound them from top to bottom. When sustained
applause finally demanded an encore he asked for Ginsberg's per-
mission to read 'Helicon.'' It was a touching gesture, and the poem
itself was wildly received. Those in the audience, who had seen the
two embrace when they first met on the stage, who perhaps did not
know that Hollander had once dismissed *Howl* as a "dreadful little
volume" exhibiting an "utter lack of decorum of any kind," understood intuitively that "Helicon" was a peace offering, a love poem
and more—a propitiation of part of himself and his generation.

Ginsberg, who followed, seemed by comparison insensitive to his
listeners or determined to throw them off balance. He began by
chanting rather than reading, and as the *Hare Krishnas* went on,
longer than anyone imagined they could, it seemed possible that he
had sloughed off language entirely. There was Allen Ginsberg, ecstatic and uncool, apparently oblivious to us, doing his spiritual
push-ups in public. It was troubling, and needless to say it worked its
effect; gradually, grudgingly, we gave up that air of facetiousness
and sophistication endemic to every college audience. Ginsberg was
there not to please us but to convert us.

But the greater surprise, for me at least, was yet to come: poems,
many of them, some better than anything he'd previously written. A
number were funny, closer to the comic self-ironies of Hollander
than to the transports we had just witnessed or the prophetic intensities of *Howl* and *Kaddish*. Had I forgotten, or never noticed, the
Ginsberg of "To Aunt Rose" and "America" and "The Lion for
Real," bittersweet parables at once madcap and sentimental? Well,
here was "This form of Life needs Sex," in which the man who had
shocked television interviewers by introducing Peter Orlovsky as his
spouse explored his new interest in women and procreation.

There was more, poems too various to be classified, and when
Planet News: 1961–1967 was published later in the year they were
there on the page, they hadn't evaporated. Ginsberg had survived as

a poet too, as a poet above all. *Planet News* was one of the richest, meatiest offerings of the decade, no relic of the Beat movement, no longer marginal, but close to the center of a new literary consciousness. This is no doubt the secret tribute of "Helicon," home of the muses, where a young Ginsberg, the siren-like Virgil, guides a younger Hollander, his half-willing Dante, down to a modern underground, to St. Luke's Hospital to sell his own blood: the springs of inspiration run deep, deeper than the virtuosity of craftsmen like Campion or Auden could suggest. "And I know," the now-older Hollander concludes,

> That opening up at all is harder than meeting a measure:
> With night coming on like a death, a ruby of blood is a treasure.

Ginsberg had won what once seemed merely a battle of anthologies. Academic poetry and its sisters, the precious, claustral closet-novel and the well-made Jamesian short story, were as moribund as the polite essay, though some of their practitioners didn't know it. More than literary form had been at stake; at issue was the direction of our consciousness and culture. The Beat movement died too—Ginsberg himself thought it already dead in 1961 when he took off, for most of four years as it turned out,* "to fade awhile in the Orient"—but the dramatic turn American culture took around that time ushered in its unexpected legacy. Eventually the San Francisco story became a national story; a new culture was born in which the Beat life style and art styles became widely diffused. The paranoia of the middle-aged proved justified. *Now they were everywhere!*

What really happened in the sixties? The period was surely a watershed in our cultural history, and its effects will continue to be felt for a long time. Many have grappled with its meaning, but few solid and disinterested answers have been given. Two of the earliest, most brilliant attempts, from opposite points of view, showed instead how

---

* I learned this and much else about Ginsberg from Jane Kramer's charming and insightful book *Allen Ginsberg in America* (1969). This genial profile should be supplemented by the hard-edged and tough-minded Ginsberg who appears in an interview with Paul Carroll in *Playboy* (April 1969).

cultural definition can shade off into manifesto and be deformed by polemical zeal. In the concluding essay of *Against Interpretation* (1966) Susan Sontag depicted the "new sensibility" as a redemption of the senses from the mind, and consequently the displacement of literature, with its "heavy burden of 'content,' both reportage and moral judgment," by arts "with much less content, and a much cooler mode of moral judgment—like music, films, dance, architecture, painting, sculpture." In his 1968 essay on "The New York Intellectuals" Irving Howe, perhaps the sharpest critic of the new sensibility, was only too glad to concur in this description, but found the results shallow, escapist, and nihilistic—built upon a simplistic faith in innocence and instinct, a "psychology of unobstructed need," that is indifferent to morality and impatient with ideas. He wondered whether such an attitude "is compatible with a high order of culture or a complex civilization." He deplored those who wished to put aside the tragic burdens of the twentieth century for a period of "relaxed pleasures and surface hedonism."

Now Sontag and Howe are two of the most penetrating essayists we have in this country, but the furious polemics of the late sixties led them into distortion and simplification, from which they have since tactfully retreated, so that they tended to confirm each other's stereotypes. Susan Sontag's essay "One Culture and the New Sensibility" is marred by a heavy-handed account of the moral and ideational content of literature. "The Matthew Arnold notion of culture," she says, "defines art as a criticism of life—this being understood as the propounding of moral, social, and political ideas" (which literature does in a "gross" way, with "discursive explicitness").

Parts of Irving Howe's essay perversely approximate this caricature of the traditional idea of culture. This sometime Marxist declares a *Kulturkampf* in defense of absolute "moral imperatives" and calls upon "traditional Christianity and modern Freudianism" to testify to the original sin of our biological natures. Like the Defender of the Faith of some severe humanist church he examines and rejects the moral credentials of Norman Brown, Marcuse, McLuhan, the

9

Gates of Eden

New Left, the *New York Review of Books,* the Columbia students, drug-takers, Robert Brustein and his "theatrical grope-ins" (no point in making distinctions here, as Brustein once did, until his own polemical bent got the better of *him*), as well as Susan Sontag and many others. Speaking for a complexity of consciousness ("the idea of the problematic," "nuance and ambiguity," etc.) and against simplistic "neo-primitivism," he collapses everything together, tars everyone with the same brush. One hadn't imagined that the culture of the sixties was so much of a piece.

What was there about the new sensibility that could drive an old radical into the arms of the church, so to speak? It's clear that this sensibility, far from being cool and content-less, had much to do with politics, morals, and even religion. This is where Allen Ginsberg comes in, not only as an irreducible individual but as the richest possible emblem of that whole cultural period. The Howe of 1968, afire with his mission of defending Culture against barbarism, would probably have dismissed him along with the immoralists and drugtakers as another "neo-primitive." (Even Leslie Fiedler got associated with the potheads because he wrote a tentative and notably balanced essay, "The New Mutants," that failed to condemn them. Woe unto those who actually turned on!) Yet Ginsberg didn't readily fit Sontag's qualifications either. He not only published unashamed *literature,* but he was too preachy and spoke too directly to our moral and emotional sensibilities.

In Ginsberg we can make out some of the traditional roots of the "new" culture of the sixties. He himself was at pains to enlarge our sense of the poetic tradition, and to underline his affinities with Blake, Whitman, Rimbaud, William Carlos Williams, and other poets who found little favor in the academy during the forties and fifties. ("Before I met Williams," Jane Kramer quotes him as saying, "I was all hung up on cats like Wyatt, Surrey, and Donne. I'd read them and then copy down what I thought poetry like theirs would be. Then I sent some of those poems to Williams, and he thought that they were terrible. . . . He told me, 'Listen to the rhythm of your own voice. Proceed intuitively by ear.' ")

But Ginsberg belongs to other traditions as well. It was the singular virtue of Diana Trilling's condescending essay on Ginsberg at Columbia to treat him not as a crazy visionary or an irresponsible dropout but as the remnant of an evangelical left-wing culture of the thirties. His poem "America" is full of sentimental invocations of the Wobblies, Tom Mooney, the Spanish Loyalists, the Scottsboro boys, Sacco and Vanzetti, all set in an ironic fifties context.

> America when will you be angelic?
> When will you take off your clothes?
> When will you look at yourself through the grave?
> When will you be worthy of your million Trotskyites? . . .
>
> America I used to be a communist when I was a kid I'm not sorry.
> I smoke marijuana every chance I get.
> I sit in my house for days on end and stare at the roses in the closet.

The juxtapositions are ingenious, like Blake's "Proverbs of Hell." Obviously this is not agit-prop poetry; Ginsberg is also a drug enthusiast and a visionary, not least out of disappointed political and messianic expectations. His mother was a Communist who happened to go mad, or a madwoman who once had been a Communist. The demons that haunted her fantasies were half political and half personal. Her last letter to him, which he received two days after her death and transcribed in the *Kaddish* he wrote for her, was at once visionary poetry and the stern advice of a concerned Jewish mother:

> The key is in the window, the key is in the sunlight at the window—I have the key—Get married Allen don't take drugs—the key is in the bars, in the sunlight in the window.
>
> > Love,
> > your mother

The poignant combinations of "America" and of Naomi Ginsberg were those on which all Ginsberg's work was based, and point to the ways he foreshadowed and then incarnated the culture of the sixties. Only the "tranquillized" fifties (as Lowell then called it), with its stringent sense of decorum and its political complacency, could have considered the Beat movement a dropout culture without social or artistic point.* The social point did not begin to be heard until *Growing Up Absurd* finally found a publisher in 1960. Until then the Beats were what a famous piece in *Time* had made of them, a "pack of oddballs who celebrate booze, dope, sex, and despair." The aesthetic point took longer to get a serious hearing, though *On the Road*, unlike *Howl*, had gotten some enthusiastic middlebrow reviews when it first appeared. Serious critics remained hostile to both, and their taste in poetry was enshrined in the Pack-Hall-Simpson anthology, *New Poets of England and America* (1957), which excluded not only the Beats but also the Black Mountain poets, the New York School, and every other note of incipient experimentalism, all of which, like most such "experiments," had a rich but neglected literary ancestry. Even the public behavior of the Beats, which was correlative to the inertia and resistance of the age, had its forebear in the *épatisme* of Dada and the surrealists. In the sixties this and many other germs blossomed side by side. How did the period contrive so unique a mixture of twenties bohemianism and thirties politics? The young were promiscuously drawn to both Marx and the occult, Mao and the *I Ching*, politics and pot, revolution and rock. In the arts the cultural upheaval at large opened the gates not only to sexual frankness but also to a general revival of experiment the likes of which we had not seen, at least in literature, since the first generation of modernists. (This is not to say that the experiments were as ambitious or as successful, only that they asked, and still ask, to be taken seriously, critically, instead of being dismissed under some rubric like the "culture industry" or "neo-primitivism.")

If I speak of literature it is not only because I know it best or

* Here and there in the fifties there were dissenting voices, mostly political, who assaulted the prevailing tendencies. One thinks of *Dissent* and Irving Howe's essay "This Age of Conformity," which later seemed to embarrass him slightly; of Harold Rosenberg's essays, especially "Couch Liberalism and the Guilty Past" and "Death in the Wilderness"; of Richard Chase's 1958 book *The Democratic Vista*, whose best pages offered a stinging but balanced critique of the fifties and a prescient anticipation of the new politics of the sixties. By 1959 and 1960 the trickle became a flood, and within a short space many of the founding books of the new sensibility were published. I'll examine these transitional and prophetic works in the third chapter of this book.

because other arts, such as painting, more insulated from society by their own modern aesthetic, nurtured vigorous experimental movements in the forties and fifties, but because I can't see any evidence for the notion popularized by McLuhan that books have been displaced. Literature, even popular literature, has always been the province of a more conscious minority. If books in the sixties learned to compete for their audience with films and politics and popular music, the dispersion was a healthy one (even as far as "content" goes).* It was wrong to have accused the young of not reading and also of reading the wrong books. If they traded in Eliot for Blake, this may have been a mistake, but it should have caused less panic among those who once traded in Swinburne for Eliot, or Shelley for Donne. During the sixties at Columbia, shortly before the famous upheaval, I twice conducted an undergraduate course on Blake, in which even those who came to get high stayed to sweat out the intricacies of the system. With *The Four Zoas* in one hand and Frye's *Fearful Symmetry* in the other, they could hardly be accused of intellectual laziness.

Young people in the sixties, with a great deal of sophistication, tolerance, and eagerness, were looking *for* something in literature (as Pauline Kael said at the time of young movie audiences), not just looking *at* it. And their demand for "relevance" is still relevant, an instinctive part of every good teacher's thinking, ludicrous only when it becomes too narrow and literal. So often misapplied, especially by blockheaded radicals, the slogan of relevance finally took on a comical air in the late sixties, and then expired with the decline of student activism. But the pitfalls of scaling down literature rather than scaling up our demands upon it are more visible in the narrowly personal art of the fifties, exemplified by *The Assistant* and *Seize the Day*, than in the expansive historical mythmaking that gave us *Catch-22* and *V.* and *Cat's Cradle*. Novelists in the sixties recovered

* In *Making It* Norman Podhoretz described the urgency that attended a new novel in the fifties, even a single review of a new novel, which he traced to a "tyranny of taste" that gets out of hand in "politically quiescent periods." Which of us is nostalgic for literature to have *that* kind of primacy?

the gift of fantasy and imaginative excess, as well as an adventurousness of form and technique that rivaled Joyce (though not without some loss, as with Joyce himself, of direct human appeal).

The sixties novel was a hybrid literature, a dialectical literature, like Ginsberg's poetry. Heller's *Catch-22* was an odd cross between *No Time for Sergeants* and Dostoevsky, between a joke book and Kafka. Like Kafka's own work it was a perfect expression of the Jewish imagination of disaster, which means paranoia confirmed by history. Pynchon's *V.* combined a jazzy schlemiel story with a staggering range of pseudo-Conradian adventures, which are scattered around the book like the pieces of a jigsaw puzzle whose improbable whole takes the shape of our century; or is it just a game? Neither book proceeds directly, both harbor secrets (the secret of Snowden, the mystery of V.), both expand in widening ripples of enigma and disclosure. Similarly haunted by this sense of intricate connection and hidden meaning are Vonnegut's novel *Cat's Cradle*, as clean and spare as a diagram, and Pynchon's *The Crying of Lot 49*, where the game feels more threatening. With their cartoonish characters and weird parodic sects and conspiracies, these novels walk a fine line between what Pynchon calls the "orbiting ecstasy of a true paranoia" and the terrible blankness of the quotidian, between the imagination of disaster and no imagination at all. These black-humor fantasies were deeply political, not only because their Kafkaesque anxieties so fully expressed the sensibility of those who grew up with war and cold war, the CIA and the bomb, but because their half-mythic appropriation of large chunks of contemporary reality spoke to our political imagination as no propagandist literature could.

Take Donald Barthelme's story "Robert Kennedy Saved from Drowning" side by side with Mailer's journalism. Who could have predicted that fiction and political reportage would grow together as they did in the sixties? The progress of the literary mind from the anti-Stalinist radicalism of *Partisan Review* in the thirties and forties to Trilling's still-engaged critique of liberalism in the name of imagination in 1950 to the "tyranny of taste" and the triumph of the New

Criticism was toward an increasing disengagement from politics. Somehow Trilling's (and Matthew Arnold's) insistence that the political and literary minds had much to teach each other turned into the notion that they were fundamentally inimical, perhaps because most of the lessons flowed in one direction. Arnoldian disinterestedness came to justify a disdain for ideology and an aloofness from all political commitment, whereas in Arnold it is a mode of cultural criticism, of deeper engagement, directed above all against social complacency and self-congratulation. "Wragg is in custody," people are being quarantined and dehumanized—this is Arnold's prime example of the function of criticism.

Very much marked by this atmosphere of withdrawal, the novels of the fifties oscillated between minute personal concerns and abstract mythic ones; problems of alienation and identity were referred either to the private moral will, to the mysterious chemistry of human interaction, or to metaphysical necessity. Only the ethnic novel, rooted in a small but definable community, preserved a remnant of the social substance of literature. Malamud, Bellow, and Baldwin came through honorably if not grandly in their novels. Baldwin's essays and Ellison's *Invisible Man* went further, and adumbrated the new journalism and fiction that followed.

In poetry the forties and fifties embraced a neo-conservatism of form and an emotional solipsism that went beyond that of the novel. The chief technical models, in addition to the seventeenth-century poets that Eliot had done the most to revive, were Auden and the early Lowell, and the chief theorists were the New Critics. Poets like novelists were retreating from modernism in despair of surpassing it, resuscitating traditional forms as if they were bold new discoveries. Beat poetry, bad as much of it was, made an important break with this constriction of mind, this involution of the self into a distanced object, a well-wrought urn.

One of the New Critics had erected irony, ambiguity, and paradox into a Holy Trinity of the well-made poem. In this rhetorical hall of mirrors, direct self-expression and *its* complexities counted for little. In *Howl* Ginsberg reached for what critics once called the Sublime, but John Hollander could only see "a hopped-up and improvised tone" that compared poorly with Ginsberg's "profound and carefully organized earlier writing." This astounding and revealing judgment was reiterated by Theodore Roszak, supposedly an enthusiast of the new culture, in his ignorant treatment of Ginsberg in *The Making of a Counter Culture*.

As Paul Zweig said in a review of *Planet News*, "what Ginsberg forced us to understand in *Howl*, twelve years ago, was that nothing is safe from poetry." More of the world flowed through the poem again in all its variety; but also the spirit, the imaginative appetite, that greeted the world turned out to be larger than we had allowed, as large as Whitman had boasted, able to contain multitudes. After Ginsberg we knew, but still didn't know that we knew: there was real poetry, and then there was what the Beats were doing, which was fun but wasn't Art. When Robert Lowell's *Life Studies* came out in 1959—the same year as Mailer's *Advertisements for Myself* and Brown's *Life Against Death*—it should have been clear that the game was up: not only was the shape of the poem broken open again, but the self was about to get a new kind of currency that would thrust American literature back into the Romantic mainstream. But some of Lowell's admirers abused his method: where he had been gritty, prosy, and imaginatively personal, they were literal and "confessional," making histrionic inventories of their inner lives.

It's important to stress that the main direction of American poetry in the 1960s was not "confessional," as has often been supposed, but toward the same dialectic of fantasy and fact, politics and vision, that marked the new novel. Poetry moved toward open form and the plain style, away from "poetic diction" yet towards a wild adventurousness of imagery and a Whitmanesque spiritual intensity. We saw the birth of a new surrealism—the intense, vatic, turned-on association of images of Ginsberg; the visionary kaleidoscope of Bob Dylan's *Blonde on Blonde* songs, much influenced by Ginsberg's style, as by his anger and tenderness; the whimsical surrealism of Kenneth Koch's poems and plays, with their hilarious disproportions of scale and their irrepressible, child-like verbosity; the new pastoral poetry of Roethke and his brood, feeling its way back to a new innocence and quietness, exploring the tangled, irrational roots of the self in the landscapes of nature and the mind.

I refer especially to Robert Bly and others loosely associated with him and his magazine *The Sixties,* such as James Wright, David Ignatow, and Galway Kinnell, who seem to me among the most interesting poets who emerged during the decade. They are Wordsworthians all, seeking the eye of the storm, what Wordsworth in *The Excursion* called

> Authentic tidings of invisible things;
> Of ebb and flow, and ever-during power;
> And central peace, subsisting at the heart
> Of endless agitation.

It is hardly their fault that the contemporary world and their own burdens of identity within it turned these men largely into poets of disappointment. It was the pastoral poet in Bly (and a touch of the old public bard) that compelled him to confront the Vietnam war by organizing a massive campaign of readings and even by writing strikingly original political poems,* free of sentimental platitude and direct appeal. Used often on the stump and finally included in *The Light Around the Body* (1967), these poems are angry, charmless mixtures of bizarre fact and surreal metaphor. If the ingredients sometimes fail to coalesce, especially in print, it is nonetheless remarkable that a poet from Minnesota, populistically mistrustful of New York intellectuals, with an unambiguous sense of both his literary vocation and social responsibility, should have brought politics back into poetry, where *Partisan Review* and the New Criticism had so long insisted it could not tread.

When these poets do break through to quietness and "central peace," it is tenuous and fragmentary. The self-accusing serenity that James Wright achieves in the beautiful poems of *The Branch*

---

* Not quite original: Herbert Leibowitz pointed out the influence of Neruda, whom Bly has frequently praised and brilliantly translated. Leibowitz's review, which appeared in the *Hudson Review* (Autumn 1968), made a challenging case for the failure of these poems.

Gates of Eden

Will Not Break (1963) is purchased at the expense of all volitional intensity and personal hope. "I have wasted my life," one of these poems concludes, unexpectedly and matter-of-factly. This mood of resignation makes small epiphanies possible, as when, in the same poem,

> In a field of sunlight between two pines,
> The droppings of last year's horses
> Blaze up into golden stones.

"Spring Images," which I'll quote in full, is no more than the witness, the enacted process, of three such momentary redemptions, in which perception and language transfigure everyday reality:

> Two athletes
> Are dancing in the cathedral
> Of the wind.
>
> A butterfly lights on the branch
> Of your green voice.
>
> Small antelopes
> Fall asleep in the ashes
> Of the moon.

If the imagination's alchemy succeeds for a moment in turning manure into fiery gold, the victory remains a limited one. This is a poetry of failure which also courts failure as poetry. Its purity may be mere constraint, its transfigurations confusions. It is pared down, protectively hunched over; its faults are the opposite of those of Ginsberg, whose expansiveness often hovers at the edge of rhetoric.

Both poets are in the end saved by their spirituality and their concreteness, qualities rarely found together. The poetry of the sixties could take as its epigraph the words of Jacob Boehme that Bly affixes to the first section of *The Light Around the Body:*

> For according to the outward man, we are in this world, and according to the inward man, we are in the inward world. . . . Since then we are generated out of both worlds, we speak in two languages, and we must be understood also by two languages.

The section is called "The Two Worlds," and both Boehme and Bly seem to indicate that they must remain separate. But an innovative, questing impulse in both literature and social life during the sixties tried, often futilely, often beautifully, to interanimate them, to capture not only the nimbus but the light *within* the body—without disembodying it.

For this reason I have refrained from emphasizing "the sexual revolution" as the center of the new sensibility. Of all the simplistic explanations of what happened in the sixties, that perhaps does the most violence to what actually occurred. There's no question that the period saw dramatic changes in American sexual behavior—above all in public sexual expression—and especially in the younger generation. Here the taboo-shattering antics of the Beats were but one straw in what became a great rushing wind.

But as Paul Goodman argued in 1970 in *New Reformation,* the deeper insurgency of the sixties was spiritual and religious. The American way of life in the 1950s, of which sexual duplicity and repression were but one facet, was called to the bar of plausible human values and found wanting. Or worse still, it was ignored entirely. This spiritual seriousness was what took the place of ambiguity, wit, and literary allusiveness in the poetry of the sixties. Poets as different as Ginsberg and Wright aimed to make things new again, to see with an innocent eye. This innocence cannot be reduced to Irving Howe's primitivistic "psychology of unobstructed need." It has more to do with the sentences of Boehme and the famous words of *The Marriage of Heaven and Hell* (which develop Plato):

> If the doors of perception were cleansed every thing would appear to man as it is, infinite.
>   For man has closed himself up, till he sees all things thro' narrow chinks of his cavern.

To this one could add the Wordsworthian (and Blakean) sentence of Freud that serves an another epigraph in *The Light Around the Body:* "What a distressing contrast there is between the radiant intelligence of the child, and the feeble mentality of the average adult.'' To call this a flight from maturity and moral responsibility would be beside the point. It chooses not instinct over consciousness but intelligence over mentality; these poets sought new intelligence of the two worlds and the two languages. Their attitude was not based on an indifference to morality but was an attempt to freshen the petrified sources of moral behavior. Irving Howe did battle for the encrusted moral mentality of the ages because he felt threatened by what might replace it, or by what might break out if its constraints should weaken. The history of our time made his qualms understandable, but these constraints *have* weakened; they cannot be restored by sermon or fiat. Nor have Auschwitz and *Heart of Darkness* necessarily said the last word about human nature.

All in all the culture of the sixties was a liberating one—too liberating, many have said—an opening up, not least through what Blake calls ''an improvement of sensual enjoyment.'' But Ginsberg, like Blake and Whitman before him, always enmeshed sexuality in spiritual, political, even cosmic complications. In his *Playboy* interview, Ginsberg described how his homosexuality, which set him apart from the beginning, not only ''served as a catalyst for self-examination'' but also contributed to his political consciousness, by making him sensitive to the element of hyper-masculinity and aggressiveness in the American mentality. He revived Whitman's vision of a society whose communal ties are based on a renewal of personal tenderness. And of course he was delighted at ''the reappearance in the form of long hair and joyful dress of the affectionate feminine in the natural Adamic man, the whole man, the man of many parts.'' In the same vein, at the end of ''Who Be Kind To,'' he dreamed,

> That a new kind of man has come to his bliss
> to end the cold war he has borne
> against his own kind flesh
> since the days of the snake.

At the other extreme from this apocalyptic declaration yet complementing it was the figure of Ginsberg himself, whom Jane Kramer described as ''a comfortable, avuncular presence—a rumpled, friendly-looking man with a nice toothy face, big brown owl eyes behind the horn-rimmed glasses and a weary, rather affecting slouch.'' What made Ginsberg especially important to the youth culture of the sixties was less his mantic ecstasies than the complex generosity of his presence and his values. Just as his poetry encompasses both the visionary Blake and the realistic density of Williams ("no ideas but in things"), so his sympathies embraced and transcended both the hip scene and the New Left. Ginsberg, who had come on in the fifties as a flaming prophet screaming "Moloch" at contemporary America, emerged in the sixties as a figure of patience, charm, and conciliation. "Put it this way," Jane Kramer quoted him as saying to a young activist, "the hippies—that is, the psychedelics—have got the consciousness all right, but they have the problem of how to manifest it in the community without risking the pitfalls of a Fascist organization. You people—the radicals—have a real vision of the material and social ills of the society, but you've got pretty much the same problem. The hippies have deeper insight into consciousness, the radicals more information about the workings and the nature of consciousness in the world.''

All this seems quaint and distant today, when both the hip scene and the New Left are little more than memories. But it reminds us of the hopeful and affecting vision that animated the sixties at its best, before the travesty of Manson and Altamont, the Weathermen and the SLA. Call it Romantic socialism: the Romantic vision of the redemption of the self, the libertarian socialist dream of a community of redeemed selves in the real world. This was not a position that Ginsberg achieved easily, as the autobiographical stages of *Planet News* made clear. The book moves from wild and often opaque drug visions to the pivotal 1963 poem "The Change," which is in the line of the great Romantic poems of crisis and self-recognition. The poem describes a conversion from drugs to selfhood,* from the expansion of consciousness to its concentration on "the foul rag-and-bone shop of the heart" to which Yeats reconciled himself at the end

* Ginsberg has commented fascinatingly on this transformation in his *Paris Review* interview with Tom Clark. See *Writers at Work*, Third Series.

of "The Circus Animals' Desertion." It is this later Ginsberg, *our* Ginsberg, whose warm and chastened voice we hear in the naked language of "Who Be Kind To":

> Be kind to your self, it is only one
>   and perishable. . . .
> Be kind to the fearful one at your side
>   Who's remembering the Lamentations
>   of the bible
> the prophesies of the Crucified Adam Son
>   of all the porters and char men of
>   Bell gravia—
> Be kind to your self who weep under
>   the Moscow moon and hide your bliss hairs
>   under raincoat and suede Levis—
> For this is the joy to be born, the kindness
>   received through strange eyeglasses on
>   a bus thru Kensington. . . .
> Be kind to the heroes that have lost their
>   names in the newspaper. . . .
> And be kind to the poor soul that cries in
>   a crack in the pavement because he
>   has no body—

"A little more than kin, and less than kind," mutters Hamlet in his first line, punning bitterly, since Claudius has addressed him as cousin and son. Ginsberg's poem sets out to bridge this fissure of words and feelings. Be kind to your self and to others means not only be good to them but also be kin with them, related, natural, close. Ginsberg's millennial proclamation of a "new kind of man" no longer warring on "his own kind flesh" may have been premature, if utopian visions can be called premature, but his advocacy of a politics of exorcism, celebration, and public joy rather than violent confrontation belonged to the most appealing side of the culture of the sixties, its spiritual hunger and its spiritual comedy. Unable to shake Goliath by politics alone, fearful of fighting him at all because of the corruption involved in using his own techniques, many radicals took refuge in what Ginsberg called "magic politics": "a kind of poetry and theater sublime enough to change the national will and open up consciousness in the populace."

This is utopian indeed, and as such is likely to be scorned by more hard-nosed political types. But it preserves its appeal as a vision even as its practical possibilities seem, for the present, to be wanting. It's based on the feeling that certain kinds of political action deform the agent more than they change society, and on a shrewd awareness of the role the media play in altering contemporary opinion. To what extent consciousness was in fact opened up in the populace we'll never know. Undoubtedly the American people eventually turned against the war in Vietnam. Whether they did so because we failed to win, or because of the steady drumbeat of the evening news, or because of the antiwar movement, or because of exhaustion with the war's sheer endlessness we may never discover. The sixties survives in our minds most vividly as spectacle, as an experiment in political theater—one which, because of its failures and frustrations, is not likely to be repeated on a similar scale in the near future, yet also one which, having once been tried, should remain permanently available as an avenue of protest and dissent. After Ginsberg and his friends, left-wing politics should never again become so solemn and humorless.

1975. An April evening a few days before the fall of Saigon. Ginsberg, Corso, and Orlovsky return to McMillin Theater to mark their still-remembered reading of sixteen years earlier. They are joined by an old friend, William Burroughs, and by a full house of more than 1,600 people, only three or four of whom, on a show of hands, own up to having been at the earlier event. Where have all the flowers gone?

Despite the best exertions of the four writers and their brave insistence on sticking to newer material, the reading turns into an exercise in nostalgia rather than a living event: a piece of history for kids who were two years old when the first reading took place. Corso seems wrecked and embittered, envious of Ginsberg's success and rather hostile to everyone else. Only at moments do we see some flashes of his boyish humor and ineffaceable charm. Orlovsky is predictably infantile and impossible to dislike, but both he and Ginsberg read poems that are so explicitly and aggressively homosexual that even a liberated audience begins to cringe in discomfort. Moreover, Ginsberg himself seems ill and exhausted (a week or two later he winds up in the hospital with a bad bug); evidently his work has not been getting any better, and the passion and the pain that once fired his reading of *Kaddish* now seem reduced to a routine.

The upshot of the reading was yet another piece of evidence that the sixties were long over. This was why Ginsberg seemed adrift, without the cultural matrix that had only recently kept his work at the center, and that had turned his appearances into rituals of communion for a whole generation. This was why Burroughs stole the show, for his was a completely imagined world, in a unique and unmistakable style, diabolically self-sufficient in its solipsism. With his beaky, prim, business executive's appearance and his chill, astringent voice he seemed a reincarnation of the aged T. S. Eliot (his fellow St. Louisan), a voice from the other side.

In many ways Burroughs was a more appropriate writer for the seventies than Ginsberg, and his new writing seemed as good as anything he'd ever done. For this looked to be a period more suitable to the surreal, fragmentary, Wasteland vision Burroughs and Eliot shared than to Whitmanesque expansiveness. For Ginsberg the wheel had come full circle; an outsider once, he was an outsider again, though honored and famous. A moment had passed, and the culture in its bleak descent had passed him by. A follower of Blake who had sketched the modern version of Blake's marriage of heaven and hell, he now seemed destined, like so many others in the grey seventies, to learn the meaning of limbo.

2

Cold War Blues:
Politics and Culture
in the Fifties

I

The recurrent flurries of nostalgia for the 1950s—and the eerie feeling that, but for the economic crisis, we might already have become the 1950s—have not yet stimulated any deep interest in what actually happened then; I don't mean the names and dates but what life felt like to those who were there. As the sixties recede and go out of fashion, as month by month the atmosphere becomes more pinched and constricting, the fifties become the blank screen on which many project fantasies of an alternative, as the thirties were then to some who cared about alternatives.

But such nostalgia works only by distortion and historical invention, whose effect can be perverse and self-destructive. If rock music seems to have lost its innovative edge, if it seems to founder in a decadent sophistication, we look back to the banal but energetic simplicities of fifties rock 'n' roll. If poetry goes too far toward free form and undisciplined subjectivity, we reach for a hair shirt, as Robert Lowell did in his immense sonnet sequence, *Notebook* (1970), which has gone through numberless revisions without ever becoming a poem. If our political life becomes too violent and problematic we grasp at something more orderly, as a writer in *Commentary*, John Mander, did when he eulogized the fifties as "the happiest, most stable, most rational period the Western world has known since 1914."

This is perhaps a more exact analogy than Mander cared to acknowledge. The "long summer's day" of the Edwardian peace was also the frozen smile of countless social and political hierarchies. Nearly all of Europe welcomed the war with a sense of release, as long as the thrill of letting go obscured the accumulated debt. In retrospect, the explosive conflicts of the sixties, agonizing as they often were, unmasked another Old Regime whose convenient symbol was Eisenhower, whose substance was the increasingly decayed and irrelevant traditions of rural or small-town America, and whose stability was grounded in a suppression of grievances and new energies that could be suppressed no longer.

The political atmosphere of that time is hard to recall today. The period was shadowed by a fear of thermonuclear war yet was suffused by a mood of business-as-usual, everyone in his niche. Its legislative monument was the interstate highway system, which helped transport an ever more rootless population from the farms to the cities, from the cities to the suburbs, from the South to the ghettos, from the midwest to California. While hymning the praise of traditional values people were learning to live without a past, on a roller coaster of technological novelty that had already begun to Americanize the world.

This whirl of social movement found no echo in the political arena. The hallmark of both foreign and domestic policy was the extremely narrow range of permissible debate. Formal democracy thrived while the real issues of the day were excluded from the domain of choice. When Adlai Stevenson raised questions about the draft and about nuclear testing in the 1956 campaign he was said to have exceeded the perimeters of mainstream opinion. Obviously he was not a serious candidate. High school students could debate ad nauseam whether Red China should be admitted to the UN but no one in public life could risk a similar freedom. Allied to this was the mania of national security which ruined the lives of some, touched many others with the cold hand of fear and conformity, and helped foreclose the political options of all. Much later, the domestic achievements of Johnson's Great Society and the dramatic coups of Nixon's foreign policy were but the thawed-out imperatives of this twenty-year freeze in the political process.

I enumerate these things not to close off the question of the fifties but to underline its importance. The fifties were the seedbed of our present cultural situation and the ground against which the upheavals of the sixties sought to define themselves. The challenge of these upheavals has yet to be met, and we are still living with the consequences. The lure of the fifties hints that history moves like a pendulum; it speaks to our wish to have done with these problems; it tells us we can return unscathed to an idealized time before life grew complicated and we grew older. What happened in the fifties really matters, not only for what it gave rise to but for what it seems to offer us, for the way we shall choose to live.

For that reason it is impossible to limit one's evidence, as Mander in *Commentary* does, to the often unreal world of foreign affairs. My own alternative, "what life felt like," is precarious but essential, for the culture gives our lives a tone and quality that may not be reflected by diplomats and presidents, that may be more truly expressed in the work of artists and intellectuals. Despite what seemed like the interminable bloodbath of Vietnam, and because of it, the great changes of the war's decade were ones of sensibility, awareness, and attitude, not of institutions. For all the alarm of entrenched liberals and conservatives, the political changes of the sixties—as opposed to shifts of rhetoric and mood—were nothing if not gradual and melioristic.

The cataclysms of the moral landscape were quite another story, harder to discern because changes in sensibility resist ready generalization. At stake is a fiber of assumptions and feelings that link the individual to the wider public realities of his time. Artists and intellectuals, for all their supposed alienation from prevailing social values, often articulate these assumptions most subtly. They are daily awash in a medium of feeling and opinion, and where they do take dissident positions their resistance to the age may turn out to be crucially *of* the age. Even the formal concerns of the artist, which, like the quarrels of the intellectuals, often seem parochial to the world at large, usually reflect that world in intense miniature. The culture of an age is a unified thing, whatever its different strands and apparent contradictions. Touch it anywhere and it can reveal its secrets: the texture exposed, the part betrays the whole.

One example I'll use extensively here is the cold war anti-Communism that predominated among intellectuals of the late forties and fifties, which weirdly refracted the political tenor of the nation at large. Later on in 1967, in the wake of revelations that leading periodicals and cultural organizations of the postwar period had been secretly funded by the CIA, apparently as instruments of the cold war, *Commentary,* itself in the last throes of its newfound sixties liberalism, invited some of the best-known intellectuals of the fifties to rethink their past political behavior, in a symposium on "Liberal Anti-Communism Revisited." The result was a revealing lesson in the varieties of self-exculpation. Some intellectuals were penitent to varying degrees, some impenitent, others indignant at being asked to reconsider, as if the Vietnam war and the CIA exposure could have any effect on the timeless truths of political philosophy.

What nearly all shared, however, was a tendency to minimize the scope and effect of their past opinions, and to make distinctions that few had been so precise about in the previous period. We were anti-Stalinist, they insisted, not anti-radical or anti-Communist. Nothing disgusted us more than the garden variety of Red-baiting that followed both world wars. We were libertarians and free minds, not witch-hunters or kept men. Our independent position made us a small dissident group with little influence either on national policy in the fifties or on the climate of opinion that later made the Vietnam war possible. (At least no one bothered to add, Some of my best friends were blacklisted.)

Yet for all these protestations what future historian who examines the vagaries of intellectuals during the period will fail to observe the correspondence between the views published in *Encounter* magazine and the government policies that made the covert support of *Encounter* by the CIA a good investment? Nor should our historian fail to note that at a low ebb of American civil liberties Mary McCarthy wrote a novel about a faculty Machiavel who tries to save his job by *posing* as a victim of political persecution; that Robert Warshow and Leslie Fiedler wrote essays attacking the Rosenbergs and their sympathizers rather than the men who had just executed them; that Irving Kristol and others minimized the importance of McCarthy while criticizing liberals and intellectuals who were alarmed by him; that an influential group of social scientists antipathetic to McCarthy tried to blame him, in a sense, on the Left rather than the Right by associating his demagoguery with populism and the presumed dangers of ideology;* that Sidney Hook supported the firing of supposed Communists from schools and universities *on libertarian grounds,* since such centers of independent thought had no room for those whose minds were *by definition* unfree; that many teachers and academics stood by quietly while some of their colleagues became unpersons; that Elia Kazan and others went before the House Un-American Activities Committee to beat their breasts, swear fealty, name names, tell all—the "all" being mainly trivial gossip many years old, the detritus of left-wing political life of the thirties and early forties. These episodes but skim the surface and isolate a few conspicuous individuals, yet they tell us enough to know that our future historian may abridge certain fine distinctions intellectuals love to make, especially when they are in bad faith. Hindsight will not fail to connect their opinions with certain gross actualities of the time, including blacklists, union purges, jail terms, university firings, the McCarran and Smith acts, and supinely cooperative Supreme Court decisions, to say nothing of a much wider range of political intimidation that these events helped to enforce, as the range of public policy and private opinion grew ever more narrow.

* See the essays in *The Radical Right,* edited by Daniel Bell (1955, 1963) and a critique by Michael Paul Rogin in *The Intellectuals and McCarthy* (1967).

I I

The details of these cold war episodes are hardly new and despite their maleficence I don't wish to belabor them, though I'll soon return to some of them in greater detail. My other field of evidence is not political but literary: the curious emergence of the Jewish novel into a central position in American fiction. This is not to say there was a purely Wasp hegemony over American letters before the fifties, but earlier Jewish writers like Henry Roth, Daniel Fuchs, and even Nathanael West did not gain substantial recognition until they were republished in the wake of the Jewish-American renaissance of the fifties (championed by an aggressive new generation of Jewish critics like Howe, Fiedler, and Kazin, themselves no mean flowers of that awakening).

If the Jewish writers of the thirties, as writers, failed even to survive the decade, the generation of the forties remained in its own way *maudit* and unfulfilled—and hardly acknowledged today except for its star performers. In a sense they were writers too talented but also too restless and unconfident to pursue a single line of work. Like many of their non-Jewish contemporaries—Randall Jarrell comes to mind—they were intellectuals and men of letters, not strictly novelists or poets. Several—including Delmore Schwartz, Paul Goodman, and Isaac Rosenfeld—made their mark as critics and essayists, and in fiction they tend to assume a no-nonsense tone of plain talk that, despite a leaven of whimsy and fantasy, reveals a distrust of the imaginative process when it gets too far from "real life." They gravitate toward small forms and big ideas, which they sometimes manipulate so brilliantly that they overwhelm the fictional context. They distrust eloquence and Art but remain beautifully close to the vital facts of experience, especially the experience of intellectuals caught in a wild, unsettling rush of acculturation, a crazy quilt of America. For all their attraction to ideas, they never forget that intellectuals have mothers and fathers, friends and lovers, and that ideas are hatched by people, who can be elated, changed, or even destroyed by them.

Bellow is a characteristic member of this generation, its only survivor, its only "success" as a novelist. His friend Isaac Rosenfeld is its fallen soldier, but Delmore Schwartz remains its most fascinating and least appreciated prophet. A *wunderkind* who never fulfilled his matchless promise, he descended increasingly into paranoia and isolation during the latter part of his life. By the time of his terrible, anonymous death in a shabby hotel in 1966 he had entirely faded from public view. The ripples of interest that followed his death and the publication of a thick volume of selected essays in 1970 consisted mainly of testimony from old friends to his extraordinarily vital personal presence. Berryman's *Dream Songs* and Bellow's novel *Humboldt's Gift* have provided literary versions of these private memories; understandably, they continue to emphasize the man rather than the work.

As a writer he is hard to characterize or pin down, and few have tried. The young have scarcely heard of him, though his work is one long brooding adolescence, and a scholar like Allen Guttmann, whose book *The Jewish Writer in America* aims at a certain comprehensiveness, gives him no space at all. The finale of Guttmann's work is a long section on "Mr. Bellow's America," with chapters on every one of Bellow's novels, but Schwartz's great stories "America! America!" and "In Dreams Begin Responsibilities" evidently don't belong to the semi-official canon of explicitly "Jewish" writing. Yet, as much as Bellow's first book, *Dangling Man* (1944), they do introduce themes that would become decisive in the Jewish literary renaissance of the fifties.

Even a background has its background: behind the awkward new sensibility of the 1940s lay not only the disruptions of the war but the adventures and sorrows of Marxism. "Marxism is in relative eclipse," wrote Edmund Wilson in 1940, after nearly a decade of immersion in it. "An era in its history has ended." Nowhere is that eclipse more visible than in the work of the young writers. The introspective diarist whose mask Bellow wears in *Dangling Man* begins by attacking his age as "an era of hardboiled-dom" dominated by a belief in action rather than self-knowledge. He is writing in 1942, when the obligations of wartime patriotism had replaced the pressures of social activism, but the thrust is broadly aimed. In keeping a journal and keeping to his room, Joseph—whose name recalls Kafka's anti-hero—announces a new turn in the direction of the novel, away from Hemingway and his followers and from the proletarian writers who had appropriated his tight-lipped manner to their own ideological purpose. *Dangling Man* is the strangest, most claustral of war novels, a late, mild flower of the Underground Man tradition, morosely ideological in its refusal of all ideology.

Dangling Man would probably have been forgotten today if Bellow's later work had not kept it in view. *The World Is a Wedding* (1948), a collection of Delmore Schwartz's stories of a decade, *has* been forgotten, and is perhaps *the* neglected gem of the fiction of the forties. Schwartz received recognition mainly as a poet, but neither his poetry nor his criticism has worn well—which is to say, survived the period of uncritical adulation of the great modernist writers. Everything he wrote shows a good deal of stiffness and self-consciousness, but when the hermetic, elliptical intensities of Rilke, Eliot, and the symbolists merged with the gauche poeticism of his own language and sensibility the results could be disastrous. Where his poetry is alternately hermetic and "sincere," his critical manner is uniformly earnest and labored. Except for a few first-rate pieces like "The Duchess' Red Shoes" (a critique of Lionel Trilling), his longer essays offer access to his mind more than they illuminate the object. Only in his stories does that mind become conscious of itself, for only there does his strange ruminative voice work dramatically. Instead of donning the robes of abstract cultural authority he makes his style and personality part of his subject, part of the problem.

I can't resist quoting an example of this style from "New Year's Eve," one of three stories that concern "a youthful author of promise" with a name—Shenandoah Fish—even more improbable than the author's own: "Shenandoah and Nicholas travelled crosstown in a street-car, standing up in the press and brushing against human beings they would never see again. They continued their argument which on the surface concerned the question, should Nicholas go to a party where he would for the most part be a stranger? This was a type of the academic argument, since the street-car slowly went cross-town, bearing the young men to the argument's conclusion.'' The awkward, chiseled quality of Schwartz's critical prose is evident here too, but the tone is wry rather than earnest, a volatile mixture of irony and affection. A moment later the argument deepens and we see the other passengers ''listening in amazement to their virtually ontological discussion of character.'' Schwartz's own boyish mind is just the sort that bears down on experience in an ''ontological'' way, risking absurdity in an effort to both express and overcome its own sense of isolation, its singular intensity. His stories are populated by images of himself, named like himself, who become both the meat of his satire and the vehicles of his aspiration to art, genius, and fame. Such stories as ''New Year's Eve'' and ''The World Is a Wedding'' dwell lovingly on the preciosities of urban intellectuals and artists *manqués* whose quasi-bohemianism is generally enforced by the Depression rather than founded on talent or creative energy. Contemptuous of a middle class which refuses to bow down to them, cut off from their origins yet without much inward direction, they devolve into a brittle cynicism and cliquishness that leaves them cut off from ''real life,'' trapped in their own anxious feelings of superiority.

Delmore Schwartz's attidude toward these characters is complicated: there must be a great deal of himself and his friends in them, yet he lays bare their weaknesses with a scalpel. Surely *he* is the ''youthful author of promise'' whose name betrays his own divided soul. Ironically, the stories as a whole are hobbled by the same sort of claustral self-involvement for which he tellingly indicts his characters, as if the Hemingway code of action had been replaced by a cult of sensitivity so stringent that no action whatever is possible. Taken by themselves, these stories would seem to confirm Irving Howe's suggestion that the sensibility of the New York intellectuals was too nervous and special for major creative work.

The major action of the stories is conversation: despite his irony Schwartz lovingly orchestrates his characters' talk. We are told of Rudyard Bell, who presides over a circle of would-be geniuses in

"The World Is a Wedding," that "the volley of the conversation, as at a tennis match, was all he took [away] with him. For what he wanted and what satisfied him was the activity of his own mind. This need and satisfaction kept him from becoming truly interested in other human beings, though he sought them out all the time." It's been said that Rudyard is based on the young Paul Goodman, but surely Delmore Schwartz is exposing himself as well, for in his own talk he too "was like a travelling virtuoso who performs brilliant set-pieces." But through this diagnosis the author becomes a Rudyard who knows and transcends himself. Like Rudyard, Delmore is an Artist and talker but one who tries to connect, whose bohemian contempt for the middle class is superseded by a fascination with his origins and identity. After Schwartz's death Dwight Macdonald, with his usual amiable obtuseness, wrote that he could never understand his friend Delmore's "obsession with his Jewish childhood." Paradoxically then, his self-involvement forced him to become truly interested in other human beings. Only they could help him decode his own secret, and it's precisely this obsession that propels his fiction from random satire and self-dramatization to an entirely different order of material.

In "America! America!" (his best story) and "In Dreams Begin Responsibilities" (his most famous one) Schwartz turns from the narrow circle of his contemporaries to the enigma of the previous generation. Both stories focus on the formative bonds between parents and children and the infinite abyss that separates them, that especially separates the immigrant generation from its "American" offspring. "America! America!" is about the declining fortunes of the Baumann family, which devolve from the father's prosperous importance in the immigrant social world to the chronic failures of his clever, maladaptive, ne'er-do-well sons. As in Joseph Conrad's novels, however, half the interest of the story comes from its teller, in this case Mrs. Fish, Shenandoah's mother, to whom he seems to be listening for the first time, thunderstruck by the complex world from which he came (which lies accusingly outside his ken as an artist), struck too by the sensitivity of the speaker, whose intuitive insight into "the difficulties of life" shames him for his arrogance and self-importance. "Shenandoah was exhausted by his mother's story. He was sick of the mood in which he had listened, the irony and the contempt which had taken hold of each new event. He had listened from such a distance that what he saw was an outline, a caricature, and an abstraction. How different it might seem, if he had been able to see these lives from the inside, looking out."

The whole story is brilliantly punctuated by such notations, by the undulations of self-awareness in this writer as he is flooded by the past and by the alien world of the middle class. "He reflected upon his separation from these people, and he felt that in every sense he was removed from them by thousands of miles, or by a generation, or by the Atlantic Ocean. . . . Whatever he wrote as an author did not enter into the lives of these people, who should have been his genuine relatives and friends, for he had been surrounded by their lives since the day of his birth, and in an important sense, even before then. . . . The lower middle-class of the generation of Shenandoah's parents had engendered perversions of its own nature, children full of contempt for every thing important to their parents." *

Schwartz's theme has more than a personal dimension. He is sounding a note that goes back 150 years to the first stirrings of romanticism in Europe: the alienation of the artist from middle-class society. This was an especial dogma in the wake of the modernist movement of the 1920s, whose difficult art, addressed to a purified elite, was sometimes built on an attack on modern life in toto, and in the wake of the radicalism of the thirties, which identified the middle class as the special villain of contemporary society. A staggering number of contemporary writers were strangers in a strange land: Americans in Europe, Poles writing in English, Anglo-Irishmen liv-

* Compare the following reminiscence by Alfred Kazin in *A Walker in the City:* "It was not for myself that I was expected to shine, but for them—to redeem the constant anxiety of their existence. I was the first American child, their offering to the strange new God; I was to be the monument of their liberation from the shame of being—what they were. . . . Our families and teachers seemed tacitly agreed to be a little ashamed of what we were."

ing by their wits, self-exiled questers like D. H. Lawrence, seeking a new spiritual home. Such deracination could be a source of strength. As Isaac Rosenfeld argued in 1944, "marginal men" could have a perspective on modern society unavailable to the insider. Delmore Schwartz echoes this theme in an essay on Eliot: "Modern life may be compared to a foreign country in which a foreign language is spoken. Eliot is the international hero because he made the journey to the foreign country. . . ."

Where this view of modern life prevails the Jew, especially the secular Jewish intellectual, becomes the quintessential modern man: doubly alienated, from the prevailing national culture and from his own traditional culture, uprooted from the European pale and yet cut off from his own uprooted parents. But the artist who is truly interested in other human beings—and has some concern for his own sanity—soon comes to the limits of alienation as a viable ground for his work. (This is why so many modernists, like Eliot and Yeats, like Lawrence in Mexico, eventually fell into eccentric nostrums of pseudo-tradition in religion or politics.) This is what Schwartz's Shenandoah recognizes as he hears his mother telling the story of the Baumanns, and surely no writer has inserted a more crushing insight into the strengths and limitations of his own work: "Shenandoah had thought of this gulf and perversion before, and he had shrugged away his unease by assuring himself that this separation had nothing to do with the important thing, which was the work itself. But now as he listened, as he felt uneasy and sought to dismiss the emotion, he began to feel that he was wrong to suppose that the separation, the contempt, and the gulf had nothing to do with his work; perhaps, on the contrary, it was the center; or perhaps it was the starting-point and compelled the innermost motion of the work to be flight, or criticism, or denial, or rejection."

Delmore Schwartz's best stories move away from this starting-point, toward an empathy for other lives, but they never fully evade these limitations. They are exquisitely wrought but excruciatingly self-conscious. No one would call them expansive. Their main theme remains that of the isolated self and the mysteries of identity that can never be solved but never evaded. For the author himself the final paranoia and anonymity, the trail of broken friendships and brilliant memories, to say nothing of the deterioration of his work, were the final seal of the same failure.

I I I

The very title of Saul Bellow's first novel suggests its kinship with Delmore Schwartz's work, almost more than the book itself does. As William Phillips aptly remarked, Bellow's Joseph dangles "with both feet on the ground." (His resemblance to the Underground Man is skin-deep.) Not until *Herzog* (1964), his retrospective summation of the cultural life of the postwar period, would Bellow fully convey the glory and anguish of the deracinated Jewish intellectual of that time. What makes *Dangling Man* prophetic of a new literature and sensibility is its intent focus on the theme of the isolated self. Where Herzog and Tommy Wilhelm (in *Seize the Day*) will desperately reach out to people to overcome their almost unbearable sense of disconnection, Joseph attenuates all human connection in order to experiment on himself, to sound every inward note. *Dangling Man* is literally a book about a man who keeps a journal ("to talk to myself"): "and if I had as many mouths as Siva has arms and kept them going all the time, I still could not do myself justice." Severed from his job, not yet in the army, out of touch with wife, friends, and family, scarcely able to read, Joseph is performing an ontological experiment on the self, acting out a dream of absolute freedom that is the flip-side of the coin of alienation. In its small and weightless way *Dangling Man* foreshadows the metaphysics of the self, the elusive mysteries of personality, that would dominate the fiction of the fifties—the legion of small novels which would recoil from the Promethean extremes of modernism and naturalism to take refuge in craft, psychology, and moral allegory.

One ingredient of these new novels of sensibility would be the abandonment of the public world that had provided much of the terrain of the great novels, to say nothing of the terrain of Jewish millennial aspirations: politics, class, manners and mores, even the very feel of the streets. In a shrewd and ambivalent review of Bernard Malamud's marvelous collection of stories *The Magic Barrel* (1958), Alfred Kazin commented that "his world is all too much an inner world—one in which the city streets, the houses, the stores, seem, along with the people who broodingly stand about like skeletons, some with flesh, always just about to fold up, to disappear into the sky. . . . People flit in and out of each other's lives like bad dreams."

How different from this or from any other Jewish fiction of the forties and fifties is a book like Daniel Fuchs's *Summer in Williamsburg*, first published in 1934, ten years before *Dangling Man*. When Fuchs's novels were reissued in the early sixties, much was made of the fabulistic, "poetic" side, as if they could only be appreciated in the wake of a moral allegorist like Malamud. Actually, the great strength of the books is their feeling for the life of the streets, the Runyonesque "low company" of youthful gangs in Williamsburg and Jewish mobsters in the Catskills, a chapter of social history quickly forgotten when the Jews became more respectable and the Jewish novel more morally austere. In Fuchs the moral temperature is low: he is notably ham-handed in portraying the religious life of his Jews, a more inward subject. He is a folklorist, an anthropologist of street life rather than a purveyor of moral parables. For all his freedom from the cant of proletarian writing, he remains in essence a 1930s realist; for him life is with the people.

Well, Daniel Fuchs folded up shop after three novels and went off to make his fortune in the great world—Hollywood. Delmore Schwartz's characters need have no truck with the world because they are Artists, too pure to be responsible, or responsive. Bellow never allows his characters that exit. His Joseph is explicitly *not* an artist, despite his diary-writing; he claims no higher moral license to drop out, adheres to no adversary community of the alienated, finds no salvation in "acts of the imagination": "I have no talent at all for that sort of thing. My talent, if I have one at all, is for being a citizen, or what is today called, most apologetically, a good man. Is there some sort of personal effort I can substitute for the imagination?'' But this is precisely the talent Joseph never uses, the effort he can never make. Compared with Fuchs, Bellow is deeply involved in the moral and communitarian strain of the Jewish tradition. Joseph claims to seek the social equivalent for the most profound commitments of the artist. But the final gesture by which he abolishes his alienation is ominous: he puts himself up for induction. Of course this is no Vietnam but a ''just'' war, one Joseph says he believes in, but the satisfaction he expects is quite different from that of defeating the Germans. The bittersweet last lines of the book make clear that the dream of freedom has given way to an equally absolute dream of adhesion: ''I am in other hands, relieved of self-determination, freedom cancelled. Hurray for regular hours! And for the supervision of the spirit! Long live regimentation!''

There is a good deal of self-irony in these lines, and Bellow could hardly be said to endorse their vision of the good life. But I call them ominous for they anticipate a great deal in Bellow's later work, from Augie March's opening chant that ''I am an American, Chicago bred,'' to Herzog's polemics against ''the Wasteland outlook, the cheap mental stimulants of Alienation,'' to Mr. Sammler's tract against the moral and political radicalism of the sixties, his defense of ''civilization'' against the ''petted intellectuals'' who attack it ''in the name of perfect instantaneous freedom.'' Bellow's turn in the fifties toward accommodation with American society and his increasing hostility toward intellectuals who criticized it are quite well known, though few have noticed that the pattern of self-immolation goes back as far as his first book. This would be of little importance except to students of Bellow's development were it not representative of the whole intellectual climate of the fifties. The *Partisan Review* symposium on ''Our Country and Our Culture'' in 1952 is only the most famous indication of this new mood, which spread at just the time our country was prosecuting its most dubious adventures: the cold war and its domestic correlative, the mania of internal security.

It's true that some intellectuals, especially literary intellectuals, did try to maintain an adversary stance. Delmore Schwartz, for example, ever faithful to the modernist mentality, contributed to the symposium a defense of "critical nonconformism" (a term suggested by the editors) as against the new spirit of accommodation. But the whole brief, like the term itself, is lamentably abstract and typically confined to the cultural sphere: a defense of highbrow values against the incursions of mass and middlebrow taste. This was the usual tack of "adversary" intellectuals of that day; it suggested a strict hierarchy of cultural values with you-know-who at the top. (Even Harold Rosenberg accused sociologists of "mass culture," of secretly *liking* the stuff! Gasp!) Only the smallest handful of independent intellectuals effectively focused their criticism where it was most needed: on political decisions, on aggregations of social and economic power, on questions of civil liberties which then affected so many lives.

Thus it would be fair to say that the residual intransigence of some (mostly literary) intellectuals and the newfound Americanism of other (mostly political) intellectuals amounted to the same thing. The political intellectuals sang the virtues of American life, with its pluralism and pragmatism, its procedure by consensus, and its presumed freedom from ideology and moralism—this in the age of John Foster Dulles!—and excoriated the illusions of liberals, radicals, Popular Front types, and strict constructionists of the Bill of Rights (like Justices Black and Douglas). The literary intellectuals, while maintaining the cult of alienation, simply abandoned politics to pursue private myths and fantasies, to devote their work to the closet intensities of the isolated self or isolated personal relationships. The concept of alienation lost its social content and took on an increasingly religious and metaphysical cast. European existentialism and crisis theology became an incalculably great influence on the mood of the fifties—shorn, however, or their political matrix. The moral and psychological Sartre of the forties was admitted. The political Sartre of the fifties was ignored or ridiculed—then replaced by Camus, whose emphasis on the absurdity of the human condition and nostalgia for a lost simplicity of being were more painlessly assimilated, and answered to the dominant mood.

I V

What makes all this poignant is the simple fact that though the intellectuals lost interest in politics, politics itself went marching on, shamefully—desperately in need of critical scrutiny and principled antagonism. In exploring the climate of opinion of the fifties I don't mean to blame America alone for the cold war or to slight the terror of the Stalinist monolith and the fatuity of its American apologists. I don't mean to suggest that intellectuals should have made common cause with the Party, as Sartre did for a brief period in France, a party that was at once servile and manipulative, philistine and morally and politically bankrupt. Yet, as the historian Allen J. Matusow has written, "the great irony of McCarthyism is that it developed in the absence of any real internal Communist menace; for by 1950 Communism in America had lost whatever influence it once possessed."

However true this may be for the country at large it does not quite apply to the intellectuals. For them the internal menace was real, within the culture, within themselves, like their Jewishness, always threatening a return of the repressed. This fear helps explain the vengeful confessional tone of some political writing during the period ("couch liberalism," as Harold Rosenberg dubbed it). Behind the guilt and animosity looms a burning memory of the thirties, the inculpation in a Great Lie. Even those who were still in knee-pants then felt that they had somehow been taken in, that all radicalism, all politics, had been tainted irrevocably by Stalinism, and that all intellectuals were potential dupes unless ideology gave way to "realism" and complicity were absolved by confession.

It would be hard to find more vicious examples of serious political writing than the first three essays in Leslie Fiedler's *An End to Innocence* (1955), devoted in turn to the Hiss case, the Rosenberg case, and to "McCarthy and the Intellectuals." Fiedler's involvement in the political life of the thirties was practically nil—though in a later book, *Being Busted* (1969), written in a different political climate, after he himself had fallen victim to what he claimed was an official frame-up, he fondly wheels out some schoolboy adventures in radicalism—yet in his fifties essays he endlessly harries his subjects with their failure to confess and takes a confessional tone himself, with nothing to reveal except some "illusions," which quickly turn out to be the illusions of others. Joseph K. in Kafka's *Trial* is charged with no crime but rather stands "accused of guilt"; Fiedler is not content to malign the guilty: he indicts a whole generation for its "innocence."

What lies behind this puzzling assault on language and sense is a psychodrama on the theme of "growing up," in which radicalism and social hope equals childishness, while maturity demands the acceptance of middle-class values, society as it is, the tragic ambiguity of all worldly commitment, all action.* This coming to maturity for the once-alienated intellectual requires the traumatic *rite de passage* of public repentance. Thus Whittaker Chambers qualifies as a tragic figure, the "scorned squealer" who deserves our empathy since he suffers for all of us. Alger Hiss, on the other hand, is a "hopeless liar," "the Popular Front mind at bay." Why? Not simply because he is guilty, though Fiedler hasn't the faintest doubt of that, but because he refuses to put away childish things: unwilling to "speak aloud a common recognition of complicity," he cuts himself off from "the great privilege of confession."

The religious (and markedly Christian) tone and fervor of these bizarre comments is even more intense in the essay on the Rosenbergs, which after twenty pages of vituperation concludes that "we should have offered them grace," yes grace—not mercy or clemency but grace, "even to those who most blasphemously deny their

---

* A glance through the back volumes of *Commentary* or *Encounter* would disclose many curious playlets on this theme, for instance Alan Westin's "Libertarian Precepts and Subversive Realities: Some Lessons Learned in the School of Experience," *Commentary* (January 1955), an article whose very title speaks volumes. Many civil liberties, it suggests, are fine abstractions, but must bend to meet the hard realities of subversion. Libertarians, however well intentioned, who insist on "an absolutist framework," who are "unwilling to make the necessary compromises," risk leaving society "without the means of *making necessary judgments and distinctions* in coping with the formidable problem offered by the agents, *conscious or otherwise*, of a hostile foreign power." (Italics mine.)

own humanity" (that is, by refusing to confess). The Rosenbergs should have been spared not for *their* sake but to ratify our own godlike virtue and superiority. America! America! indeed.

Fiedler refuses even to entertain the possibility that Hiss or the Rosenbergs might not have all that much to confess. 'Twere to consider too curiously to consider so. To consider it would shatter his faith in American institutions: "One would have to believe the judges and public officials of the United States to be not merely the Fascists the Rosenbergs called them, but monsters, insensate beasts." But the record, even the record available when Fiedler wrote, provides abundant evidence for the most extreme judgment. There is no more horrifying document of cold war hysteria than Judge Kaufman's notorious remarks as he sentenced the couple to death. Full of inflamed rhetoric about the deadly struggle with Communism, the "challenge to our very existence," he accused them of "devoting themselves to the Russian ideology of denial of God, denial of the sanctity of the individual and aggression against free men everywhere instead of serving the cause of liberty and freedom":

> I consider your crime worse than murder. . . . I believe your conduct in putting into the hands of the Russians the A-bomb years before our best scientists predicted Russia would perfect the bomb has already caused, in my opinion, the Communist aggression in Korea, with the resultant casualties exceeding fifty thousand and who knows but that millions more of innocent people may pay the price of your treason. Indeed, by your betrayal you undoubtedly have altered the course of history to the disadvantage of our country.

Never mind that scientists then and since have labeled the A-bomb charge simplistic nonsense. All the frustrations of postwar foreign policy, all our fantasies of an enemy within to which this nation of immigrants has proved especially vulnerable, demanded a scapegoat. President Eisenhower went even further in his last-minute refusal of clemency: "I can only say that, by immeasurably increasing the chances of atomic war, the Rosenbergs may have condemned to death tens of millions of innocent people." * Who can establish in-

* I take these quotations from Walter and Miriam Schneir's excellent brief on the case, *Invitation to an Inquest* (1965).

nocence for what has not yet happened? Who dare ask mercy for the destruction of the world?

What these judges and public officials do so grossly, what Fiedler and Robert Warshow—whose essay on the Rosenbergs is a companion piece to Fiedler's—do more ingeniously, is to completely dehumanize the Rosenbergs and turn their execution into an impersonal act, almost a merciful one. (This casts a rather sickly glow on Judge Kaufman's banner of "the sanctity of the individual." As individuals the Rosenbergs were accorded not much more sanctity than the defendants in the Moscow purge trials.) In line with the strategy of blaming the victim, they accuse the Rosenbergs of having destroyed themselves—by adhering to ideology, by becoming a "case." Both Fiedler and Warshow analyze the published prison letters of the couple to demonstrate their vulgarity of mind, "the awkwardness and falsity," says Warshow, "of the Rosenbergs' relations to culture, to sports, and to themselves." The supposed meaning is that "almost nothing really belonged to them, not even their own experience." The implicit moral is that they were so empty, so crude, so bereft of style that there was nothing for the electric-chair to kill. It takes Fiedler with his talent for blatant absurdity to announce this message clearly: "they failed in the end to become martyrs or heroes, or even men. *What was there left to die?*" (Italics mine.)

What all this postmortem textual criticism, with its vengefulness and personal animosity, tells us about the issues in the case is hard to fathom, but from our vantage point it tells us much about the cold war mentality of 1953 (especially as expressed in the two leading journals of intellectual anti-Communism, *Commentary* and *Encounter*, where the articles first appeared). For all their political, even propagandistic intent, both essays show an eerie displacement of politics into aesthetics: issues of power and justice—indeed, of human life itself—are argued in terms of taste and style. For these two clever critics the Rosenberg letters are a godsend, a text, life in an orderly bundle. In their mixture of high-minded platitudes about politics and middlebrow cultural opinions, the letters provide an ideal foil for the myopic fifties highbrow with an axe to grind, for the literary mentality with a tendentious cult of style. The unity of personality—in this case the Popular Front personality—that E. L. Doctorow would grasp so beautifully in his novel about the case, *The Book of Daniel*, completely eluded Fiedler and Warshow, or proved too threatening for them. The strange synthesis of Communism, Judaism, idealism, and Americanism, so characteristic of the Popular Front period (with its stress on Communism as "twentieth-century Americanism"), they could only read as proof of insincerity, though it's familiar enough to anyone who grew up with an uncle in the Party or a parent in a CIO union.

For Fiedler and Warshow the vulgar middlebrow Jew is a cultural embarrassment who must be exorcised so that the highbrow critic can confirm his place in the kingdom of art. The Jewish radical, the quaint Popular Front "progressive," will be sacrificed so that the children of immigrants, the despised intellectuals with their foreign ideas, can become full-fledged Americans.

Years earlier Warshow himself had criticized a novel by Lionel Trilling for its failure to portray the "deep psychological drives" involved in the Stalinist experience and its aftermath, and for suppressing the dominant Jewish involvement in the radical politics of the thirties. That was in 1947. By 1953, when the Rosenbergs were finally killed, that Jewish element had been trumpeted for years in the world's headlines. The deep psychological drives of a Warshow or a Fiedler are as understandable, however unforgivable, as the quiet terror of many ordinary Jews that a pogrom was in the works (despite the thoughtfulness of the courts in providing the Rosenbergs with a Jewish judge and Jewish prosecutors). What was buried with the Rosenbergs, a few months after Eisenhower took office, was two decades of American (and Jewish) Marxism, and two centuries of a different innocence from the kind Fiedler attacks: the innocence of a nation convinced it could play the world's good citizen and moral arbiter. "Watch out!" wrote Sartre the day after the executions. "America has the rabies!" If the substance of idealism was shattered, however, the rhetoric and its illusions lived on to fight another day. It took the Vietnam war to expose the emperor's clothes and shake his righteous self-assurance.

V

I have put such emphasis on the Rosenberg case not only because of its magnitude but because by the early fifties the Jew was well on his way to becoming the American Everyman, as the black would be in the early sixties. In the wake of the Holocaust the fate of the Jew, to many, had become a parable of the human condition: a drama of pointless, horrendous suffering that revealed the modern dimensions of terror and evil. Now, in the postwar period, the relentless hunt for traces of Communism in American life was bound to have an inordinate effect on the Jews, who had been as deeply implicated as any group in the radicalism of the thirties and the fellow-traveling of the forties. In the essays of Fiedler and Warshow, as in the fiction of Bellow and Delmore Schwartz, we feel the impact of these new shocks: we see evidence of the Jewish psyche taking stock of itself, revising itself, recoiling from its recent historical role.

Red-baiting did not begin with Senator McCarthy, a latecomer who appeared when some of the battles had already been fought. The forgetting of the thirties and of the wartime Russian alliance had been in full swing in American society since 1946, with liberals like Humphrey vying with right-wingers for initiative on the issue. It was President Truman who created a massive loyalty-review apparatus for government employees early in 1947, though this probably affected Jews less than the purge of left-wing unions in the CIO and the hearings of the House Un-American Activities Committee on the entertainment industry. It was Truman's attorney general who created a list of "subversive" organizations, which circumvented due process, undermined constitutional rights, intimidated dissent, and became a boon to every witch-hunter and blacklister in the land. By 1949 the leaders of the Communist Party had already been prosecuted under the dubious terms of the Smith Act, which had been passed with Communist support in 1940 as an instrument against fascism.* When McCarthy made his famous list-waving debut as a

* On this point and others see the spirited and generally fair-minded history of the American Communist Party by Irving Howe and Lewis Coser, published in 1957.

Red-hunter in Wheeling, West Virginia, in February 1950, he was seizing and exploiting—and soon personifying—a situation that had been years in the making and was especially ripe for a right-wing demagogue.

It happens that 1950 was also the year in which Bernard Malamud began publishing the stories that were eventually collected in *The Magic Barrel*. Nowhere do we see the revised version of the Jewish psyche more clearly expressed, more poignantly imagined, than in Malamud's work. Needless to say, his books show no trace of the McCarthy period, no trace of politics of any sort (at least until the flawed historical novel *The Fixer* in 1966); this is one thing that helps make him one of the quintessential writers of the fifties. "Revised" is an odd word to apply to Malamud since he is the most deeply traditional of the Jewish novelists, traditional in his unrivaled grasp of the Jewish imagination of disaster, traditional in his authentic stock of immigrant and second-generation characters, traditional above all in the very feel of his stories—his preference for moral fables and realistic storytelling over modernist experiments in technique and narrative consciousness. In fact it is Malamud's genius in *The Magic Barrel* and in his best novel, *The Assistant* (1957), to combine a distilled accuracy of urban Jewish speech and scene with a mode of poetic parable reminiscent of Hawthorne, or of his older Yiddish contemporary, I. B. Singer. But this succeeds only within a narrow imaginative range. Malamud's best work is built around a few obsessive metaphors and situations. From the pathetic little grocery store in *The Assistant* to the actual prison in *The Fixer* to the abandoned tenement in *The Tenants* (1971), he sees the world in Pascal's terms as a prison-house from which we are led off one by one to die. His protagonists, whose names are as similar as his titles, are all rooted in the schlemiel figure of the Jewish folk tradition: anti-heroes thwarted at every turn, sometimes comically, sometimes horrifically—ordinary souls with a rare talent for catastrophe. To be a Jew is to suffer—this is the simple moral equation at the heart of *The Assistant*—and the only proper response to suffering is quiet stoicism and stubborn if hopeless decency. Morris Bober, the grocer, is a Good Man, for all the good that does him.

If the prison-house metaphor suggests the influence of existentialism (or a parallel to it), the theme of suffering and endurance is more authentically Jewish, distilling as it does much of the grimmest of Jewish historical experience, so apocalyptically renewed in this century with the destruction of the European communities. But it is one thing—though perhaps too limited—to convey the experience of suffering, to capture the banal, grinding agony of the small shopkeeper eking out a marginal living; this is a heartrending achievement (though I feel that, intent on an allegory of Man Alone, he screens out the compensatory joys of religious, communal, or family life). But it is quite another thing to put a high moral valuation on this agony; there is a strain in Malamud's work that is more Christian than Jewish, an emphasis on bearing the cross, on suffering-for-others, on salvation through suffering. When Frank Alpine, the Italian assistant, asks the old storekeeper, "Why do you suffer, Morris?" he calmly answers, "I suffer for you." At the heart of Malamud's work is a quasi-religious theme of salvation, as when Alpine finally becomes a Jew and takes on his back the same wretched store, the same wretched life, that had crushed his dead employer.

What do these timeless patterns of suffering and redemption have to do with the 1950s, when they were conceived? There is little sense of specific historical time in *The Assistant*. Though nominally set in the 1930s, its historical matrix is as shadowy as its New York milieu is claustral and specter-like. Yet I believe this tells us a great deal about the period when it was written. As Ruth Wisse shows in her fine study *The Schlemiel as Modern Hero*, the schlemiel character became dear to Jewish folklore as a vehicle of spiritual transcendence amid constrained and sometimes desperate social circumstances. As in farce, where the most extreme violence is rendered harmless and absurd, the schlemiel, usually a comic figure, provides a catharsis of catastrophe and pain, a way of coping. Wisse says that Sholom Aleichem, in adapting this folk-motif, "conceived of his writing as a solace for people whose situation was so ineluctably unpleasant that they might as well laugh. The Jews of his works are a kind of schlemiel people, powerless and unlucky, but psychologically, or, as one used to say, spiritually, the victors in defeat." Maurice Samuel makes a similar point about Sholom Aleichem's "application of a fantastic technique that the Jews had developed over the ages . . . a technique of avoidance and sublimation. . . . They had found the trick of converting disaster into a verbal triumph, applying a sort of Talmudic ingenuity of interpretation to events they could not handle in their reality." The schlemiel (or the schlemiel people) achieves a victory of mind or heart, even in the shadow of the iron fist.

Yet such a strategy can be deeply quietistic and evasive—quite literally "fantastic," as Samuel says—especially in circumstances less constricting than the Russian pale or the Polish ghetto. Even there, as currents of socialism, Zionism, and the Hebrew Enlightenment spread among the people, some of Sholom Aleichem's contemporaries were scornful of these folk attitudes and psychological habits. Wisse suggests that the most famous schlemiel story in Yiddish literature, Y. L. Peretz's "Bontshe the Silent," which is "now widely regarded as a study of sainthood, is actually a socialist's exposure of the grotesquerie of suffering silence; Chaim Nachman Bialik's response to the infamous Kishinev pogrom was outrage against the *victims* who flee or hide, pretending that vengeance will come from God." The controversy that has flared repeatedly over Jewish behavior under Nazi occupation and in the death camps is an extension of the same quarrel, the same anguish, on an immensely more horrific scale.

In its own way then, Bernard Malamud's work can be seen as one kind of response to the frozen and quietly fear-ridden political atmosphere of the McCarthy and Eisenhower years. This is not to say that it's not deeply imagined, with profound roots in the Jewish psyche and the Jewish moral tradition. Yet that tradition has many branches, not simply its line of Jacob—sensitive, wily, domestic, passive, fed by mother-love—but also its thwarted line of Esau—hairy hunter, "activist," doomed favorite of the father. The Jewish novel of the 1950s is a reversion to the line of Jacob, *an atonement for Jewish radicalism* that is also perfectly in tune with the wider currents of the age: ruminative, private, morally austere and self-conscious, apolitical.

Finally, the literature and politics of the period are one. There is no special "key" to the sensibility of the age: almost anything works if we turn it right and press it hard. But the Jewish novel works especially well. The fifties were a great period for home and family, for getting and spending, for cultivating one's garden. All that is reflected in its writing. But its spokesmen also called it an Age of Anxiety; behind its material growth hovers a quiet despair, whose symbols are the Bomb and the still-vivid death camps and a fear of Armageddon that rings true even in the monstous phrases of a Judge Kaufman. But this anxiety is metaphysical and hermetic, closed in upon itself: the Bomb evokes despair rather than anger or opposition. The Jewish novel reflects this spirit and ministers to it, for it is literally overwrought—anguish hemmed in by form—offering finally the uneasy absolution of art for a torment whose origin it cannot know and whose course it cannot alter.

3

The Rise of
a New Sensibility,
or How the Fifties
Broke Up

I

The sensibilty of an era may be unified but it's never uniform. The retrospective observer can make out the dominant themes, the key lines of influence. If he does this grossly, he can easily flatten each phase of history into a false unity; if he does it with any sense of the complexity of life and the dynamics of change—as Hegel does in writing history or Malraux in art history—he can take pleasure in singling out the minor theme that will become major, the aberration that will serve as a carrier to the next generation, or what D. H. Lawrence described as "the new shoots of life springing up and slowly bursting the foundations."

Certainly one of the dominant notes of the 1950s was its moralism, which I have described as the displacement of concrete political issues into abstract moral ones. With an eye on the human condition as a whole, the fifties moralist could hardly lower his olympian sights to attend to the individual lot of man-in-society. In this context

Norman Mailer was a particularly significant dissenting figure. For a time he remained rooted in the residual political culture of the forties, which distinguished his fiction but also proved to be something of a dead weight. Gradually, like the rest of America, he shifted from a Marxian to a Freudian terrain. Like other fifties radicals he was most effective, and most prophetic, in the psychosexual sphere rather than in the old political one. He became adept at invoking the official values of the fifties against the lived reality. In essays like "The White Negro" he took the moralism of the fifties seriously but inverted its content. He took the individualism of the fifties seriously too, but without its stoical overtones. Where repression was, let liberation be: this was the message not only of Mailer but of a whole new line of Freudian (or Reichian) radicalism, which did so much to undermine the intellectual consensus of the cold war period.

"These have been the years of confirmity and depression," Mailer wrote in 1957 in "The White Negro." "A stench of fear has come out of every pore of American life, and we suffer from a collective failure of nerve." The men of the fifties prided themselves on a moral depth beyond the duplicities of politics, yet their period will surely be known for its ultimate moral cowardice, as a time when, in Mailer's words, "one could hardly maintain the courage to be individual, to speak with one's own voice." Yet only after three groping, questing, fascinating novels did the young writer manage to break through into *his* own voice.

Mailer's emphasis on courage does not primarily refer to the courage to oppose what we now think of as the most specific vices of the fifties: blacklists and union purges, the cold war, the intimidation of dissent, and the jailing of supposed Communists. Beleaguered liberals were caught between fighting these abuses and joining them, to prove their own purity. Mailer asserts that the collective opposition has failed, that "the only courage, with rare exceptions, that we have been witness to, has been the isolated courage of isolated people." Mailer himself, a celebrated young author, had made his debut in politics campaigning for Henry Wallace and the Progressive party in 1948. In a sense all three of his early books were political novels.

But he insists that by 1957 "the years in which one could complacently accept oneself as part of an elite by being a radical were forever gone."

Instead the courage that Mailer honors—his totem is Hemingway—is the courage to be, the strength to face up to death and violence, including the death and violence in oneself. The Mailer of "The White Negro" is nothing if not a man of his time. For him too the political nostrums have failed, the only salvation is individual and religious. Every age has a tendency (as Hegel and Plato long ago demonstrated) to cultivate its own principle of decay, to foster the spirit that will eventually overthrow it. The hipster figure who stalks through Mailer's manifesto is a typical product of the existentialist brooding of the fifties. The hipster cuts through and exploits the hypocrisy of the period, the rampant cynicism about honor and social role-playing that lies just beneath the surface of its official pieties. The Organization Man of the fifties, like the con-man intellectual living off the foundations, knows that the old dreams and ideals are finished, that it's all a game, just as Mailer's hipster knows from Hemingway that "in a bad world there is no love nor mercy nor charity nor justice unless a man can keep his courage . . . that what made him feel good became therefore The Good."

In "The White Negro" Mailer calls on the myths and values of the fifties only to undermine them. Where the fifties had substituted the isolated man, the competitive capitalist monad, for the radical dream of collective man in a just community, Mailer brandished the figure of a Nietzschean adventurer seeking experience beyond good and evil. Where the fifties had substituted religion for Marxism, Mailer discovered "the American existentialist" who transcended the sham of suburban religiosity and churchgoing. Where the fifties theorized about totalitarianism in far-off places, Mailer found a creeping totalitarianism here at home, "a slow death by conformity," he said, "with every creative and rebellious instinct stifled." Mailer's psychopathic hero is a bomb that explodes beneath the bland surface of the fifties, constructed out of all its repressed violence and rebelliousness, composed of the longings for personal autonomy and extreme experience that could not be satisfied by respectability, domesticity, maturity, and competitive success. The fifties also believed in love, if its popular plays, songs, and books are to be credited, and here too Mailer expropriates the decade's values for his own purpose. "At bottom," he says, "the drama of the psychopath is that he seeks love. Not love as the search for a mate, but love as the search for an orgasm more apocalyptic than the one which preceded it. . . . But in this search, the psychopath becomes an embodiment of the extreme contradictions of the society which formed his character. . . ." At bottom Mailer's purpose is to explore those contradictions—and the contradictions in himself—not to recommend violence. The key works of the new sensibility are all disguised or overt critiques of the fifties, written during that time but suffused with a sense of isolation unparalleled in our cultural life since the first stirrings of modernism.

The appearance of stridently rebellious works like "The White Negro" in the late fifties inevitably complicates our picture and makes it more difficult for us to treat the whole era as a single entity. In fact of course the sensibility of any period is plural, its strands diverse and contradictory. What we in hindsight call change is usually, as I have noted, the unexpected swelling of a minor current as it imperceptibly becomes a major one, and alters the prevailing mood. We can now see that such a change was occurring in the late fifties, and it was prophetic of Mailer and Paul Goodman (in *Growing Up Absurd*) to seize on the beat and hip phenomena, as well as the plague of delinquency and youthful anomie, as cracks in the whole system, harbingers of a new spirit they themselves only dimly anticipated. Though dissent during the period remained strictly theoretical, the late fifties saw the publication of a number of books, creative as well as analytical, that were deeply hostile to the dominant spirit of the age. A number of them became canonical works of the sixties, much to the surprise of their authors, who often failed to do work that was nearly as good once the winds had shifted in their direction. Whatever this reveals about the uses of alienation in the life of the mind, it remains fascinatingly true that the cultural revolution of the sixties was one of the startling instances of the precedence of theory over practice. The immediate intellectual underpinnings of the sixties appear in the dissident works of the late fifties. It is this ferment of criticism and theory and its connection to later developments in art and society that I wish to explore here.

I I

Whatever the virtue of alienation in fostering originality, no thought or imagination occurs entirely in a vacuum; the decline of the cold war consensus in the cultural sphere in the late fifties runs parallel to a gradual dismantling of the cold war itself. The heyday of McCarthyism in the United States coincided with the Korean War and the last psychotic phase of Stalinism in the Soviet Union. But Stalin died in 1953, the war ended in 1954, and by December of that year McCarthy had been censured by his colleagues in the Senate. Eisenhower, the general-turned-president who frequently expressed his desire to go down in history as a man of peace, met with Stalin's successors in the first of a series of summit conferences, which signaled the first gingerly steps of a military and political détente. When the Russians launched their Sputnik satellite in 1957 our competitive furies found a new peaceful channel. Washington woke up to a "crisis" in education, and soon "defense" money, aimed at a crash program in foreign languages, was inadvertently helping to fund departments of comparative literature. As William Leuchtenburg has written: "What a generation of liberals clamoring for federal aid to education had failed to achieve, the cold war accomplished almost overnight."

There were other portents in the political sphere, such as the 1954 Supreme Court decision against segregated school systems. But it wasn't till 1957 that the Court saw the consolidation of a thin liberal majority on other issues, especially civil liberties, which had been dangerously eroded, thanks to "judicial restraint," during the

McCarthy period. And in Montgomery, Alabama, a bus boycott organized by a young minister named Martin Luther King not only extended the challenge to segregation beyond the educational sphere but inaugurated the tactics of direct action that were to play a fateful role in the politics of the sixties.

These were only portents, however, and some of them took fifteen years to come to fruition. The rigidities of the political arena continued to make it impossible for serious issues to get a hearing or find a reputable sponsor. John Kennedy campaigned for the presidency in 1960 as a "realist," though this did not prevent him from hammering away at a nonexistent "missile gap" or from promising a more "flexible" military posture which—by turning from nuclear deterrence to tactical strategies—would eventually get us into the longest war in our history. In his television debates with Nixon, Kennedy took an especially hard line on Castro's Cuba, then still in its pre-Communist stage, and the two could find little to disagree about except for two offshore islands near China. Like so many American elections it became a contest of images, with Nixon's runny makeup and shifty, thug-like appearance deciding the show. As for the issues the *New York Times* (October 16, 1960) commented that the contest had "come more and more to focus on one question. . . . Which nominee would provide the nation with the best leadership in the cold war?" (In that respect the campaign resembled Roosevelt's performance in 1932, *plus royaliste que le roi,* with the candidate attacking Hoover for failing to balance the budget, yet somehow managing to signal a new sort of energy and concern.)

Yet by 1960 a growing body of opinion in the United States had ceased to accept the suppositions on which the cold war was based. How widespread this shift was in the public at large is hard to gauge, for the politicians offered little direct choice, and more than ten years of propaganda had muffled every trace of dissent. But Kennedy's narrow victory showed that "downgrading America" (as Nixon called it) was no longer necessarily fatal for a national candidate. The beginnings of a new critical outlook can be traced much more clearly among intellectuals, who in the early fifties had largely succumbed to the pro-American, anti-Communist, anti-political attitudes of their countrymen.

This ferment was especially marked among the New York intellectuals, where anti-Stalinism had spilled over into anti-radicalism, depoliticization, a bland pluralism, and sometimes even art for art's sake. Yet even in reaction the New York intellectuals retained more Marxism than most other Americans had ever had. No one was a more eloquent defender of the autonomy of art—and critic of Marxist criticism—than Lionel Trilling; but like Edmund Wilson he remained fundamentally a historical critic, a breed that the New Criticism had presumed to abolish; at moments he seemed to embody a more subtle, revisionist Marxism—a Marxism fed on the tradition of English cultural criticism from Burke and Coleridge to Ruskin and Arnold, in its own way a deeply historicist tradition.

In one form or another this sort of quirky personal synthesis characterized many of the New York intellectuals: their work maintained a political cast, and often a radical rhetoric, even in flight from politics, and they tended naturally to think of literature and the arts in political terms. Yet often they remained shackled by their long struggle with Stalinism, so that their passion for general ideas could never again accept any systematic theory, could express itself only in a cult of brilliance (as Irving Howe noted), or in a hidden tendentiousness that vitiated their claims of objectivity. As C. Wright Mills, the quintessential fifties maverick, said of those who proclaimed the End of Ideology:

> Practitioners of the no-more-ideology school do of course smuggle in general ideas under the guise of reportage, by intellectual gossip, and by their selection of the notions they handle. Ultimately, the-end-of-ideology is based upon a disillusionment with any real commitment to socialism in any recognizable form. *That* is the only "ideology" that has really ended for these writers. But with its ending, *all* ideology, they think, has ended. *That* ideology they talk about; their own ideological assumptions, they do not.

As Mills intimates, and as his own work shows, it was not those who had been most deeply involved with Stalinism who first made a sharp break with the fifties consensus, but rather those who had been too young in the thirties, or had maintained an isolated radical position all along, such as Goodman and Harold Rosenberg, or those who had been driven to new positions by the barren spirit of the fifties itself, like Mailer and Mills. Characteristically, these men wrote for *Politics* in the forties, *Dissent* in the fifties, and *Partisan Review* occasionally, but remained isolated even within these small circles. Their roots and allegiances were more idiosyncratic, going back not to Stalinism or even classical Marxism but to anarchism or Trotskyism, to Reich or Weber, Herzen or Kropotkin. These models made them philosophers and (usually) libertarians, but only the world of the fifties made them prophets and important social critics.

III

I can well remember the impact that C. Wright Mills' work had on us as undergraduates in the late fifties. He seemed like the one bold spirit in the gray, gray crew of American social science. As it happens I wasn't much interested in social science but Mills' polemical tract of 1958, *The Causes of World War Three*, captured the irrational atmosphere of that era perfectly: the cold war, the Dulles policy of armed deterrence and "massive retaliation," the cheerful preparations for nuclear Armageddon. When Mills (like Sartre) also took up the cause of Castro's Cuba—against an increasingly hostile American policy there—we cheered. (Castro in his pre-Leninist phase was another of our idols: the compleat hippie revolutionary.) I knew that my elders at Columbia considered Mills shallow and unsound, a dangerous simplifier—and the part of me that was innoculated against ideology, that considered the world too ambiguous and complex for any sweeping theories, shared their misgivings. Later, after his death, when his collected essays were published in 1963, one reviewer could assert complacently that poor Mills had disintegrated well-meaningly from a crack professional to a crude polemicist in his last years.

Somehow, though Mills' work was widely taught in the decade that followed, the judgment stuck. He was no longer around to develop his position and keep in touch with the new culture he had fostered (as Paul Goodman and Herbert Marcuse could). But a glance at a late essay like "Culture and Politics" (1959) shows the weakness of such a schematic view of Mills' career. Far from revealing the decline of a good sociologist into a bad editorialist, the essay more than makes up in pointed generalization for what it lacks in empirical data. From early on in his career Mills was no statistics man swimming in jargon but an almost novelistic observer of social change and the distribution of social power, the kind of observer who is also a citizen, who is committed, who makes judgments. He concludes *White Collar* (1951) with a troubled analysis of the political indifference of the men of the "new middle classes" (who are "not radical, not liberal, not conservative, not reactionary; they are inactionary; they are out of it"). In the chapter on intellectuals, "Brains, Inc.," he shows how more and more of the educated have become technicians and corporate hired hands, "unable to face politics except as news and entertainment," while "the remaining free intellectuals increasingly withdraw . . . they lack the will."

He goes on to attack "the cult of alienation" (the cherished despair of the literary culture) and "the fetish of objectivity" (the pose of the technician in the social sciences). The *Angst* of the former, he says, is a rationalization of political defeat, "a fashionable way of being overwhelmed," while the "narrowed attention" of the latter is uncritical: it bespeaks the man "who assumes as given the big framework and the political meaning of his operation within it." Mills himself is the prototype of the advocacy intellectual of the sixties, self-conscious about the social role of his profession and imbued with an old-fashioned sense of the moral and political responsibility of the intelligentsia (a commitment that differs from that of the Old Left in its loyalty to the truth, not simply to the Cause).

In "Culture and Politics" Mills takes up one of the chief themes of his earlier work: the growing inadequacy of liberalism and socialism, our two chief social models, to account for the changes in

American (or Soviet) society in the last decades. Both models, he says, presume a degree of citizen rationality—whether we call it political awareness, class-consciousness, or economic self-interest—that could bring power in society under the sway of the popular will. But in both major nations democracy has been thwarted by overdevelopment, the expansion of corporate, state, or military power, the growth of bureaucracy, and the proliferation of unheard-of means of manipulating opinion.

In *White Collar* Mills had zestfully analyzed our departures from the classical models, from small-scale competitive individualism and the traditional proletariat; his aim was to bring the nineteenth century up to date. But Mills' later work is darkened by the increasing irrationality of the rationalization of the system: something has gotten out of hand that defeats analysis, defeats planning, destroys the possibility of choice. He fears that "the ideas of freedom and reason have become moot; that increased rationality may not be assumed to make for increased freedom." Mills' chief targets are the highly rational—and insane—preparations for a third world war, the gradual convergence of the policies and social systems of the two superstates, and the dominance of both by powerful elites who make of democracy "more a formal outline than an actuality."

This last point would be further developed by Marcuse in the sixties, though not from Mills' more libertarian perspective. Perhaps dominated by his experience of German totalitarianism, Marcuse would depict the individual entrapped in a Kafkaesque vise, in which every apparent increase in freedom would actually signify another turn of the screw. Mills, like Paul Goodman, was basically an optimist in the American mold. (It took many years for Marcuse to acknowledge the "new spirit" among the young, which Mills and Goodman were already writing about in 1960.) Mills considered himself a "radical humanist" whose faith was that man makes his own history, and even the rise of powerful elites he took, quite inconsistently, as evidence that "the scope and the chance for conscious human agency in history-making are just now uniquely available."

Within a year after he wrote these words in "Culture and Politics,'' Mills was emboldened by the first signs of a New Left awakening in many countries, for 1960 was a year of worldwide student outbreaks: riots that shook anti-Communist governments in Turkey, Japan, and South Korea; the Aldermaston march against nuclear weapons in England; the beginnings of civil disobedience in the United States—which did not yet conform to this global pattern of student politicization—from lunch-counter sit-ins in the South to a massive sit-in against the House Un-American Activities Committee in San Francisco, during which more than 600 people were arrested.

In his famous letter to the *New Left Review* in England that year Mills welcomed these developments, and disagreed with those in the New Left who clung to the working class as the agent of historical change. ''Such a labor metaphysic,'' he said, ''is a legacy from Victorian Marxism that is now quite unrealistic.'' Instead he nominated ''the young intelligentsia'' as the harbingers of a new society.

In time Mills' antagonists, the spokesmen for the end of ideology, would seize upon another intelligentsia, the technical intelligentsia, as the agents of their own brand of social change—''technetronic'' rather than humanistic, elitist rather than participatory. In 1961 the reign of the expert and the whiz-kid would begin in Washington, the anointing of the intellectual-as-technician whose ominous emergence Mills had noted ten years earlier. Cased in his own ideological blinders, impervious even to intelligence data, this whiz-kid would do what Eisenhower and Dulles, for all their cold-war rhetoric, never had done: take us to war to save the world from Communism. The home-front battle between these two intelligentsias in the sixties would reveal an America caught at a crossroad of history, torn between two violently conflicting social ideals.

I V

The ascendancy of the technocratic forces in the sixties would fuel the dissidence of academic intellectuals, the New Left, and the counterculture, until that dissidence would break up on the rocks of its own frustrations—its inability to affect policy, to elect candidates, or even to preserve its own integrity in the face of failure and backlash. The theoretical anticipations of the new sensibility in the late fifties had no such problems. Lacking any likelihood of objective change they were utopian leaps-in-the-dark, full of the *bonne conscience* of enlightened alienation, brilliantly waspish in their critique of the mood of the fifties, and boldly speculating in the grand manner on what Norman O. Brown called "the nature and destiny of man."

In retrospect we can see that—apart from the repressive politics of the age, which do have their own malign distinctiveness—the fifties were less a distinct cultural period than the last phase, the decadent, academic phase, of the modernist sensibility of the twenties. Nothing could have been more at variance with the cautious and well-bred atmosphere of the fifties than the volatile mixture of critique and speculation that we find in its dissident utopian theorists. Commenting on his own contemporaries in 1957, Norman Podhoretz saw "a certain justice in regarding the young generation as a non-generation, a collection of people who, for all their apparent command of themselves, for all the dispatch with which they have taken their places in society, for all their sophistication, for all their 'maturity,' know nothing, stand for nothing, believe in nothing." He also saw this false and willed maturity, this premature adulthood, as the characteristic flaw of the literature of the period, "a literature of an unearned maturity, a maturity almost wholly divorced from experience, an expression, really, of the fear of experience."

Podhoretz's article on "The Young Generation" provides a shrewd insight into the intellectuality of the period, a style of mind so different from the more critical and apocalyptic noises that were already beginning to disrupt it. "Everything that happens to these young people seems immediately to be milked of its 'meaning' before it has a chance to make an impact; everything must be understood before it gets out of control." This helps explain the enormous prestige of criticism—i.e., interpretation and cultural dogmatics—in a period that had after all very little of the critical spirit. It also casts light on the single greatest paradox of the literary culture: the wor-

shipful acceptance of modernist literature—its academic canoniza-
tion—combined with a tactical retreat from the radical, experimental
edge of modernism, into a literature of limited risks, smooth surfaces, and small, poetic intensities. Podhoretz's article concludes
with a canny prediction; deep down his generation has grown restless, he says, and "it is beginning to feel cheated of its youth. . . .
Since this is a generation that willed itself from childhood directly
into adulthood, it still has its adolescence to go through—for a man
can never skip adolescence, he can only postpone it." In the event,
the impetus for change certainly did *not* come from the sophisticated
young intellectuals of the fifties; but in its perception of the culture at
large, the comment would prove to be prophetic.

Richard Chase's almost forgotten book *The Democratic Vista*
(1958) developed, in its good-natured way, an even more withering
critique of the prevailing mood. Chase was the only writer of the fifties to grasp fully the "interim" character of the period. He saw
clearly that the withdrawal of thinking men into domestic or material
concerns could not last, for the action on the historical stage would
continue, and ultimately affect the private life in drastic and unsettling ways. True to the spirit of Whitman invoked in his title,
Chase's attack is neither wholly political nor strictly cultural, but a
rich if sometimes contradictory mixture of the two. Chase sees the
parallel between two of the most confident assumptions of the fifties— the end of ideology in politics and the death of the avant-garde
in art—and demolishes both. "Why should we think of ideology as
coming in 'ages'?" he asks. "It is one of the natural and perennial
weapons of the mind and is generated anew whenever the mind
applies itself, not just to 'the art of living,' but to social realities as
they are working themselves out in history. I doubt if either social reality or history has disappeared. . . ." And similarly in the cultural
sphere: "It is the custom nowadays to pronounce the avant-garde
dead. But the fact seems to be that under modern conditions the
avant-garde is a permanent movement." *

* I quote this passage from its original version in Chase's essay "The Fate of the
Avant-Garde."

Gates of Eden

Despite what he calls the "literary academicism" of the forties and fifties, Chase saw that the urge to experiment with new forms and new modes of consciousness would not disappear simply because it had been wished away. But what interested him even more was the polemical spirit of the avant-garde, its critical, even hostile relation to prevailing social norms. In an age of little political hope, Chase sought to appropriate and to politicize the prestigious but emasculated spirit of modernism. If his contemporaries had retreated from politics into art, Chase would recall them to a more intransigent, less accommodating vision of the relations between art and society; he would revive radicalism by redefining it in cultural terms. If there was no *party* of truth or change, there could at least be a revival of the critical spirit.

Unfortunately Chase's book missed its mark. By casting his message in the form of polite and unconvincing dialogues, including much trivial banter, he weakened the force of the argument and yielded too much to the genteel spirit he took pains to criticize. But Chase's book dulls its cutting edge in still another way: by putting such stress on the cultural sphere Chase ratifies the absence of political hope, and concedes too much to the aestheticism of the fifties and to the notion that—unlike the crisis-ridden thirties—*our* political and economic system is a great success ("illusory as this may eventually prove to be"). But Chase, like Whitman, contradicts himself, and in the conclusion of his discussion of ideology he catalogues the sources of social malaise that lurk beneath the affluent facade. This is the most moving passage of the book, and also the most prophetic:

> Of what value is the new competence in family life if, while we have achieved it, we have surrendered control of the material development of the country? It is time to ask ourselves if a fruitful and humane life will be possible at all in an America full of the flashy and insolent wealth of a permanent war economy, brutalized slums, rampant and dehumanizing Levittowns, race hatred, cynical exploitation and waste of natural resources, government by pressure group, by executive abdication and by Congressional expediency, vulgarization and perhaps the destruction of the schools, not to mention the sporadic flash and fall-out of "nuclear devices." Here are enemies enough. Here is the seedbed of new ideologies.

All these points seem self-evident today, but it took both courage and insight to pursue them in the fifties, when accommodation was the order of the day and militant gestures seemed embarrassing and old-fashioned. Chase disposed of the canard that the problems were all being solved, that there were no more enemies to fight, no evils grave enough to evoke a radical response. While other would-be radicals merely pined nostalgically for the thirties as if nothing could be learned from the Stalinist debacle, Chase directed his attention to the here and now, "dimly imagining the future," he said, "rather than trying to relive the past." "Shall we not hope, at any rate, that the great experience of alert minds in the next decade will be the shock and exhilaration which will follow from our suddenly asking the question, What was happening on the great stage of history while we have been playing our closet dramas?" (Two years later Paul Goodman would put it even better: "One has the persistent thought that if ten thousand people in all walks of life will stand up on their two feet and talk out and insist, we shall get back our country.")

If Richard Chase anticipated the cultural form that the radicalism of the sixties would take, with its emphasis not on political economy but on the quality of the human and natural environment, Harold Rosenberg's work in the fifties also rested on a vision of the interplay of culture and politics. His 1959 collection of essays, *The Tradition of the New,* combined a defense of the avant-garde, especially in painting—the only game in town in the traditionalist fifties—with a witty and devastating assault on the political confusions of the intellectuals, especially the breast-beating ex-liberals like Leslie Fiedler. Along with his friend Goodman, Rosenberg was probably the smartest of the New York intellectuals, the most diversely learned and gifted, the most independent, the most consistently radical. But like some of the others his work abated in interest (though not in brilliance) once he achieved wider recognition. After becoming art critic of *The New Yorker* in the sixties, he almost ceased to write about literature and politics; and the decline of abstract expressionism left him isolated and querulous, the perpetual outsider, even on the art scene, where he continued to exert great influence.

By 1960 even Leslie Fiedler became a small harbinger of cultural change. Without renouncing the venomous anti-Communism of his McCarthy period he stopped writing about politics and turned his Freudian gun-sights on the history of American literature, where genteel standards still largely prevailed and even the pioneering criticism of D. H. Lawrence, let alone the psychology of Freud, had yet to be assimilated. Fiedler's Freud, like that of Marcuse, Brown, and Reich, was the early prophet of sexual fulfillment rather than the old philosopher of stoic renunciation. (Quentin Anderson reviewed *Love and Death in the American Novel* under the heading "All Discontents and No Civilization.") Much in the finger-pointing way he had carried on his political inquisitions, Fiedler summoned the American novelists to the bar of sexual enlightenment and genital maturity (where of course nearly all were found wanting, poor benighted souls). Critics have often haplessly tried to show that they were more intelligent than their subjects—it's hard not to know more than someone who wrote two centuries ago!—but Fiedler was the first critic to try to prove he was more *macho*. Combining loose plot summaries, flimsy generalities, historical half-truths, errors of detail, and ad hominem invective, Fiedler managed to say very little about each of the novels he discussed, as if in reaction to the New Critical explicators, who had tried to say too much. Yet Fiedler did help to break the hold of these blinkered exegetes on American literature, and to introduce Lawrentian psycho-critique into academic criticism. If Mills practiced advocacy sociology Fiedler created his own style of advocacy criticism, though it remained more a style than a workable set of ideas. Nevertheless, his book foreshadowed some of the mutations of literary criticism during the sixties, when the pose of objectivity and the obsession with internal structure and imagery would give way to something wilder, more personal, more intense and apocalyptic—a breakthrough which had its parallels everywhere else in the culture.

Whether Fiedler's book itself made any larger cultural contribution is open to doubt. A few years later in his essay "The New Mutants" Fiedler was one of the first to shed insight on the new sensibility of the sixties, especially on the shifting explorations of sexual identity among the young. But the sexual ethic of *Love and Death* was basically conservative; its Freudianism was tame compared to the speculative work that Marcuse, Brown, and even Trilling had already done. At the time its insistence on sexual explicitness, on the physical realities of passion, seemed then like another blow for liberation from the Victorian literary pruderies of the fifties, a moment which also saw the belated publication of *Lady Chatterley's Lover* and Henry Miller's *Tropic* novels. In retrospect, however, Fiedler's obsession with genital maturity—his inquisitorial, cultural commissar's eye for any trace of adolescent or homoerotic attitudes—seems more closely allied to the would-be sobriety and maturity of the fifties than to the polymorphous perversity—the playful experimentalism—of sex in the sixties. And Fiedler's *literary* preference for the Gothic and the irrational did not extend into any interesting social doctrine to replace the socialism he had once found so tainted. (Later on, long after "The New Mutants," Fiedler's total identification with the youth culture seemed like a desperate attempt to find a charismatic role, to become a guru without really having a message.)

V

The important theoretical works of the new sensibility were the product of a more radical Freudianism than Fiedler was then willing to entertain. Freud had insisted that all civilization was built on repression, but American society in the forties and fifties was far more repressive than the common good required. Freud had made a similar point about the late Victorians, but, as Herbert Marcuse was fond of pointing out, advanced industrial society had perfected methods of manipulation and control—what Marcuse called "surplus-repression"—undreamt of by our straitlaced grandfathers. Marcuse's favorite example was the mass media, especially the electronic media, which had been honed by the Nazis into a unique intrument of propaganda and totalitarian domination, and which (according to Marcuse) served as a subtle weapon of conformity even in the democratic countries, making a hollow shell of our formal liberties and representative institutions.

Without accepting this anlaysis we can acknowledge that America in the early fifties was something less than an open society. The dominion of puritanism in the arts and in domestic and social relationships existed side by side with widespread intimidation in public life, in business, and in the professions. Men who had spent thirty years as movie directors, union officials, or university professors disappeared from their jobs without a trace, became unpersons, a solemn warning to others; those in less exalted positions were undone even more anonymously. The pressure of this environment on the intellectual life can be observed in Marcuse's best book, *Eros and Civilization* (1955), an attempted synthesis of Marx and Freud in which the magic word "Marx" is never mentioned. It's hard to tell how much this self-censorship is due to the paranoia of the refugee, how much to prudent calculation, and how much to Marcuse's own desire to reach an audience inoculated against radicalism.

It's worth asking ourselves why the Freudian radicalism in Marcuse's book, and in the work of Paul Goodman and Norman O. Brown, came to fruition at the time it did, in a period so unsympathetic to radicalism of any kind, and why it had such a dramatic influence on the intellectual life of the sixties. After all, the most striking quality of the cultural life of the sixties, the combination of political militancy and cultural bohemianism, the thirties and the twenties, was precisely in line with those earlier theoretical conjunctions of Marx and Freud. This is not to say the Marcuse was responsible for the counterculture, any more than Mills created the New Left or Goodman fomented the campus uprisings. (Goodman would later be amused and dismayed by young people who spouted his ideas but seemed never to have read a book, spouted them *at him*.) What happened was more than intellectual fashion or Mephistophelean influence. Our society changed for its own deep-seated reasons; society responded in its massive and lumbering way to the same grievous conditions that had first provoked certain intellectuals into critical protest and utopian speculation. As Auden said of Yeats, "Mad Ireland hurt him into poetry."

It's safe to say that few kids became radicals, hippies, or freaks in the sixties from reading *Eros and Civilization* or *Growing Up Absurd*. Similarly, the rioters of Watts, Detroit, and Newark had not learned their discontent from LeRoi Jones, Stokely Carmichael, or even Martin Luther King. Like the children of the white middle class, they were acting out the logic of their own lives, though it sometimes took the language of ideology to convince them that their discontent mattered. The tremors of the sixties, which shook institutions in so many remote corners of society, were generated from society's own deep core, from all those problems neglected in the fifties that could no longer be wished away, the same problems that men like Mills, Chase, Goodman, and Marcuse—to say nothing of sociological popularizers like Vance Packard and William Whyte— had already gone far toward identifying.

What complicated this parallel between thought and practice is that so many of the disaffected in the sixties were the products of affluence and education rather than deprivation. Their predecessors, the younger generation in the fifties, had played hard to win, but *they* were challenging the rules of the game or refusing to play at all. The intelligentsia of the fifties, centered in a few cities and a few universities, were a self-conscious elite disdainful of mass society and middlebrow vulgarity. But the "young intelligentsia" whom Mills had identified as agents of change were to become an amorphous mass spread out across thousands of colleges and communes, in the country and the city, whose culture enshrined music and films and drugs more than books, but who adopted certain books that rationalized their discontent and gave it a structure, books that helped them articulate a new set of values. Some of these writers in turn adopted them, visibly surprised that their own ideas, deemed unpublishable in the fifties, should suddenly find a mass echo.

I wish to single out Marcuse, Goodman, and Brown as the

Gates of Eden

theorists whose work had the greatest impact on the new culture of the sixties. Their work responded deeply to the social and moral impasse of the Eisenhower era but also went beyond criticism into a new vision of the social order and its possibilities. The impasse of an era is reflected in the impasse of its criticism. The ills of American society in the fifties were rivaled by the decadence of Marxist criticism, which had degenerated into a metaphysic of brittle slogans and rigid historical hopes, none of which could hide two generations of moral and political compromise. For Old Leftists, society was an engine with certain parts, going in a predictable direction. For ex-Leftists, now under the sway of Burke, Tocqueville, or Weber, society was a delicate organism whose parts could not be tampered with without grave risk of damaging the whole. Both points of view were peculiarly fatalistic, and unresponsive to what actually could be done in society. The Marxism of the former group was "economic" and "scientific"; it sought "iron laws" in history and—unlike the Marxism of Marx—left little room for the agency of the individual or for his claims to happiness in the here-and-now. On the other hand, the anti-Marxism of the latter group put all its emphasis on the individual, but saw his fate as gloomy and tragic, impervious to change, hedged by necessity. (In both cases, social science and political philosophy shade off into branches of religion.)

What provided a way out of this impasse of social thought was a peculiar blend of Marxian and Freudian revisionism, which can be observed distinctly in the seminal works of Marcuse, Brown, and Goodman. The end of the fifties saw the first publication in English of Marx's early writings, which emphasized "alienation" rather than the laws of political economy, and which gave much impetus to the development of a new humanism that would steal Marx away from his orthodox keepers. Similarly, the Freud who emerged at the same time was not the Freud of the fifties whose dark view of human nature and the necessity of restraint provided the underpinning for a new social quietism, a new version of original sin. Nor was it the liberal revisionism which, in departing from Freud's instinctual theories, tended to de-emphasize sex and to find happiness in the successful "adjustment" to society's demands.

70

The new Freudian radicalism stressed the repressive character of society, but without the later Freud's tragic and stoical belief that these repressions could never be transcended, that the "realm of necessity" could never give way to the "realm of freedom." For Marcuse the key change since Freud's death is the tremendous expansion of technology which, despite the threat it poses of greater manipulation and control, also points toward greater freedom. This is to be achieved through the diminution of human labor, creating the possibility of a society built more on leisure and pleasure. What is paradoxical here is that Marcuse, though criticizing the structure and priorities of the advanced industrial society of the fifties, largely accepts its technological optimism, its faith in an ever-increasing economy of affluence and abundance. Indeed, he even scales new heights:

> Automation, once it became *the* process of material production, would revolutionize the whole society. The reification of human labor power, driven to perfection, would shatter the reified form by cutting the chain that ties the individual to the machinery—the mechanism through which his own labor enslaves him. Complete automation in the realm of necessity would open the dimension of free time as the one in which man's private *and* societal existence would constitute itself. This would be the historical transcendence toward a new civilization. [*One-Dimensional Man*]

Much could be said about this passage as an illustration of the strengths and limits of Marcusean dialectics. The style of argument, familiar from orthodox Marxism—Marcuse is actually building upon a passage in Marx's *Grundrisse*—suggests that though things seem to get worse they're actually getting better, for they're moving toward a dialectical reversal that will shatter the whole game. Elsewhere in the same book Marcuse insists that though things seem to be getting better (more freedom and leisure, higher standards of living) they're actually getting worse, through what he calls "repressive desublimation," in other words, the distractions of bread and circuses to keep the masses content and in their place.

Both these arguments imply that common sense is a trap, that the surface of things is very different from the reality, that society is never quite what it seems. This tack enables Marcuse to expose the genuinely paradoxical character of some recent social trends and "democratic" institutions. It enables him to develop a notion of freedom that is in some ways deeper than the liberal one, which Matthew Arnold described as "doing as one likes." It enables him to think in a utopian way, to conceive of transcending the social given. But it also leads him into a lofty German contempt for empirical reality, including the expressed needs and wishes of most individual men. "In the last analysis," Marcuse says, "the question of what are true and false needs must be answered by the individuals themselves, *but only in the last analysis; that is, if and when they are free to give their own answer.*" (Italics mine.) Since by his definition individuals in our society are not free, he feels obliged to tell them what their real needs are. Moreover, we suspect that they could only be considered "free" when their wishes came to accord with his analysis. "As long as they are kept incapable of being autonomous, as long as they are indoctrinated and manipulated (down to their very instincts), their answer to this question cannot be taken as their own." Marcuse explicitly rejects totalitarian dictation, but often he writes more in the spirit of a conservative elitist than a democratic radical. Though Marcuse will not force men to be free, he has little respect for the way they live, work, and play.

The same can be said of many of Marcuse's former colleagues in the Frankfurt school, out of which his work emerged in the twenties and thirties. As brilliant theorists who evolved a humanistic, Hegelian Marxism and applied it to many areas of contemporary life their work was of inestimable value. They refashioned a profound synthesis between dialectical materialism and the Western cultural tradition which Nazism had overshadowed and Stalinism had ruptured. But their writings on popular culture—T. W. Adorno on jazz, for example—reveal the extent to which their critical perspective belongs not to Marxism but to the long and honorable line of conservative attacks on modernity. By attacking the "culture industry" they affirmed an allegiance to high culture and the autonomy of art that Stalinism had betrayed. But they also left little room for new perspectives on either mass culture or the avant-garde, of the sort we find in more "democratic" theorists like Brecht or Walter Benjamin.*

The style of these men expresses the same elite viewpoint. The nimble and elegant ping-pong of Adorno's dialectics affirms its author's contempt for the common sense of empiricism and the bureaucratic sloganeering of the Stalinists, and announces his adherence to the German philosophical tradition; but the language is opaque to all but the most subtle and highly trained reader. Marcuse's cruder and more accessible style is equally insulting to the empirical mind. The conceptual "transcendence" that he gains by his play of abstractions fails to compensate for the loss of concreteness, the lack of observed reality. Words like *liberation, domination, transcendence,* and *reification* sometimes take on a mechanical trajectory of their own in his prose, become reified, as it were, into opaque verbal blocks that relate only to each other, not to the world. Robert Frost compared free verse to playing tennis with the net down; at his worst Marcuse plays philosophy with the world down, and triumphs in a hollow kingdom of words. Even his major work of social criticism, *One-Dimensional Man,* shows what difficulty he has keeping his eye trained for long on society. The famous analysis is nearly all in the first two chapters, after which he turns in relief from society to ideology, where a purely philosophical critique will get by. (Even *Eros and Civilization,* a much greater book, disintegrates into a paraphrase of Schiller and other poets and philosophers when it comes to deliver its own message, to tell us how a new life can be lived.)

This sort of abstraction and distance from society is traditional in German *Kulturkritik* and metaphysics, the very mode of philosophizing Marx sought to overthrow. In Marcuse's case it was surely compounded by a felt distance from "the American way of life," including the university scene. Both *One-Dimensional Man* and *Eros and Civilization* are full of comments that tacitly apply with special force to the alienating circumstances of the fifties. He sees the age as

* See Adorno and Horkheimer, *Dialectic of Enlightenment,* first published in 1947, and Adorno's later reflections in "The Culture Industry Reconsidered," written in 1963.

one in which "the social controls have been introjected to the point where even individual protest is affected at its roots. The intellectual and emotional refusal 'to go along' appears neurotic and impotent." An even more personal comment (especially if we recall Marcuse's controversial academic career) occurs later in *One-Dimensional Man,* in the course of his lively and ingenious assault on Anglo-Saxon "ordinary language" philosophy (whose methods he compares to those of the congressional committees):

> The intellectual is called on the carpet. What do you mean when you say . . . ? Don't you conceal something? You talk a language which is suspect. You don't talk like the rest of us, like the man in the street, but rather like a foreigner who does not belong here.

There is a strain of hedonism in Marcuse that must have found America's Puritan work ethic particularly jarring. For Marcuse all labor is alienated labor; satisfaction comes only through erotic activity, leisure, or play. Nothing in Marcuse is so distinctly un-Marxian as this refusal to envision the possibility of satisfaction through work, through unalienated labor. It takes us back instead to the utopian speculations of the early Marx, as in the famous attack on the division of labor in *The German Ideology,* where he envisions communism as a society "which makes it possible for me to do one thing today and another tomorrow, to hunt in the morning, fish in the afternoon, rear cattle in the evening, criticize after dinner, just as I have a mind, without ever becoming hunter, fisherman, shepherd or critic."

V I

In comparison with Marcuse, Paul Goodman was a man who seemed at home in America, a Jeffersonian rather than a Hegelian, and one who especially emphasized the value of satisfying work—though he himself lived a variegated life that fit Marx's description rather neatly. Like Marcuse he was also something of a conservative; he identified Coleridge and Arnold among his forebears (in other words, the same tradition of Tory radicalism that had fostered Trilling and Chase, as well as Leavis, Hoggart, and Williams in England). I find, however, that it's extremely difficult to talk of him in these impersonal terms, though I knew him only from a distance. Like Allen Ginsberg, Goodman was more than a writer in the sixties: he was a pervasive and inescapable *presence*. During the sixties both poetry and theory made a pact with the devil and descended into the street, following Marx's admonition to change the world, not merely to interpret it. Goodman was a fixture at all these public rituals—the protest-meetings and teach-ins, the marches and demonstrations —but not because he was a great orator or politician. My own impression on the few occasions I saw him in action was that he was above all a great teacher, the most tireless and incandescent Socratic figure of the age. This came out not only in his passion for the young, which was fueled by his sexual need, but also in the relish with which he took on alien audiences that were by no means ready to cheer his gospel. As if haunted by unhappinesses that made private life unbearable, he never seemed able to say no to any public occasion. At the end of *New Reformation,* his moving and bittersweet retrospective on the sixties, written when he was already very tired, he asks himself: "Why do I go? Ah, why do I go? It's not for the money and it's not out of vanity. I go because they ask me. Since I used to gripe bitterly when I was left out of the world, how can I gracelessly decline when I am invited in?" The occasion in question was a seminar at Dartmouth for "American Telephone and Telegraph executives who were being groomed to be vice-presidents." Most Leftists, old or new, had they deigned to go at all, would have seized the occasion to denounce the audience as exploiters, fascists, robber barons. Instead, Goodman's contribution was a list of practical suggestions, some so practical as to be radical and unadoptable, but no doubt sufficient to provoke hours of heated talk.

Goodman behaved the same way with audiences that were prepared to idolize him. The team-man's pep talk was alien to him. He was incapable of flattery, though he could be gratuitously brutal. He tended to hector his audiences, to galvanize them within their immediate situation. He always spoke *to* them, not out of some private dazzling soliloquy of his own. The first time I saw this happen was at Columbia in 1960 or 1961, when some of us connected with the undergraduate newspaper tried to organize a series of speakers. We had no money to offer; everyone was busy, busy—all our culture-heroes turned us down. All except Paul Goodman, of course. The talk he gave seemed based on no more than impromptu jottings scribbled on the subway, but it was about us, about where we were, especially about Columbia and the poor citizenship, the civic irresponsibility it had always displayed toward its immediate community and toward his beloved city. In short, Goodman gave a complete analysis of the Columbia student uprising—seven years before it occurred! It wasn't carping, it wasn't rhetorical, it wasn't even eloquent; it was simply practical, but also utopian, since it was based on a grand vision of the role a university could play in a great urban scene, and on his sadness and anger that it did not choose to play that role.

A few years later I watched him do the same thing for three days nonstop at a conference of graduate students somewhere in western Massachusetts. Even when he was not lecturing officially he was surrounded by people, and he gave himself to them completely; as a continuous Socratic performance it was so impressive it was scary. I myself was disappointed that I couldn't get him more interested in some of the clever and brilliant things I was saying. My bright-young-man's ego was bruised. I wasn't used to it. Later when he published his journal *Five Years* to show the world that he was not a good man but one driven and debased by sexual hungers and humiliations, I was able to guess at what happened: I simply hadn't turned him on. Sex and pedagogy were intertwined for Goodman, along with citizenship, abstract ideas, family feelings, religious feelings, and so on, as they were for the Greeks. He could turn people on when he too was turned on; he needed to take as well as to give.

Far from being a weakness in his work this vulnerability and naked need gives his writing an emotional charge missing from most social criticism; it binds together his stories, novels, and poems with his essays and critical writings into one unfolding personal statement. Whatever their differences of texture and form they remain the testimony of one spirited citizen and man of letters. At the end of *New Reformation* he was glad to find himself "thinking from where I breathe." To this reader he always seems to be speaking from where he lives. Nowhere is this more evident than in *Growing Up Absurd* (1960), his masterwork in social criticism and a book that did much to inform the whole frame of mind of thinking people in the sixties.

The immediate subject of *Growing Up Absurd* is the young, mainly those who have dropped out into the Beat subculture and the others whose delinquency has dropped them into the hands of the law. Its real subject is the America of the Eisenhower age, a society which, in Goodman's view, gives its youth no world to grow up in. The world seems "absurd," meaningless; it fails to provide satisfying roles and models. Hence the young do not simply drop out; rather, "they act out a critique of the organized system that everybody in some sense agrees with." Goodman is here applying existential and psychological concepts that are usually excluded from social analysis. He aims to produce an account of youth and of society that is impermissibly inward, novelistic, even subjective. Since his concern, like that of the nineteenth-century English culture critics, is more with the *quality* of life than with material well-being, he needs above all to convey the *feel* of contemporary experience both for himself and for his youthful subjects.

In retrospect we can see how much Goodman's personal situation contributed to this bold and moving analysis. His passionate feeling for these young male outcasts no doubt is grounded as much in his homosexuality as in his general humanity, especially since he felt he was an outcast himself, a sexual nigger.* The condition of the outsider, the reject of the "organized system" with an "addiction to forbidden haunts and vices," runs like a thread through the whole book, not only because of the author's sexual habits but also alluding to twenty-five years of near-poverty and neglect as a writer. Unlike

---

* "My homosexual acts have made me a nigger, subject to arbitrary brutality and debased when my out-going impulse is not taken for granted as a right." (*New Reformation*)

Marcuse, Goodman was not taken in by the myths of contemporary affluence. Well before Michael Harrington's book *The Other America* he concentrated on the marginal and the unemployed, the pockets of victimization; like Harrington he had sometimes lived in them. Goodman considered himself a prime reject of the organized system of literature, which had little use for an all-purpose "man of letters" who couldn't settle down. Thus like other fifties intellectuals, like the epigones of the Frankfurt school, Goodman attacks the promoters and hucksters of popular culture, and complains of "an organized system of reputations that is calculated statistically to minimize risk and eliminate the unsafe."

I don't mean to suggest that *Growing Up Absurd* is mainly a personal gripe, only to explore how Goodman—without being in the least "confessional" like many later sixties writers—brought his own visceral feelings to bear on the social reality. He challenged the period's sacroscanct myth of value-free objectivity in criticism and social science, putting together a book that's part anecdote, part philosophy, part griping, part sociology, and part visionary moral statement, all set down in a deceptive manner of ungainly informality that only *seems* casual. All this helped get the book rejected by a dozen publishers including the one who had commissioned it, before *Commentary* magazine picked it up to inaugurate its new leftish sixties regime. Today the book is still described by friendly observers like Henry Pachter as "loosely written" and "poorly researched," platitudes that miss the cunning and originality of its style.

Goodman's stance is a strange combination of the polymath who knows a lot and the plain speaker who is just your ordinary informed citizen raised to the nth power. It's directed against not only the false neutrality of the social scientist but also the hyper-cultivated Brahmin tone of the literary intellectuals of the fifties. For their air of ironic sophistication and world-weariness Goodman substitutes straight talk, honest indignation, little homilies and emotional outbursts, and an appeal to corny values like nobility, honor, community, patriotism, and faith, each of which casts a subversive light on our current social arrangements. Like the Victorian social critics

Goodman shows how radical (yet traditional) it can be to hold an inhumane society to its own professed values. To him this is a society that ignores the human cost in its rush toward modernization and profit.* Like the Victorians Goodman emphasizes the paradoxes of "progress," the loss of human scale in our physical and social environment, "the present waste of human resources," the devaluation of both work and leisure.

But Goodman is no machine-breaker at war with modernity and efficiency. As a good anarchist he can easily demonstrate the *inef-ficiency* of a quack modernism mindlessly attached to bigness and waste. "There is probably a point of complexity at which, cut off from the country, the city ceases to advance beyond country backwardness; it becomes impractical and begins to induce its own kind of stupefaction and ineptness." He goes on to list ten or twelve ways the city has changed since his youth, with some practical alternatives. No Jeremiah prophesying ruin, Goodman earns his nostalgia and indignation by being concrete. His is practical optimism that values the subject over the product and puts "animal ardor" and a messy vitality above the illogical wisdom of the machine and the social conglomerate.

All this is conveyed in Goodman's style, which, like Wordsworth's, is artful in its moral and emotive simplicities; at its best it achieves a uniquely plebeian kind of eloquence, a populist rhetoric of "plain talk" behind which the avant-garde artist is almost effaced. Norman Mailer was one of those who was famously unimpressed by this style (at least after Goodman had attacked *him*); in *The Armies of the Night* he labels it merely pedestrian but also admits that his antipathy to Goodman is more personal and sexual than literary. They are rival "sexologues," he explains, and he accuses Goodman of holding a hygienic, permissive view of homosexuality (and "onanism"!), whereas he, Mailer, knows that all sex is fraught

* "All the great words, it seemed to Connie, were cancelled for her generation: love, joy, happiness, home, mother, father, husband, all these great, dynamic words were half dead now, and dying from day to day." (D. H. Lawrence, *Lady Chatterley's Lover*)

with guilt and sin, and some kinds are simply wrong, soul-destroying.*

Politically, too, the differences between Goodman and Mailer were important: during the Kennedy years, Goodman, an advocate of decentralization and "community control," attacked Mailer's Carlylean attraction to the Great Leader. But this was preceded by their sexual quarrel, which goes back to "The White Negro" and *Growing Up Absurd,* goes back even beyond that, to the impact of Wilhelm Reich on literary intellectuals in the 1940s. A close look at the sexual and political implications of "The White Negro" and *Growing Up Absurd* would tell us a good deal about the cultural radicalism that emerged at the end of the fifties.

VII

Earlier I took note of how prophetic it was for Mailer and Goodman to draw serious attention to the new bohemian subculture of the late fifties, in tandem with the upsurge of youthful delinquency and rebelliousness. In retrospect, those developments foreshadowed a great deal of the communal utopianism, urban restlessness, and street violence of the sixties, but at the time they were treated with no such seriousness. The media played up both the Beats and the juvenile hoodlums as isolated spectacles of inarticulate exhibitionism. Mailer and Goodman undertook to become spokesmen for this discontent, interpreters of all the "acting out," who could read in withdrawal and youthful anomie a complex critique of the system and its values. For some of us who were in college then these men instantly became heroes, as did Norman O. Brown. I can recall no public event more inspiriting and electrifying at that time than Brown's vatic, impassioned Phi Beta Kappa oration at Columbia in 1960

* It's also rather obvious in *Armies* that Mailer envies Goodman's youthful New Left legions, just as he confesses his jealousy of Robert Lowell's name, fame, and literary eminence. The book was a complex bid for both—political leadership *and* literary standing; in its own way it very nearly succeeded.

(later published under the title "Apocalypse: The Place of Mystery in the Life of the Mind"). Because these men were intellectuals, because we were budding intellectuals, they had made a startling conjunction for us—which they also embodied—between the world of ideas and a new mode of experience, a new consciousness. We recognized that none of them had been minutely faithful to his subject, that they had seized on the hipsters or on psychoanalysis as the occasion for a personal breakthrough rather than as a problem of interpretation. But in doing so they had discovered not only new and transfiguring ideas but a new intellectual style—committed, inspiriting, prophetic—rich with the promise of salvation and the dream of a new world. Unlike the ordinary discourse of academics, it spoke to the ultimate issues of culture and personal destiny.

I think it's fair to say that these men spoke with special urgency to our newness to the world of ideas—we who knew their vocabulary but had never seen it used with such animating directness—and to our late adolescence, for we knew that at bottom their gospel was a sexual one, that sex was their wedge for reorienting all human relations. And for us at that moment the sexual hunger was paramount, for all our self-conscious intellectuality. It was our breakthrough they were talking about, enacting—our worldlessness and coming-into-being, our absurd growing up. It mattered little that Mailer stressed the *macho* and violent side of the hipster figure while Goodman—perhaps in line with his own sexual struggle—stressed the anxiety and displacement, the lack of any experience that felt real. To us they were two sides of the same coin, and spoke equally to our lust for deep experience and for transfiguring sex (for which transfiguring ideas were a not quite adequate substitute, though they were a passionately intense sublimation). The rationality and intellectuality of the fifties had helped to form us, but when Mailer wrote of love as "the search for an orgasm more apocalyptic than the one which preceded it," I was enthralled, while the qualified homage to violence a few lines earlier, which has angered moralists like Irving Howe, made no such impact. I had no need of it, and took no notice.

If a certain wryness has crept into my tone it's because I'm surprised by the distance between the person I was and the person I am. Rereading "The White Negro," *Eros and Civilization, Life Against Death,* and other works I've referred to in these pages I'm impressed anew at the intelligence and style, the prescience and passion, of all this literature of cultural change, yet I find that it's lost much of its power to animate me. Partly this is because the sixties are long over. So much of what these men advocated has either been obscenely, obstinately frustrated or, worse still, has come to pass, with the mixed results we have come to expect in all human affairs. Commune life, the death of the family, open marriage, the politics of confrontation, educational reform, participatory democracy, mind-changing chemicals—all these promises have been simultaneously fulfilled and undermined. In some respects our society will never be the same; in other ways it never really changed.

Sexual liberation was surely one of these promises, and nowhere have our public values—and perhaps even our private conduct—changed more noticeably than here; but the sexual apocalypse at the end of the rainbow has not yet occurred, nor do I know what would happen if it did. Life goes on in the old way. I suspect even adolescents suffer in the old way, despite the evident new freedoms. Today when I read "The White Negro" or *Life Against Death* I can recall how much excitement I once felt, and feel some of it again, but it's distressingly hard to know just what the excitement was all about. Mailer's orgasm to end all orgasms, his hipster-psychopath's decision "to try to live the infantile fantasy," Brown and Marcuse's attack on the "tyranny of genital organization" and their paean to the "polymorphous perverse" sexuality of the infant (along with their fascination with Freud's death instinct)—I find it difficult to imagine what these things meant to me, who had scarcely attained to the tyrannized state that they were attacking. To me they meant not some ontological breakthrough for human nature but probably just plain fucking, lots of it—in other words, just the opposite of what they said. I was sexually starved, though I hardly knew it, and these men seemed to promise that good times were just around the corner. Under the cover of grand ideas grand needs were making themselves felt. To recapture completely my feeling for these books would be to recapture my adolescence. It would be something of a sham. The sixties coincided with my own coming of age; I cannot depersonalize them, I cannot extricate them, try as I might.

VIII

I certainly don't mean to reduce enormously complex books like *Life Against Death* or *Eros and Civilization* to moments in my private history, but surely it was crucial for me that their exploration of "the ambiguities of sublimation" appeared at the time I was sublimating most ferociously—above all in the passion with which I threw myself into books like theirs. Furthermore, their animus toward Freud's notion that civilization must inevitably be founded on repression came toward the end of one of the most repressive periods in American history, which both of them as old Marxists must have experienced with special force. Marcuse's allusions to the domestic cold war are veiled but unmistakable, and in a sense the whole social model he analyzes is a generalized form of American society in the forties and fifties, when the classic expectations of revolution have defaulted, when "the goods and services that the individuals buy control their needs and petrify their faculties," when "they have dozens of newspapers and magazines that espouse the same ideals," when the "foe appears as the archenemy and Antichrist himself: he is everywhere at all times; he represents hidden and sinister forces, and his omnipresence requires total mobilization." Even Brown, whose book is far less political, writes in his introduction of having "lived through the superannuation of the political categories which informed liberal thought and action in the 1930's," but of being "temperamentally incapable of embracing the politics of sin, cynicism and despair" that followed. Clearly he sees the book as the prophetic and utopian equivalent of his former Marxism. Like Richard Chase but far more ambitiously, he was trying to bring the thirties up to date.

The difference between Brown and Marcuse must nevertheless be stressed. Where Brown takes Marxism as one more set of symbols and categories, another anthropological system to be merged with Freud's, Marcuse sets out genuinely to historicize the Freudian categories, to turn them from absolute and timeless truths into a critical account of a specific phase of our culture. Like the neo-Freudians they attack, both of them aim to complete the social psychology that Freud himself only began to sketch in his last two decades. Both undercut the merely therapeutic use of Freud that prevailed after his death, yet neither is able to make the step from utopian theorizing about "the nature and destiny of man" to a more specific vision of the way people might actually live. This barrier helps explain why both writers later retreated from Freud: Marcuse into more conventional social criticism and Marxist militancy, Brown into Christian "body mysticism" and then back to sublimation, especially the conventional sublimations of the poetic imagination, which Marcuse too had fallen back on for the content of his future state.

However much we may criticize Marcuse's later work, at least it represents the development of a position, something we can differ with; Brown's later career is in prose poetry, not in conceptual thinking. The rhetoric of the "Apocalypse" oration was breathtaking, the best Nietzschean writing since *Zarathustra* itself. Though we may legitimately ask just what Brown means by mystical phrases like "holy madness" or "second sight," as a trumpet-call to renewal in the academy it is a worthy successor to Emerson's "American Scholar," with its message (which Brown quotes) that "the one thing in the world, of value, is the active soul." But *Love's Body* (1966) is as far beyond the renewal of institutions as it is beyond consecutive thinking. Instead it comes on as a new gospel, in which a vulgar-Freudian mode of symbolic analogy gets applied indiscriminately to every corner of life, every institution in culture. Now and then the book makes some brilliant, witty conjunctions. But if everybody in space is a phallus surrounded by a vagina, then this symbolism has lost all hermeneutic value; it becomes an unwitting burlesque of a certain post-Freudian rhetoric of interpretation. (Some recent

French Freudianism has extended the caricature; it makes Brown look like a piker.)

The ingenuity of Brown's later poetics, however dubious, is sufficient to indicate how much of the success of *Life Against Death* stemmed from its own different but daring rhetoric. Brown is a devastating polemicist, a lucid expositor and critic, and a remarkable synthesizer of material from different disciplines. His reading of Freud has a fervor and dramatic excitement that Freud's own work eschews; it comes to us not as dry science, an analysis of the given, but as an evangel, a Bringer of Truth. After reading it I became a convert of sorts, and heroically preached what I hoped was a subversive doctrine of vitalism and sexual liberation in all my undergraduate and graduate term papers, finding such a message (not without some justification) in texts as diverse as *The Rape of the Lock, The Beast in the Jungle,* and *Hard Times.* Poor disciple that I was, I remained quite oblivious to Brown's attack on the "program of oversimplified sexual liberation" which he attributes to Reich and early Freud. If the real message was "polymorphous perversity" I must have had a hard time making use of it. And by 1962, when I heard Brown himself (in a lecture at Wesleyan) allude disparagingly to "the academic author of *Life Against Death,*" I knew the game was up. He had become a guru, hemmed in by flatterers, enveloped by pregnant silences, beyond ordinary discourse. *He* would never answer the questions he had helped to raise.

Marcuse's reading of Freud was less complex and drastic than Brown's; he seized and brilliantly appropriated only a few central strands of the Freudian system, and his political anchor kept him from getting utterly lost in cultural speculation, as Brown does by his last chapter. For all of Brown's rhetorical and synthesizing power, it was Marcuse who came closer to unifying the themes of personal liberation and social change, authenticity and justice, in a way that anticipated the new heterodoxies of the sixties. Both the militants and the bohemians could fairly claim him as an ancestor. Marcuse himself was unable to maintain this remarkable balance. With the revival of the Left in the sixties, his cultural interests receded before his political ones. Two later prefaces to *Eros and Civilization*, written in 1961 and 1966, become increasingly strident in trying to reorient the book in a purely political direction. He may have been right in stressing that only politics provided an avenue for true change, but in his excitement at the revival of radicalism he all too readily identified his politics with the insurgent forces of the moment, whatever their aims and tactics.* Again and again he retreated from social analysis and from his own daring ideas into revolutionary clichés, the realm of the publicist rather than the philosopher.

In truth Marcuse had always been stronger as a theorist than as a social analyst or forecaster. *One-Dimensional Man* (1964) provided a valuable conceptual framework for looking at society, but like his other work it wasn't itself close to what was actually happening. Thus Marcuse's well-known oscillation between optimism and pessimism over the last twenty years, though it expresses certain interesting ambiguities at the heart of his thinking, is peculiarly empty in relation to the world at large. The optimism of *Eros and Civilization* in 1955 was a utopian leap, based on an abstract reading of certain historical forces like the growth of technology. Though a speculative work, it remains more concrete and humanly specific than anything else he wrote. Despite the language of liberation, however, Marcuse did not anticipate the general liberalization of society that began to occur in the mid-fifties, especially in the sphere of sexual behavior and political expression. Later, in *One-Dimensional Man*, when Marcuse does take note of these changes, he is desperate to dissociate his own predictions from what he finds happening. By 1964, with everything beginning to open up, Marcuse is most deeply pessimistic. He dismisses all signs of new freedom as "repressive desublimation" and finds absurd or trivial real-life examples that supposedly show whole spheres of human activity being "de-eroticized." Similarly, he dismisses the early countercultural man-

---

* By 1974 he would theorize that feminism (or "feminist socialism")—previously unnoticed in his system, but now the last active remnant of sixties radicalism—was ordained to be the next stage of "the Revolution." See his lecture on "Marxism and Feminism" published in *Women's Studies* 2 (1974).

ifestations, such as "Zen, existentialism, and beat ways of life," as "modes of protest and transcendence [which] are no longer contradictory to the status quo," and which therefore "are quickly digested by the status quo as part of its healthy diet." Nor does he take any note until his last page of the new political forces mustering on the margins of social power. Whatever seems better is objectively worse. In this book Marcuse's lumbering conceptual apparatus becomes his defense against the obvious; if at moments it keeps him from being taken in, it all too often prevents him from seeing straight.

In *An Essay on Liberation* (1969) the exact opposite occurs. The youth culture that society had digested in the previous book now became the agent of historical change, just when its disintegration began to be apparent to others. Reviving pre-Marxist theories of human nature, Marcuse now seeks "a biological foundation for socialism," grounded in the mores of the counterculture. The same dialectical machinery that previously found futility everywhere now finds revolutionary potential in every accidental trait of the young, including their use of dirty words, their dress, music, supposed bathing habits, and so on. Aching to recapture his lost utopianism, Marcuse hitches his star to that of his young followers, translating their behavior into the language of German philosophy, often with ludicrous results. For social observation he substitutes a purely journalistic perspective; instead of theory he offers political rhetoric; ephemeral matters of fashion are hypostatized into world-historical developments in a way that, at its worst, rivals the fatuities of *The Greening of America*.

I'm well aware that I've applied harsher standards to Marcuse than to anyone else I've written about here. This is because he promises so much. Of all the theorists who influenced the sixties Marcuse alone seemed capable of bringing Marxism up to date. That he failed to do it is no disgrace. At the very least he created a framework of analysis through which the cultural and personal dimension—the arts, the media, sexual mores, the use of leisure—could be integrated into social theory and political awareness. If his analysis could be mindlessly parroted by the new academicians of the Left, it would also remain a touchstone for those who could constructively refute or adapt it. Without rejecting Marxism Marcuse helped radicals break with the old Marxist orthodoxies and think freshly about the novelties of their own modern situation.

With these last comments on Brown and Marcuse I've gone far afield from that transitional period when the fifties began to break up in the realm of cultural theory. The late fifties were a fertile period, a seedbed of ideas that would burgeon and live in the more activist, less reflective climate that followed. A comparable breakup and transition could be traced in almost every sphere of American society during the same period: in politics, in education, in advertising, in popular culture, and in each of the creative arts. Sometimes the roots of change were not American at all. In film, for example, the influx of the new European directors—Godard, Truffaut, Chabrol, Fellini, Antonioni, Bergman—inaugurated a golden age that included a rediscovery of these sophisticated artists' own American models. In literature the changes in national sensibility were reflected even more turbulently, as experiment and innovation jostled the conservative conventions of the postwar period. The end of the fifties saw the publication of Ginsberg's *Howl* and *Kaddish,* the best poems of Corso and Ferlinghetti, the first books of the so-called New York school of poets, *On the Road* (Kerouac's picaresque tribute to Ginsberg and Neal Cassady), John Barth's parodic revival of the big Shandean anti-novel in *The Sot-Weed Factor,* Lowell's *Life Studies,* Mailer's *Advertisements for Myself*—besides the many works of social theory and criticism we have considered here (some of them as artful and eloquent as anything in the creative literature). For those of us in college at that time the changes of adolescence—and the exhilarations of intellectual adolescence—superseded yet became interwoven with the problems of cultural change. It was an exciting time to be growing up: less stable than the fifties, less hectic than the sixties, but alive with possibility, rich with eerie dissonances between a still-living past and a dimly apprehended future.

II

BREAKING THROUGH:

THE HIDDEN HISTORY

OF THE SIXTIES

Once more unto the breach, dear friends, once more. . . .
Shakespeare, *Henry V*

4

Black Humor
and History:
The Early Sixties

A FEW YEARS AGO any critic who suggested that writing fiction had been a central imaginative activity during the 1960s might have been asked to have his head examined. Had he added that the fiction of the period also tells us a great deal about what was happening then, he would have been written off entirely as a crank. It was axiomatic then to assert that the electronic media had entirely displaced the printed word; that young people in the sixties didn't read, let alone write; that all the most talented of them went into film, or politics, or rock; that those who did write novels simply turned away from the gaudy carnival of contemporary life, as Tom Wolfe said in *The New Journalism,* "gave up by default," leaving the way clear for the hip new journalists and rhetoricians. According to Wolfe, novelists became "Neo-Fabulists" entranced by myth and parable understandable only to themselves, and lost interest in reality.

Today the enthusiasts of fiction are far less likely to be on the defensive, for the creative impulses in the novel have proved more durable than facile McLuhanite explanations of cultural change. But there is more than a grain of truth in Tom Wolfe's simplistic account. The sixties were a moribund period for the realistic novel, and perhaps in consequence the commercial market for fiction declined precipitously. Novelists who did sustain a realist method, such as Updike, Bellow, and Malamud, were weakest when they dragged in blacks or hippies, or worried about the war, or unisex, or the future of the moon—topical subjects on which Wolfe's journalists were strongest. Yet the journalists themselves, not only Wolfe but Capote and Mailer, insistently invoked the prestige of the novel to validate their work, much as the early novelists of the eighteenth century had coyly rejected the idea of fiction and masked their work as journals or case histories. The eighteenth-century novelist had to insist that he was artless; the sixties journalist had to prove he was an Artist. In each case the rationale was a relic of an outworn cast of mind that the work itself would help to superannuate. What died in the sixties was not the novel but the mystique of the novel, its critical prestige, its wide and loyal audience, its status as the royal road to cultural success.* The dream of the Great American Novel disintegrated, as did the line between high art and other kinds of cultural performance, but the novels that continued to be written were some of the most staggeringly ambitious that America had produced. The second coming of modernism in American fiction, which Tom Wolfe deplores and misunderstands, may have narrowed the audience for the novel and limited its ability to deal with the immediate carnival aspect of contemporary fashion, but it gave the dream of the novelist a new kind of grandiosity and range. In a topsy-turvy age that often turned trash into art and art into trash, that gaily pursued topical fascinations and ephemeral performances and showed a real genius for self-consuming artifacts—an age that sometimes valued art too little because it loved raw life too much—novels were written that are among the handful of art-works, few enough in any age, that are likely to endure. It's a bizarre prospect, but the sixties are as likely to be remembered through novels as through anything else they left behind.

Yet Tom Wolfe is right in one respect. The future readers who

---

* "In that far-off time," says Gore Vidal of the late forties, "the people one met talked about novels and novelists the way they now talk of movies and directors. Young people today think that I am exaggerating." (*New York Review of Books*, May 30, 1974)

Black Humor and History: The Early Sixties

look to the novels of the sixties to learn about society are sure to go awry. The kaleidoscope of fashion, the spectacular changes in morals and manners, which Wolfe claimed as rich new territory for the journalists, evoked scant interest in writers of fiction. There was little good sociology in sixties novels, even among the realists, who were schooled not in the great tradition of social realism that goes back to Balzac, Stendhal, and Jane Austen but in a minor Jamesian variant on that tradition. The novelists who admired (and misread) Henry James in the forties and fifties saw reality less in terms of money, class, and social ambition than as an infinitely complex web of personal relationships, of subtle shades of consciousness. Neglecting the interplay between individuality and history, between desire and social determination, which had been essential to the social insight of the great realists, they kept to problems of domestic entanglement, personal identity, and private moral choice. And if they sometimes shaded off into fable or allegory, it was only to stress the timeless and perennial quality of these moral issues. If Bernard Malamud and other Jewish writers are the perfect examples of this sort of moral allegorist, one could just as easily adduce the fiction of James Baldwin, William Styron, J. D. Salinger, Jean Stafford, and many others. The ghosts of Henry James and Nathaniel Hawthorne did not always come decked out in caftan.

The younger realists who succeeded these writers, such as John Updike (in *Rabbit, Run* and the small but impressive *Of the Farm*) and Philip Roth (in *Letting Go* and *When She Was Good*), continued to stress the familial and amatory entanglements of their characters, often using a standard locale familiar from their childhoods, and only lightly sketching the social milieu in a ready satirical way. "We didn't much think of politics," Updike recalled much later in an interview. "We were much more concerned with the private destiny that shaped people." Updike said this in 1971, at the publication of a remarkable Janus-faced sequel, *Rabbit Redux,* in which a brilliant depiction of a confused, pathetic marriage is followed by a wobbly attempt to haul in a topical theme, The Sixties—personified by a young hippie girl and a black militant, and concluding in a great symbolic fire. (The book is also set at the moment of the first moon walk.) Yet in his interview Updike instinctively reaffirms his older credo: ". . . . you introduce topical material into a novel at your own peril. I am convinced that the life of a nation is reflected, or distorted, by private people and their minute concerns."

Only in *Couples* (1968) did Updike try to fill in a broader social scene. Taking full advantage of the new license in sexual matters, he tried to do a full-scale portrait of the changing sexual mores of middle America. But the result was more like a parody or inversion of the older novel of personal relationships, for while putting the sex in he had screened nearly everything else out. It was a minuet of couplings and uncouplings that all had a dogged sameness, a personal novel in which no one had much personality. Discreet hints of a religious allegory were perhaps meant to lend the book weight, but luckily for Updike they were not obtrusive enough to interfere with its sales. Like some other sixties novelists Updike made out best with his weakest work.

If there was little good sociology in the work of Updike and Roth, there was even less in the more central and innovative strain of sixties fiction, the so-called comic-apocalyptic writers or black humorists, whose company both Roth and Mailer would join before the decade ended. Sometimes these writers do illuminate a contemporary setting, providing news of the world that you can't get from the News. I don't know of a better account of the pre-Beat New York under-culture of the mid-fifties—the bars, the floaters and drifters, the artists and would-be artists, the talents and the hangers-on, and everywhere the jazz—than we get in Pynchon's *V.*, or a more brilliant version of the L.A. scene than we find in his next book, *The Crying of Lot 49*. But Pynchon's imagination goes far afield from these realistic bases, which themselves have been subtly transformed into Pynchonesque metaphors for certain states of mind, peculiar world-historical anxieties. Nor is Heller's *Catch-22* really "about" World War II, though it does contain a good deal of amusing but marginal satire on the McCarthy period (such as the Great Loyalty Oath Crusade and the scandal of "Who promoted Major Major?

Who promoted Major Major?''); the book's imaginative center is elsewhere. Even an exceptionally realistic piece of black humor like Thomas Berger's wryly funny *Vital Parts*, which really does try to ''do'' the sixties, gradually shifts its attention from discotheques, sexual mores, rebellious long-haired kids and black militants to . . . cryonics, the effort to cheat death by freezing and storing people—in other words, material for fantasy, pure invention, and unhindered comic bumbling (so aimless that it nearly sinks the book). As sociology *Vital Parts* does not sustain even its own author's interest for very long.

The imaginative ambitions of these novelists keep them from any sustained social commentary; they illuminate society less through their content than through their experiments in form, by which I mean not simply technique but the pressure of individual vision from which new technique must flow. Critics who use literature as social evidence tend to treat its content as documentation, ignoring the subtle ironies and modifications which transmute raw experience within an imaginative work. Part of my aim in this book is to develop analogies between social change and changes in the *forms* of the arts, especially the novel. Form can be seen as a structure of perception, a deep-seated rhythm of experience and sensibility. Thus the individual work (like the individual self) partakes of the social whole willy-nilly, without having to allude to it directly. The conservative form of the novel in the 1950s, which is reflected in Saul Bellow's comment that ''realism is still the great literary breakthrough,'' mirrors the conserving and inward-turning character of the age. Likewise the surge of modernist and experimental fiction in the early sixties is subtly related to the new feelings of social malaise and reformist zeal that set in during the late fifties, gained impetus from the urgent, high-spirited tone of Kennedy's campaign for the presidency, and burst forth during his administration with precious little concrete progress to keep it going. In those early years of the sixties there was a scent of change in the air, a sense of things opening up, of new possibilities. This was not without its dangerous side, for, by the iron law of rising expectations, forces were aroused in society that soon overshot their prescribed bounds. The New Left and the civil rights movement did not develop under Eisenhower, when things were at their worst, but under Kennedy, when inchoate promises and possibilities were in the air. And they died under Nixon, who recreated an atmosphere of utter futility and himself embodied the vengeful spirit of middle-American backlash (as if the election of 1960 were at last undone, the sixties rolled back).

To try to relate the social atmosphere of the early sixties to the key novels of the period whould seem to be a thankless task. We all know that there is no easy correspondence between the arts and society, and that all due allowance must be made for individual genius working out its own salvation. Moreover, since books like *The Sot-Weed Factor*, *Catch-22*, and *V.* are long and complex, they were also long in gestating; it's difficult to say in what sense they belong to their moment of publication. But the cultural climate of the period was also, as I have tried to show, long in gestating, and the solitary labors of these very writers were surely among the points of gestation. The new sensibility of the sixties was unusually pervasive; in retrospect we can see how it touched every corner of our culture, any one of which, examined closely, helps illuminate the general ferment, the movement of change. Without abridging the distinctive claims of individual genius we can't help but notice a similarity of purpose and form, a common breakthrough, in many of the new novels. This in turn was followed by a loss of verve and a diminution of force among several of the older writers, as the cultural center seemed to make one of its periodic (and rather cruel) shifts.

Our problem is complicated by the fact that there's no easy symmetry between the older and the newer novel, as some would like to claim. If the Jewish novel, with its beleaguered humanism and weighty moral seriousness, is characteristic of the earlier period, the black humorists of the early sixties offer no easy contrast. It's not simply that several were as Jewish and as morally obsessed as Malamud or Bellow, but because their fascination with the ironies and absurdities of existence flows directly out of the Jewish novel, though it gets expressed in a different way. The opposite of the Jewish novel is not black humor but Camp, which is a form of aestheti-cism and brittle wit directed against whatever becomes too solemnly moral and humanistic. Camp is decorative, flip, gay, and insouciant, while black humor is pitched at the breaking point where moral anguish explodes into a mixture of comedy and terror, where things are so bad you might as well laugh. This helps explain why even some of the black humorists who are not Jewish, such as Berger and Pynchon, adapt the schlemiel figure out of Jewish fiction (Berger's Reinhart, Pynchon's Benny Profane); the schlemiel inhabits the shadowy margin between the comedy of errors and a comedy of ter-rors. As a chronic loser he is indestructible, the kind of man no soci-ety can do without: he'll go on losing forever. And as a figure of fun he's a threat to no one; he's low down on the scale of Hobbesian competition, cut off from the rarefied zone of great fortunes and great falls.

Similar things are true of the other main figure at the center of six-ties novels, a cousin of the schlemiel, the picaresque anti-hero. One striking difference between novels of the fifties and those of the six-ties is that the former, which tend to be more psychological and to focus on the complexities of individual character, preserve a belief—inherited from nineteenth-century realism—in the possibilities of personal growth, a Freudian faith in the maturation of self through the formation of adult relationships. In picaresque fiction, however, the hero, who is often an indestructible naif or innocent, gets pro-pelled not into familiar human interaction but through a series of ex-ternal events that are often random, bizarre, even surreal or apoca-lyptic. Voltaire's Candide is too much of an Everyman to grow or change; he cannot learn from his "experience," he can only be inun-dated. Instead of "novelistic" development we find a structure of repetiton and intensification: the same thing always happens, but no one will ever *learn* anything. Instead of fully rounded "real-life" characters we find cartoon-like puppets, manipulated according to the author's moral purpose.

Not all the black humor novels of the sixties approximate the *Candide* pattern. Kurt Vonnegut's novels come closest, especially

Slaughterhouse-Five, whose befuddled, childlike hero, allegorically named Billy Pilgrim, is set down in a world that kills and maims in the most causal and summary way. What complicates this air of shell-shocked simplicity are the bizarre "time warps" which layer the action so that all the disasters of crazy Billy's life seem to be happening to him simultaneously. To express what he sees as the insanity of contemporary history, Vonnegut does a pop adaptation of modernist experiments with time: Billy is a holy fool who "has come unstuck in time," who keeps uncontrollably enacting different moments of his life. As such he is a kind of novelist whose control has slipped, who remembers too much of modern history and his own private sorrow; the pressure has become too great, the ache to tell must somehow be relieved. This is why *Slaughterhouse-Five* is not one of Vonnegut's best books. As a writer he works best when he can be most playful and inventive, ripping off public events in inspired burlesque, making up Borgesian religions, cultures, whole literary *oeuvres,* and writing down their texts. But faced with the firebombing of Dresden, where he himself had been a helpless bystander, a stunned survivor, he lets the intensity of his feelings overshadow the fable designed to express them. The brilliant first chapter, which tells the story straight, overwhelms the fictional version that follows.

Compared to the moving personal presence of the author in the opening chapter, there's a thinness and insubstantiality, a puppet-like quality, to Billy Pilgrim and his fellow "characters" as they jerk their way through the time warps laid down for them by the author. The other side of the inventivenss of sixties fiction is the high degree of manipulation and authorial presence we encounter, which entails a depletion of life in the thing made, the story told, the character caricatured. A writer like Barth pays for his Brechtian honesty about what he's making up by a loss of vitality, until the "story" is pared down to his own witty and self-conscious voice soliloquizing about the act of creation. This imbalance between creator and artifact is an ambiguous development. Fictional characters in the fifties can still subject life to a degree of personal control, can grow and change within the limits of their personality. But the zany, two-dimensional characters in Vonnegut, Barth, Pynchon, and Heller declare not simply their authors' departure from realism but also their brooding sense that life is increasingly controlled by impersonal forces. For the realist of the fifties character is destiny; for the comic-apocalyptic writer destiny turns character into a joke. For the fifties writer history is remote and irrelevant compared to "private people and their minute concerns"; for the sixties writer history is absurd but it can kill you. Books like *Slaughterhouse-Five* and *Catch-22* do not slowly gravitate toward death like straightforward novels with unhappy endings. Because of their peculiar structure—in which everything is foreshadowed, everything happens at once—they are drenched in death on all sides, like an epidemic that breaks out everywhere at the same time. Thanks to the time scheme of Heller's book, characters seem perpetually a-dying and reappearing—quite a joke—so that we're shocked when they finally do disappear, one by one, each with his own mock individuality, each to his utterly depersonalizing fate.* And the Army stands for fate or necessity itself; it's a machine not for fighting or killing but solely for devouring its own.

Contradicting this pessimism, however, which sees individual life as manipulated and controlled from without, is the high degree of artistic power and license that goes into accomplishing this effect. If the sense of impotence and fatality in these novels expresses one side of the sensibility of the sixties, their creative exuberance and originality points to another; something that's also crucial to the radicalism of the period, the belief that old molds can be broken and recast, a sense that reality can be reshaped by the creative will. In their inventiveness and plasticity these books are the fictional equivalent of utopian thinking. This is why we must distinguish between verbal black humorists, such as Terry Southern, Bruce Jay Friedman, and even Philip Roth, whose basic unit is the sick joke or the stand-up

---

* Heller achieves exactly the same effect through Pirandellian dramatic games in his impressive antiwar play *We Bombed in New Haven*. As in Pirandello's *Tonight We Improvise,* which the Living Theater revived at the end of the fifties, behind the game of illusion-and-reality is one bedrock reality: death.

monologue, and what I would call "structural" black humorists, such as Heller, Pynchon, and Vonnegut. The former take apart the well-made novel and substitute nothing but the absurdist joke, the formless tirade, the cry in the dark; the latter tend toward over-articulated forms, insanely comprehensive plots (the paradox that is more than verbal, that seems inherent in the nature of things). Both kinds of black humorists are making an intense assertion of self—the former directly, the latter in vast structures of self-projection—that flies in the face of the prevailing depersonalization and external control.

All black humor involves the unseemly, the forbidden, the exotic, or the bizarre. Céline shatters the class-bound complacencies of accepted literary language with argot and street-slang, bringing the novel away from high-cultural norms and closer to living speech. His fulminations express the native cynicism of the common man, especially the marginal man of the lower middle class, who knows in his gut that all ideals are a crock of shit. He speaks for the prickly, impossible individual with all his prejudices intact, whom mass society and monopoly capitalism are always threatening to grind under, but who somehow manages to look out for Number One. Black humor always plays Falstaff to the conventional novel's Hotspur or Prince Hal. Whether it stresses the nether functions of the body, as in Henry Miller, or simply the nether side of all sentimentalities and idealizations, as in Nathanael West, or even the perverse, as with Nabokov's *Lolita* or Roth's *Portnoy's Complaint*, black humor is always affronting taboos, giving offense, recalling people to their physical functions and gut reactions. (That such cynicism conceals its own sentimentalities, that it's the obvious mark of the disappointed sentimentalist, we hardly need to emphasize.) Thus black humor became an aspect of the libertarian, idol-shattering side of the sixties. Books like *Portnoy's Complaint* and Mailer's *Why Are We In Vietnam?* could never have been published before the sixties; two decades earlier the language of Mailer's first novel had to be censored for publication, despite its army milieu. Both Mailer and Roth, like all young writers, had been taught to imitate their literary betters; like so many others, both seized on the sixties as a moment for letting go, with predictably mixed results—breakthroughs don't allow for guarantees.

Eventually things reach the point, in serious writing as in pornography, where scarcely any taboos were left to be assaulted. This revealed the intrinsic limitation of the "breakthrough" conceived entirely in terms of subject matter and épatisme, without benefit of new discoveries about life or new departures in form.* With few taboos left, the older mold of the novel broken but not recast, the verbal black humorists fell quickly into decadence and self-imitating excess. *Lolita* was followed by *Pale Fire* and *Ada, Portnoy's Complaint* by *Our Gang, The Breast,* and *The Great American Novel.* The last of these books is especially indicative of one of the weakest tendencies of black humor. Tossed into its negligible plot is an amazing assortment of dwarfs, cripples, freaks, and grotesques—with a few women thrown in as "slits"—far beyond the ripest excesses of Southern Gothic. Many of these "characters" are casually assigned to monstrous kinds of deformity and death in the course of the book, and by the end their whole world, a baseball league, collapses apocalyptically in ruins. We have a duty to inquire, as Mark Shechner does in a recent essay on Roth, what unexamined impulses of aggression and sadistic cruelty have gone into the making of this type of "humor." By contrast, the earlier breakthrough book, *Portnoy's Complaint,* really does use black humor, psychoanalysis, fantasy, and even lyricism to explore a real novelistic subject, which combines sex, Jewishness, growing up, morality, and the "family romance." After *Portnoy* Roth seems to have imagined that he had found a quite different formula, that a stand-up routine of bad taste and exaggeration were enough in themselves, without any deep personal engagement or formal effort.

The black humorists are generally strong in fantasy, and Roth is

* As Susan Sontag once wrote, apropos of a play by Edward Albee: "What is wrong with Albee's work—or Tennessee Williams', for that matter, is not the emphasis on freakishness, sexual perversion, or the like. It is the insincere, shallow use of this material. The perverse situations are not really probed. They are used, rather, as a conventional device for shocking an audience. . . . [T]he only real shocks in art are those that pertain to form. The real shocks, which the American theater lacks, are those of a bold image carried to the point of a genuine sensuous assault upon the audience." (*Partisan Review,* Winter 1964)

unusual among them—much closer to the writers of the fifties—in his weakness at fantasticating materials from outside his own experience. But Roth's post-*Portnoy* books do have a typical end-of-the-sixties quality in their gratuitous violence and desperate (but unearned) extremity. They belong to what we might call the Weatherman phase of recent literature, when the utopian hopes of an earlier moment turned sour, when some of the would-be free spirits were driven to such a pitch of frustration and intense desperation that they lost touch with reality. There had been such a thread, though minor, in the politics of the period from the beginning, and even more so in the literature. As William Blake stressed in his "Proverbs of Hell," liberation finds its necessary limit only through excess, not by way of caution and prudent restraint. But the verbal black humorists test the limits of exaggeration as a useful literary strategy. Thus the later stories in Malamud's *Pictures of Fidelman* push the schlemiel character into a masochistic comedy of humiliation that is genuinely unpleasant to read. Woody Allen often comes on like Fidelman on late-night talk shows, and the effect is similar. It's no accident that his films, for all their attempts at being "visual," lack any real architectonic imagination and depend too heavily on one-liners. A writer like Terry Southern is often crass and trivial, except in rare moments like the last pages of *The Magic Christian*, where his imagination brings off an apocalyptic fantasy of large comic proportions. At the bottom of the barrel are novels like Bruce Jay Friedman's *The Dick*, in which there is no imagination at all, where instead of imagination the novelist offers up his most rancid prejudices and adolescent twitches, from a repulsive racism to a sophomoric back-alley lechery, all in the name of shock and bad taste. Even a fine writer's writer like Stanley Elkin, who can be terribly subtle in the rhythms of his language, tends to be gross in his emotional tone, tends to be hysterical and overwrought in a way that's unbearable because it's so unmodulated. The Dostoevskian extremism and desperation of Jewish black humor is hard to keep under control, even when it's deeply felt; sincerity is not enough. It's a rare book like Bellow's *Herzog* or *Humboldt's Gift* where this frantic quality justifies and fulfills itself, by serving its subject and allowing for emotional nuance. Herzog's letters especially enable Bellow to move from a merely private and psychological case to the redefinition of a whole cultural period (an ambition that boomerangs disastrously in the rank, embittered pages of *Mr. Sammler's Planet*).

Failure to make such connections is what defeats a great deal of the verbal black humor of the sixties, which makes only a marginal advance on the personal novel of the previous decade. It alters the tone of the fifties novel without expanding its horizons. It brilliantly exploits vulgar, "pop" material, often with sexual audacity, and sometimes achieves a rollicking, exuberant comic tone. But with the exception of a few books like *Portnoy's Complaint*, it rarely stakes out new social or fictional territory. It partakes of the liberated spirit of the sixties but rarely does much that's constructive with its new-found freedom.

Quite the opposite is true of the writers I've called "structural" in their black humor. Construction is their strong point, mazes of plot, astoundingly complex fictional textures reminiscent of Joyce, Kafka, Borges, and Beckett—though sometimes we may wonder to what point all the energy of formal invention. These writers make a much sharper break with the private world of the fifties novel. Characteristically, like Pynchon, they reinvent an older literary form, the historical novel, which had descended into a moribund popular genre (the costume novel), or, like Vonnegut, they do devious and inspired take-offs on topical materials (such as the Eichmann and Abel cases in *Mother Night*, right-wing lunatic groups in *Mother Night* and *The Crying of Lot 49*, Caribbean dictatorships, the Bomb, and the end of the world in *Cat's Cradle*, the politics and philanthropy of the Rockefeller family in *God Bless You, Mr. Rosewater*, all sorts of politics in the stories in Donald Barthelme's *Unspeakable Practices, Unnatural Acts*, and so on). In other words these writers of the sixties rediscover the historical world, the public world—even as they are deeply skeptical of it—just as the sixties in general rediscovers the joys and horrors of politics, even as many feel poisoned by it.

In this light the work of the only two fifties novelists who wrote effectively about politics, Mailer and Ellison, takes on a new importance. Each of Mailer's first three novels, especially that tortured fable of the Party and the Revolution, *Barbary Shore*, wrestles partly with a political theme, increasingly in tandem with a sexual one. Finally, in *An American Dream* (1965), a work of baroque style and fantasy, Mailer's interests merge as he develops and examines his own fascination with sexual *and* public power, which he had already begun to do in his essays. And later in *The Armies of the Night*, the spirit of self-examination that had flared in *Advertisements for Myself* finds its perfect cultural moment in the Pentagon march of 1967, a public spectacle of immense private resonance for Mailer and for his readers: the result is both great autobiography and great history, the sixties' best attempt at stock-taking and self-definition.

The other writer who had grappled in the fifties with the romance of Communism—Ralph Ellison in the remarkable Brotherhood sections of *Invisible Man*—also emerged as a literary prophet of the sixties, though he himself published little then. The episodic and surreal method of *Invisible Man* goes against the grain of the fiction of the fifties but splendidly foreshadows the comic-apocalyptic novels that would follow. As against John Updike and other writers of the fifties, both Mailer and Ellison seem to accept George Eliot's dictum that "there is no private life that has not been determined by a wider public life." But their particular modernity comes in the recognition—already present a hundred years earlier in Dickens and Dostoevsky—of the bizarre and extreme new forms that public life can take, the subtle, insidious modes of determination it can impose. To encompass these developments, to match them imaginatively, the heightened response of a new technique would be necessary. The gray, documentary texture of naturalism, the naked, flattening anger of agit-prop writing (the older method of literary *engagement*), simply would not do. Like Dickens in his last great period, Ellison knew that it would take a wild, undisciplined imagination to appropriate the social actualities that lay behind the Brotherhood, or Rinehart the Trickster, or Ras the Exhorter. Following Ellison, the writers of the sixties, like the political activists of the period, were determined to profit from the mistakes of the thirties, and to cast both literature and politics in a quite different mold.

In a sense the differences between the thirties and the sixties were inevitable. The Old Left really believed that history could be explained, that our problems could be solved by changing the social arrangements. The fervent Americanism of Popular Front radicals between 1935 and the death of the Rosenbergs in 1953 was for many of them wholly sincere. The Rosenbergs never challenged the government's right to try them, never mocked the instruments of "justice" and trappings of authority that held them in tow. The contrast with the political trials of the sixties—and with their outcome!—could hardly be more drastic. The Rosenbergs believed in the system, which they felt was being abused, just as they believed that history would absolve them and that individual lives, their own lives, were worth sacrificing for the "progressive" cause. If the early New Left had any theory of history, it was kept well hidden. The radicals of the sixties were committed to spontaneity and to the personal here-and-now. They turned the courtroom into a scene of political theater, to illustrate the illegitimacy of the system and the superior wit and more attractive humanity of its opponents. (Evidently it was good theater, for they convinced a surprising number of carefully picked juries that their government couldn't be trusted.)

The literary equivalent of the sixties activists, call them the fictional radicals, also held a profoundly ironic and adversary view of the historical process. Typically, "progressive" literature is muckraking literature: a ferreting out of abuses so that the system can function according to its original ideals. Sixties literature, on the contrary, has an anxious, dead-end feeling about history, a paranoid fear about how it all holds together, a restless bafflement before the puzzle and complexity of it all. One way this attitude gets expressed is in the mock-historical novel, such as Barth's *Sot-Weed Factor*, Berger's *Little Big Man*, and one or two of the more campy historical chapters of Pynchon's *V*. Rather than finding a form of their own to express this sense of historical irony, these books or segments settle for pastiche or anti-novel, for tongue-in-cheek imitation of an earlier genre (the eighteenth-century picaresque novel, the Wild West novel, the international spy novel). Without developing their own sense of history, they merely parrot or parody the historical sense of the books they attach themselves to. Though they are loving recreations, the Barth and Berger books especially miss the robust spirit of the forms they imitate, and settle for an easy if not dismissive irony. Though highly indicative of the new feeling for history that followed the private concerns of the fifties, and full of a kind of imagination alien to the fifties, they are basically a literature of latecomers to the feast of the muses, what Barth himself once called a "literature of exhaustion," of self-consciousness: "novels which imitate the form of the Novel, by an author who imitates the role of Author."

In the pages that follow I'd like to look more closely at three representative black humor novels of the early sixties, *Mother Night*, *Catch-22*, and *The Crying of Lot 49*. These books are neither antiquarian nor excessively literary; in a complex way they develop a striking and unusual sense of history that in the end tells us less about history than about the cultural tone of the period when they were written. Vonnegut and Heller return to World War II not for purposes of historical recreation, not simply because it was their own great formative experience, and certainly not to provide the vicarious thrills of the conventional war novel. Rather, it's because the unsolved moral enigma of that period and that experience most closely expresses the conundrum of contemporary life fifteen years later. Earlier writers had been able to approach World War II with a certain moral simplicity; here after all was a "just war" if there ever was one. But after fifteen more years of continuous cold war and the shadow of thermonuclear war, all war seemed morally ambiguous if not outright insane; in the prolonged state of siege the whole culture seemed edged with insanity. With that special prescience that novelists sometimes have, *Catch-22*, though published in 1961, anticipates the moral nausea of the Vietnam war, even famously anticipates the flight of deserters to neutral Sweden. Similarly Vonnegut in *Mother Night* chooses a morally ambiguous double agent as his "hero," just as he writes about the problematic Allied bombing of Dresden rather than a Nazi atrocity in *Slaughterhouse-Five*.

Like Pynchon, but in a different way, both Vonnegut and Heller are interested in international intrigue; they marvel at the zany and unpredictable personal element at work or play within the lumbering forces of history. Heller's Milo Minderbinder is a satire not simply on the American capitalist entrepreneur but also on the international wheeler-dealer, whose amoral machinations, so hilarious at first, become increasingly somber, ugly, and deadly—like so much else in the book—so that we readers become implicated in our own earlier laughter. Yet Milo is particularly close to the book's hero, Yossarian: the two understand each other. They share an ethic of self-interest that in Yossarian comes close to providing the book's moral: as in Céline, it's all a crock, look out for Number One. In the figure of Milo the book and its protagonist confront their seamy underside, a hideous caricature of their own values.

This doubling effect is typical of works of structual black humor. In the historical plot of *V.* the central character is called Stencil, and one key structural element is the pairing of fathers and sons—Hugh Godolphin and Evan Godolphin, Sidney Stencil and Herbert Stencil. The younger Stencil's quest for V., which is also a search for parents and identity, is an attempt to decipher a history whose meaning is encoded in the fragmentary remains of previous histories and earlier generations. On this point there's a striking resemblance between *V.* and the Oedipal detective novels that Ross Macdonald has been writing since *The Galton Case* in 1959. In Macdonald the mysteries of the present are always solved by decoding the past; there's an abundance of missing parents, traumatized children, and buried corpses that have been moldering for a generation, waiting for their secrets to be unearthed. In late novels like *The Underground Man* and *Sleeping Beauty* these Oedipal tangles are doubled and redoubled into a plot of appalling complexity, even repetitiveness, so that individual identity pales—it becomes hard to keep track of the characters or to separate them, and the solution comes to interest the author far less than the obsessive mesh of parallel relationships. In *V.* the detective, Herbert

Stencil, is himself a cipher (as his name implies) who merely organizes an immense range of partial perspectives into one large diagram, a pattern of possible coherence and meaning. But where detective novels really do deliver a final secret that solves and abolishes all puzzles—Edmund Wilson objected that "this secret is nothing at all" after the big buildup—Pynchon is a modernist who leaves open the possibility that this final solution may be a mirage . . . a mirage or a shocking confirmation of a plot-ridden and mysteriously over-organized world. The mystery writer creates the pattern, but the modernist makes it more truly resonant, mysterious, and contingent.

The doubling and proliferation in the plot of these novels—which approaches a point of surfeit, even nausea, in the dense, choked pages of *Gravity's Rainbow*—always points to an ambiguity of identity, to mysterious correspondences behind the plenitude of the world's surfaces. In Pynchon the ambiguity is historical, ontological: who am I, where do I come from, who's pulling my strings, how can I wrench some meaning from my hieroglyphic surroundings? In Vonnegut the ambiguity is moral: what's the relation within Howard W. Campbell, Jr., the double agent who is the protagonist in *Mother Night* (1961), between the writer, the lover, the Nazi propagandist, and the American spy? Vonnegut himself tells us that the moral of the story ("the only story of mine whose moral I know") is that "we are what we pretend to be, so we must be careful what we pretend to be." In fact the book seems more of a fictional anticipation of Hannah Arendt's thesis that Eichmann represented "the banality of evil." Campbell does indeed encounter a very banal Eichmann while both are awaiting trial as Nazi criminals in an Israeli jail. Campbell's own specific gravity is not banal but mediocre. He's a mediocre but utterly facile and amoral man with a horrible talent for survival.

If Vonnegut's fascination with the bombing of Dresden suggests a degree of survivor-guilt—he lived while 135,000 others died—*Mother Night* is a positive brief against survival and adaptability in a murderous age. "If I'd been born in Germany, I suppose I would have *been* a Nazi, bopping Jews and gypsies and Poles around," says Vonnegut. He feels no superiority to the passive, pliable Everyman. His naive persona, which many critics have reviled as false simplicity, seems to me utterly true to his view of the world. What makes Vonnegut appeal so much to adolescents is probably a certain adolescent pessimism and moral absolutism, a modern Weltschmerz, which often threatens to reduce complex human problems to simple dichotomies, easy formulas. This is especially true when he speaks in his own person, in essays, prefaces, and interviews, where the mask of the wise simpleton quickly becomes cloying.

But in the novels something else happens. Simplicity of statement begins to have a quite different function. The manner becomes flat and factual, the chapters very brief, like the précis of an action rather than a full-scale novelization. Descriptive and psychological texture are reduced to mere notation, the action to pure plot, and the plot proliferates to a high degree of complexity, taking amazing twists and turns that double back on one another. Like most writers attracted to science fiction, Vonnegut has a precise, logical turn of mind; he loves to scatter the action in twenty separate strands, some of them quite fantastic, only to loop them all neatly together at the end. In this, like Pynchon in *V.*, he resembles the genre-writer or the old-fashioned crafter of well-made plots more than the modernist addicted to problematic and open-ended forms. But Vonnegut crowds the three-decker story into a book the length of a novella so that the emphasis on plot and incident, on Aristotelian changes of fortune, becomes overwhelming, becomes in fact the meaning, not simply a device. (This is especially true of *Mother Night* and *Cat's Cradle*, his strongest books, which both belong to the early sixties.)

The result is a subtle alteration of our sense of reality, at least as we read the book. Despite the promiscuous mixture of fact and fantasy, Vonnegut's flat, declarative manner and the simple-man persona give his narrators a sort of man-to-man reliability in the mind of the reader. They put everything in the story on the same plane: the most bizarre events seem more matter-of-fact, while flat-out realities take on the glow of lunacy they would naturally have if we weren't so inured to them. Vonnegut is attracted to such subjects as the Nazis or the Minutemen not so much because of his German descent or his own participation in World War II, but because, like other garish and spectacular subjects that appeal to him, they accord better with his sense of reality. Unlike the personal novelist of the fifties, who stakes his claim on the ground of immediate experience, who desires above all to be credible, Vonnegut finds life truer in its more extreme, more lunatic manifestations. Such a sense of the modern world could be fatal to a novelist; it could make him the ringmaster of a freak show, or a trivial, harmless fantasist, as it does some of the verbal black humorists. (Alfred Kazin complains, with some justice, of their "typed extremism" and of "the passion for collecting all possible accidents, oddities, lunacies and giving them an enormous presence in one's own mind.") But the mentality of Vonnegut, Heller, and Pynchon is not the collector's mentality but a more truly novelistic one, seizing on a genuine subject, a piece of world, and finding the imaginative means for making it a separate world, a convincing, coherent artifice.

The Jewish novelists of the fifties were drawn to extreme emotional states; they saw life's problems and glories in the involutions of the self. A writer like Vonnegut is drawn to extreme conditions of reality, conditions which have addled our minds or dulled our capacity for *any* emotional response. Perhaps under the influence of the death camps or the Bomb, but responding as well to the general tenor of modern life, Vonnegut and Heller are drawn to situations in which the arbitrary, the terrible, and the irrational have been *routinized*. They find it maniacally comic that men should learn to adjust to insane conditions, cultivate their private lives, go about their business. Howard Campbell is both an American spy and a Nazi propagandist, a game he plays so well that he frequently overdoes it; if not more Catholic than the Pope he's surely more Nazi than the Führer. "How else could I have survived?" he asks his American superior. "That was your problem," he's told. "Very few men could have solved it as thoroughly as you did." (This combination of virtuosity and amorality intrigues Vonnegut; Campbell turns pliability and time-serving into a fine art.) His father-in-law Werner Noth, the police chief of Berlin, is a different sort of time-server. Though hanged summarily from an apple tree as a Nazi, it turns out that "terror and

torture were the provinces of other branches of the German police,"
that Noth's province was to keep up ordinary law and order and keep
the traffic moving. "Noth's principal offense," we are told, "was
that he introduced persons suspected of misdemeanors and crimes
into a system of courts and penal institutions that was insane. Noth
did his best to distinguish between the guilty and the innocent, using
the most modern police methods; but those to whom he handed over
his prisoners found the distinction of no importance. Merely to be in
custody, with or without trial, was a crime."

Much of the comedy of *Catch-22* comes from the same effort to
maintain business as usual under "insane" conditions. The painstaking records the Nazis kept were perhaps rooted in a similar impulse.
Werner Noth is a great admirer of his son-in-law's propaganda
broadcasts and, though a Nazi, is unconcerned that Campbell may
also have been an American spy, "because," as he tells him, "you
could never have served the enemy as well as you served us. . . .
Almost all the ideas that I hold now, that make me unashamed of
anything I may have felt or done as a Nazi, came not from Hitler, not
from Goebbels, not from Himmler—but from you. . . . You alone
kept me from concluding that Germany had gone insane." Out of
pure play-acting, unhampered by any real disorderly commitment,
Campbell has amusingly (!) become the Ur-Nazi, whose work still
turns up twenty years later as the staple of right-wing lunatic fringe
groups. You are what you do, you become what you seem to be. No
wonder Vonnegut and Heller became classics of the anti-Vietnam
generation, curious comic bibles of protest, so different from the
protest literature of the thirties, while writers like Malamud, who
took the fifties posture of stoicism and endurance, or else Jamesian
renunciation, gradually lost favor.* Vonnegut's zany, cartoon-like
plot, his distaste for violence and heroic posturing, and his affinity

* This is not to say that established writers were unaffected by the new cultural
mood; Mailer and Roth, for example, changed styles completely, as did numbers of
poets. Saul Bellow was galvanized into oppositional fury by his total loathing of the
new culture and all its works. But some fifties writers lost energy and force even when
they lamely adopted a more militant message their imagination couldn't fully sustain—notably Baldwin after *The Fire Next Time* and Malamud in *The Fixer* and *The
Tenants*.

for a few simple human verities help make his work the moral equivalent of the New Politics of the early sixties, which substituted communitarian good will, anarchic individualism, and ethical fervor for the old staples of ideology. Thus Vonnegut, in a key passage of *Mother Night*, likens the totalitarian mind to "a system of gears whose teeth have been filed off at random. . . . The missing teeth, of course, are simple, obvious truths, truths available and comprehensible even to ten-year-olds, in most cases. . . . This is the closest I can come to explaining the legions, the nations of lunatics I've seen in my time." Like the New Left, however, Vonnegut is more impressive as happening than as explanation: the "at random" seems particularly inadequate. But the ingenious reversals of Vonnegut's plots go well beyond the simple verities of his own moralizing, and provide as full a helping of moral ambiguity as any modernist could want.

The final twist of Vonnegut's book is Howard Campbell's last-minute exoneration by the system of "justice," which he refutes by committing suicide. After all, unlike Eichmann, he had surrendered to the Israelis precisely to counteract his miserable gift for survival; now he takes more definitive action. By writing this book and then taking his life he becomes his own prosecutor, judge, and executioner. Vonnegut is sure that there are no heroes, that he himself might have gone along with the Nazis had he lived in Germany, and therefore that no one has the right to stand in judgment of another. By executing judgment on himself Campbell cuts through the fog of moral ambiguity and becomes the book's true protagonist and center of value.

I said earlier that characters in black humor novels tend to be cartoon-like and two-dimensional, without the capacity to grow or change. To this we must add the qualification that the protagonist is usually different: he doesn't completely belong to this mode of reality or system of representation. As Richard Poirier has suggested apropos of Pynchon, the central character of these novels often moves on a different plane: he shows at least the capacity to become a fuller, more sentient human being, a character in a realistic novel.

In the first part of the book the "hero" is typically enmeshed in a system of comic repetition: tics of speech and behavior, entanglements of plot, all the "routines" of verbal black humor, life imitating vaudeville. Heller, for example, like Dickens, knows how to make his own comic technique approximate poignant human realities. And as the comedy in *Catch-22* darkens, the system of dehumanization becomes clearer, and the central character becomes increasingly isolated in his impulse to challenge and step outside it.

In Yossarian Heller introduces a new figure into postwar American fiction, descended from the schlemiel of the Jewish novel but finally an inversion of that passive and unhappy figure. Heller tells us he's an Assyrian, but only because (as he said to an interviewer) "I wanted to get an extinct culture. . . . [M]y purpose in doing so was to get an outsider, a man who was intrinsically an outsider." The typical schlemiel is certainly no hero, but like Yossarian has a real instinct for survival. In earlier days Yossarian had really tried to bomb the targets, as he was supposed to do. Now his only goal is to avoid flak, to keep alive. "Yossarian was the best man in the group at evasive action." This Yossarian is concerned only with saving his skin, obsessed by the things that threaten his life. "There were too many dangers for Yossarian to keep track of." And Heller gives us a wonderful catalogue of them, from Hitler, Mussolini, and Tojo ("they all wanted him dead") to all the insane and fanatical people in his own army ("they wanted to kill him, too") to all the organs of his body, with their arsenal of fatal diseases:

> There were diseases of the skin, diseases of the bone, diseases of the lung, diseases of the stomach, diseases of the heart, blood and arteries. There were diseases of the head, diseases of the neck, diseases of the chest, diseases of the intestines, diseases of the crotch. There were even diseases of the feet. There were billions of conscientious body cells oxidating away day and night like dumb animals at their complicated job of keeping him alive and healthy, and every one was a potential traitor and foe. There were so many diseases that it took a truly diseased mind to even think about them as often as he and Hungry Joe did.

Yossarian seems perilously close to the Sterling Hayden character in *Dr. Strangelove,* the general who fears that women are sapping his vital bodily fluids. The insanity of the system, in this case the army, breeds a defensive counter-insanity, a mentality of organized survival that mirrors the whole system of rationalized human waste and devaluation. The self itself becomes an army, a totalitarian body politic, demanding total vigilance against the threat of betrayal and insurrection. Each individual organ, each cell, becomes an object of paranoid anxiety. I remember as a child being afraid I might forget to breathe, holding my breath as long as I could, to be reassured it would still happen without me. Yossarian too has the "childish" wish to assert the sort of outside control that he himself feels gripped by.

The pattern of *Catch-22* is similar to that of *Mother Night:* a world gone mad, a protagonist caught up in the madness, who eventually steps outside it in a slightly mad way. The Sweden to which Yossarian flees at the end of the book is something of a pipe dream, a pure elsewhere. Yossarian's friend Orr has made it there (from the Mediterranean in a rowboat!), but Orr is Yossarian's opposite, utterly at home in the world, as idiotically free of anxiety as Yossarian is dominated by it. Orr is the unkillable imp, the irrepressible innocent, a "likable dwarf with a smutty mind and a thousand valuable skills that would keep him in a low income group all his life." Orr is the gentile Crusoe to Yossarian's Jewish neurotic; along with the diabolical Milo they form a spectrum of the possibilities of survival in extreme situations, which include not only wartime but just about all of modern life, indeed the whole human condition, for which the war is ultimately a metaphor.

But Yossarian goes through a second change before the book ends: he becomes a troublemaker and, worse still, the unwilling keeper of the book's conscience, just as Nately's whore becomes the figure of Nemesis, the haunting, surreal spirit of female revenge for the callous inhumanity of a man-made world. The earlier Yossarian saw through the no-win bind of Catch-22 and set out monomaniacally to survive. But as each of the others goes separately, uncomplainingly, to his predictable fate, Yossarian becomes more and more the somber registrar of their deaths and exits:

> Nately's whore was on his mind, as were Kraft and Orr and Nately and Dunbar, and Kid Sampson and McWatt, and all the poor and stupid and diseased people he had seen in Italy, Egypt and North Africa and knew about in other areas of the world, and Snowden and Nately's whore's kid sister were on his conscience, too.

Yossarian has come willy-nilly to brood about more than his own inner organs. Other people have become a desperate reality to him, and with it has come a sense of their common fate, their mutual essence. The secret of Snowden, who spills his guts in the tail of a plane, is revealed to Yossarian alone:

> His teeth were chattering in horror. He forced himself to look again. Here was God's plenty, all right, he thought bitterly as he stared—liver, lungs, kidneys, ribs, stomach and bits of the stewed tomatoes Snowden had eaten that day for lunch. Yossarian hated stewed tomatoes. . . . He wondered how in the world to begin to save him.
> "I'm cold," Snowden whispered. "I'm cold."
> "There, there," Yossarian mumbled in a voice too low to be heard. "There, there."
> Yossarian was cold, too, and shivering uncontrollably. . . . It was easy to read the message in his entrails. Man was matter, that was Snowden's secret. Drop him out a window and he'll fall. Set fire to him and he'll burn. Bury him and he'll rot, like other kinds of garbage. The spirit gone, man is garbage. That was Snowden's secret. Ripeness was all.

Impelled perhaps by the unconscious Jewish identification, Heller paraphrases the famous "humanizing" speech of Shylock ("If you prick us, do we not bleed? if you tickle us, do we not laugh? if you poison us, do we not die?"). But the final allusion to *Lear* is breathtaking: an impertinence to do it, the height of *chutzpah* to bring it off. The scene must be read as a whole to see how well it works—it's the penultimate moment of the book—but even the delicate texture of these pages of prose would be nothing had not the "secret" of Snowden been such an important leitmotif throughout the book. (Snowden's death had taken place before the book opened, but it's fully remembered and decoded as he lies in the hospital in the next-to-last chapter, as if its meaning, which underlies the whole book, had taken that long to be reduced to its terrifying simplicity and finality.) The somber tone of this passage—despite the necessary farcical touch of Yossarian's dislike of stewed tomatoes—is something that's not available to verbal black humor, which aims for wild incongruities at every turn, which is more at home with disgust and humiliation and absurdity than with the simple terror of the world as it is; such a poignant effect requires a more fully human respondent, which Yossarian has by now become. Heller's "structural" use of the secret of Snowden makes it a time bomb of ineluctable tragic fact ticking away beneath the book's surface of farce and rollicking insanity; except that the secret unfolds its revelations gradually, alongside the story, until it finally *becomes* the story.*

When I first read *Catch-22* I felt strongly that except for the Snowden chapter the book's final shift in tone in the last seventy-five pages didn't work, that after doing an amazing *comic* adaptation of Kafka and Dostoevsky most of the way, Heller unaccountably switched to imitating them directly in the finale, a contest he couldn't win. Rereading the book I can see why I felt that way—we miss the sheer gratuitous pleasure of the comedy—but I also see how much the somber and even ugly side was present from the beginning and how gradually the book modulates into it: for such laughter we have the devil to pay. The *Mr. Roberts* element won't carry us all the way through. I'm now sure the last section works and makes the whole book work; up against a wall, I'd have to call *Catch-22* the best novel of the sixties.

But what can we learn about the sixties from *Catch-22?* I think the popular success of the book can be attributed to the widespread spiritual revulsion in the sixties against many of our most sacrosanct in-

---

* I wonder if Heller was aware of Wordsworth's use of Snowdon, the Welsh mountain, as the penultimate scene of revelation before the conclusion of *The Prelude;* if so he inverts Wordsworth's brooding "recognitions of transcendent power" into his own more nihilistic *Lear*-like epiphany. He does refer to Villon's rueful "snows of yesteryear"—"Où sont les Neigedens d'antan?"—but not to Wordsworth. The name itself may mean "snowed-in," for the scene in the plane, with Snowden whimpering and Yossarian "shivering uncontrollably," is infused with the terror of frozen entrapment, life ebbing away in preternatural cold. Kazin aptly calls this the "primal scene" of the novel. It's surely the book's primal experience and the master-image of Yossarian's anxieties.

stitutions, including the army; to which our leaders replied by heightening just those things that had caused the disgust in the first place, especially the quality of fraud, illusion, and manipulation in our public life. Just as the response to war-protest was escalation and the solution to the failures of the bombing was more bombing, so the push for more honesty in public debate was met by more public relations and bigger lies. The Johnson administration's unshakable insistence that black was white, that escalation was really the search for peace, and that the war was being won was a perfect realization of the structure of unreality and insanity that runs as a theme through both *Mother Night* and *Catch 22*. One typical and well-deserved victim is Doc Daneeka, who collaborates with the insanity of Catch-22 until it creates the general illusion that he himself is dead (which, morally speaking, he is). Daneeka's merely physical presence is inadequate to contradict his "official" demise; he is destroyed as much by his own demented survival ethic as by the structure of unreality that is the army. "We're all in this business of illusion together," says another doctor when he asks Yossarian to substitute for a dead soldier whose parents are coming to see him die. "As far as we're concerned," the doctor says, "one dying boy is just as good as any other, or just as bad."

> "Giuseppe."
> "It's not Giuseppe, Ma. It's Yossarian."
> "What difference does it make?" the mother answered in the same mourning tone, without looking up. "He's dying."

When the whole family starts crying, Yossarian cries too. It's not a show anymore. Somehow they're right, the doctor's right, they *are* dying; in some sense it *doesn't* matter. A piece of ghoulish humor has turned into something exceptionally moving. The same point is made with the Soldier in White, a mummy in bandages whose only sign of life is an interchange of fluids. What *is* a man, anyway, when things have come to this extremity? The ground is being readied for revealing Snowden's secret. The *Lear* theme is at the heart of the book, no mere device for concluding it.

Unlike the realistic novelists of the fifties, the black humorists suggest that besides our personal dilemmas, which often loom so large in our imagination, we all share features of a common fate, enforced by society and the general human condition. Though the quest for identity must inevitably be personal, in some sense we *are* interchangeable. Furthermore, the quest will surely be thwarted if society becomes a vast structure of illusion and duplicity, and hence treats us as even more interchangeable and manipulable than we necessarily are. One effect of Vietnam and Watergate was that the official organs of our society lost much of the respect and credence they had commanded. Even middle Americans began to live with less of a mystified and paternalistic sense of Authority. The disillusionment and ruthless skepticism—really, spoiled idealism—of *Catch-22*, outlived the sixties to become a pervasive national mood. With Célinean cynics and paranoids installed in the White House, people at large became that much more cynical and paranoid themselves. And the paranoia had some basis in fact, for in a highly polarized society, where the self-imposed limitations of tradition and civility have been cast away, it's likely that somebody really is out to get you, by any means fair or foul. During the Johnson and Nixon administrations we learned that even in this country Authority's talent for abusing power is greater, or at least more nimble, than society's ability to check the abuse. The Watergate revelations showed how close we came to an internal *coup d'état*, perhaps on the Indian model, if not to the paranoid nightmare of manipulation and control foreshadowed by the black humor novel.

During the Eisenhower administration American power, though it had not withdrawn from its new world role, was quietly exercised in what seemed like a paternal and benign way. When Kennedy challenged the phlegmatic and restrained tendencies that underlay the saber-rattling of a Dulles, he called attention to American power and position in a new way. Kennedy demanded a more flexible military posture, the ability to fight two and a half wars simultaneously (a typical maniac vision), and hence the tactical power to combat so-called wars of national liberation, one of which was already in progress in Indochina. Kennedy's liberalism, like the whole liberal tradition since 1945, was internationalist, while Eisenhower and the conservatives still labored under a faint shadow of isolationism, the precedent of the period after World War I, when America had pulled back from its international "responsibilities." Hence Vietnam *was* in large measure the liberals' war, not only because many liberals were crucial in prosecuting and defending it but because its rationale emerged directly from the cold war liberalism of the forties and fifties, which accepted the worldwide mission of "containing" the Communists wherever they might appear, in whatever national form. By attacking the old general for a nonexistent "missile gap" and for overall military weakness, Kennedy seized the initiative of anti-Communism for the Democratic Party, less than a decade after McCarthy had snatched it away from Truman and Acheson. And predictably, the first two years of the Kennedy administration—from the Bay of Pigs, to the summit meeting with Khrushchev in Vienna, to the Berlin crisis of the summer of 1961, to the Cuban missile crisis of 1962—were a period of substantial intensification of the cold war, while our defense establishment was being vastly expanded and retooled for hot wars. The more soft-centered liberals like Stevenson, Bowles, Galbraith, and Schlesinger, who might have opposed this tendency, all were confined to window-dressing positions that were more or less marginal to the making of policy.

While few of these things "caused" any writers to write their books, I think this climate helps explain why black humor began its great efflorescence during the Kennedy years, in apparent contradiction to the idealism, optimism, and high style that we still like to attribute to that period. Mailer's *An American Dream* can be read as a testament about the Kennedy years, ultimately shrewder than all the tendentious memoirs and eulogies that were published after the assassination. When I first came upon the references to Kennedy in the opening pages I thought them meretricious: one more piece of megalomania for Mailer to associate his all-too-Mailerian hero with the dashing, fallen president. But Mailer's identification with Kennedy had come much earlier and ran much deeper. His first major piece of journalism was about Kennedy's nomination. A would-be courtier and counselor, he'd addressed a whole book of essays to Kennedy as president. Sexually rivalrous, he'd written an open letter to Jackie, half-scolding her but implicitly trying to woo her away. Like others Mailer saw Kennedy as some kind of union of style and power—both Irish and Harvard, moneyed and *macho*—whose classy imperial court had a use for the arts. But in the novel his hero, Rojack, complains that

> The real difference between the President and myself may be that I ended with too large an appreciation of the moon, for I looked down the abyss on the first night I killed: four men, four very separate Germans, dead under a full moon—whereas Jack, for all I know, never saw the abyss.

Recall the premise that Kennedy and Rojack are alter egos, both war heroes, both elected to Congress in the same year. (Even his name may be an amalgam of Robert and Jack.) But Mailer's Rojack has explored the nether side of violence and power, explores it again in the course of the book, coming out only "something like sane again" in the last line. The book's plot can be seen as an enactment of his fantasies, his irrationalities, his madness. Dangling over the balcony of a skyscraper to probe his courage and manhood, he hears voices that tell him he can fly. The whole book is steeped in magic and dread, the dark underside of a too-purely Apollonian Kennedy vision of power without price or penalty. Rojack is not Mailer but Mailer's ambiguous self-portrait as an archetype of the age. Only the best writers have the gift of using the accidents of their own experience, the stuff of their fantasy life, in that significant way, and we can hardly blame the book's first readers, myself included, who were still under the sway of Camelot's idealized Apollonian self-image, for seeing bad taste and confessional self-aggrandizement in its allusions to both Kennedy and the author's own recent bad-boy history.

Today time allows us quite another perspective on that period and its literature. From *Catch-22, Mother Night,* and *V.* to *Cat's Cradle, Little Big Man,* and *An American Dream,* the black humor novels of the first half of the sixties, even when conceived earlier, are like a secret history of the Kennedy years, when the terrifying specter of thermonuclear war flared garishly one last time before beginning to dim, when fond hopes for building a better society were repeatedly mocked by our inability to deal with the society we have, when a President's civilized, cosmopolitan vision helped conceal the expansion of our imperial role. Pynchon and Heller, like Mailer and Berger, are the first novelists of a new imperial America, even when they write about World War II, that just war, or about German Southwest Africa, or about the Fashoda crisis of the 1880s (which neatly foreshadows the Suez crisis of the 1950s), or about the political machinations of Argentine exiles in Florence in 1902. *V.* especially is a novel whose wide-ranging imagination, strongly influenced by European novelists of imperialism like Conrad and Graham Greene, peculiarly parallels America's new world role. Just as *An American Dream* is ambivalent toward power—sexual power, political power, American power—*V.* is ambivalent toward history, seeing in it an exhilarating if frighteningly comprehensive shape and design, but seeing it also as perhaps a fraud, an illusion, the ultimate unreality compared to the individual's humblest private need. The early sixties was itself an ambiguous period, for like these novels it did really have an exuberant and expansive side that was not mere Camelot rhetoric.

Let me stress again the positive side of that cultural moment before descending once more into the maelstrom of its hidden history. The early sixties really were a hopeful period, a dizzying time when things everywhere seemed to be opening up after the stagnation of the Eisenhower years. There were many portents of change in society. The decisions of the Supreme Court in cases of civil rights, civil liberties, reapportionment, and the separation of church and state seemed to foreshadow significant change in areas where the two other branches of government had proved cowardly, helpless, or paralyzed. A nascent civil rights movement, then still in its hand-in-hand, "We Shall Overcome" mood, was translating the stirrings of the Court into direct action. A nascent New Left, humanistic in its values, spontaneous and American in its methods, but potentially radical in its goals, seemed determined to avoid the ideological rigidity and conspiratorial mentality of the Old. In Beat poetry and the new vogue of folk music these social movements found their artistic accompaniment, as poets and folksingers reached past the academic insularity and pop commercialism of the fifties toward the positive cultural side of the left-wing heritage of the thirties, the populism of the Popular Front. When a very young Bob Dylan made his pilgrimage from Hibbing, Minnesota, to the bedside of a dying Woody Guthrie, the spirit of two epochs was symbolically joined. Songs of protest and solidarity helped create a tenuous tissue of brotherhood at every civil rights event, just as poets would later lend their bardic daimon to the antiwar movement.

But the opening up of the novel was a deeper, more ambiguous development, and I think it revealed more about the changing sensibility of the early sixties. Grandiose and experimental in form, these books partook of the imperial buoyancy of the Kennedy years. But their vision sometimes had a bleak, dead-end character that belied any official optimism. *Catch-22* had a plastic creative freedom and energy hardly present in the novels of the fifties, but it imagines a world wholly unredeemed by rational purpose or humanistic uplight. A similar ambiguity attaches to the theme of paranoia and the vision of history in Pynchon's novels. His form and language, his historical range and complexity of plot, match Heller in creative exuberance, and many in his endless cast of cartoonish characters are pure products of the comic or satiric spirit. Even his paranoid theme has its exhilarating side: it enables him to make astonishing connections and fantasize breathtaking possibilities, to subvert and intimidate our pedestrian sense of reality and causation, "to bring the estate into pulsing stelliferous Meaning" (as Oedipa Maas muses). *"Shall I project a world?"* Oedipa asks herself in *The Crying of Lot 49*, situating herself neatly somewhere between the novelist and the psychotic. She is neither, but the elaborate plot that her sleuthing gradually intuits makes for a novel that's both impressively somber in tone and yet anazingly conditional and tentative in substance. For those who entirely associate black humor with apocalyptic farce and a tone of raucous extremity, *The Crying of Lot 49* should come as a revelation. *V.* embodies more of the positive side of the paranoid vision, with its immense assortment of characters, plots, historical periods, and narrative modes, all spun together into a dazzling web of possible meanings—which still don't measure up to the pleasure of the telling, the joy of imaginative construction, where the paranoid and the novelist *do* come together. But in the spare, perfectly controlled novella that Pynchon wrote next, Oedipa, the heroine, imagines a vast plot that the author mostly doesn't care to enact. *Lot 49* is *about* plotting, and Oedipa is less the projector than the object, the possible victim. Herbert Stencil, the sleuth of *V.*, is an eccentric bird in search of his own identity, who in the process happens to construct an immense historical mosaic. Himself nothing, Stencil could only become; but since the cartoon of history is enough for him, he probably won't. But Oedipa Maas, despite her piquant Pynchonesque name, has the pulse of a full-blooded woman. The California cartoon world that surrounds her can't possibly satisfy her, but the richer baroque underworld she glimpses won't necessarily do so either. It might be a way out, but not to anything better. The ambiguity of history in *V.*—does it have no meaning or too much meaning? is it a chaos of random hints or a tightly organized totalitarian web?—becomes the more direct subject of *The Crying of Lot 49*. In trying to sort out the estate of the late Pierce Inverarity, Oedipa gets in a classic double bind, which eventually comes to represent reality itself, particularly the American reality. Either Oedipa has stumbled onto an immense plot—or into an immense hoax—that has the "secret richness and concealed density of dream" but also a dream-like pointlessness and ineffectuality, or else there is nothing, no "real alternative to the exitlessness, to the absence of surprise to life, that harrows the head of everybody American you know," nothing but the official surfaces of life, the "lies, recitations of routine, arid betrayals of spiritual poverty." Oedipa hopes none of these things is true. "She didn't like any of them, but hoped she was mentally ill; that that's all it was." Either no exit, or an exit into rich but unhinging, even appalling realities, or perhaps an exit into madness, clinical paranoia, inner space.

It's astonishing how well the book locates itself on this narrow shelf of ambiguity, this edge of contingency, beautifully epitomized in a small moment when Oedipa comes upon what looks like an ordinary trash can, hand-painted with the initials W.A.S.T.E. "She had to look closely to see the periods between the letters." It's a witty touch, for those tiny periods flickering near the vanishing-point could mean nothing at all, but might also make all the difference between a simple trash can and a system of secret communication going back centuries; she may have stumbled into the dense underbrush of a hidden reality, something she might have uncovered "anywhere in her Republic, through any of a hundred lightly concealed entranceways, a hundred alienations, if only she'd looked." "Behind the hieroglyphic streets there would either be a transcendent meaning, or only the earth."

It should be clear why Pynchon's paranoid myth makes some claim on us, without demanding that we be paranoid ourselves or give any credence to the reality of V. or the Tristero System. Pynchon's paranoia is neither a clinical paranoia nor a literal paranoid view of history but instead a metaphor for something the novelist shares with the mystic, the drug-taker, the philosopher, and the scientist: a desperate appetite for meaning, a sense at once joyful and threatening that things are not what they seem, that reality is mysteriously over-organized and can be decoded if only we attend to the hundred innocent hints and byways that beckon to us, that life is tasteless and insipid without this hidden order of meaning but perhaps appalling *with* it.

Without farce or violence, Pynchon's paranoia reveals an alienation from American life greater than that of Heller or any other comic-apocalyptic writer. Society commands no loyalty in *Lot 49*, though the freaked-out scene of California in the sixties evokes an anthropological fascination; the rest is a tissue of falsehood and spiritual deadness. The drifter ambiance of *V.*, which Pynchon himself has evidently continued to live out, has ripened in good sixties fashion into a complete rejection of official cant and the square world. Pynchon's sensibility, like that of some of the earlier Beat figures

(whom he resembles in many ways, not including his highly structured style of writing and his aversion to personal publicity), strikingly foreshadowed the mood of young people in the late sixties. For
them paranoia, like radicalism, drug-taking, and communal life, was
both a rejection of the official culture and a form of group solidarity,
promising a more fully authentic life-possibility.

For Pynchon the paranoid imagination is a special way of rebelling
or dropping out, but it's also more than that. He compares it to a
hallucinogenic drug. For him it rends the veil of life's banal and
numbing surfaces, putting him in touch with something more deep
and rich, which may also unfortunately be quite unreal. Above all it
makes him feel more fully alive, with a more intense and absolute
self than the official rational culture dares allow. It's "a delirium
tremens, a trembling unfurrowing of the mind's plowshare." It's
also analogous to the powerful sentiment of being that marks certain
religious experiences: "the saint whose water can light lamps, the
clairvoyant whose lapse in recall is the breath of God, the true paranoid for whom all is organized in spheres joyful or threatening about
the central pulse of himself. . . ." It's important that Oedipa herself
does not really have such an experience, only a glimmering and conditional intimation of it. Her mind trembles and is unfurrowed, but
down to the end she passively receives these intimations and continues to weigh and judge them, caught in her double bind:

> Another mode of meaning behind the obvious, or none. Either Odeipa in
> the orbiting ecstasy of a true paranoia, or a real Tristero. For there either
> was some Tristero beyond the appearance of the legacy America, or there
> was just America and if there was just America then it seemed the only
> way she could continue, and manage to be at all relevant to it, was as an
> alien, unfurrowed, assumed full circle into some paranoia.

Evidently Pynchon is tempted to romanticize Oedipa into a figure or
rebellion, just as he briefly inflates Pierce Inverarity's "legacy" into
an allegory of America; but this is not where the book is really
impressive. In the final scene Oedipa, "with the courage you find
you have when there is nothing more to lose," prepares to make a
final gesture to expose the Tristero secret. But she's far from a heroic

figure, only—like Yossarian, like most of Vonnegut's heroes—a modest center of value in a world where human values have been misplaced or forgotten; she's caught between two worlds, the conventional and the paranoid, that each have gone amok in their own way. Oedipa is not simply the drifter and the bumbling amateur sleuth on loan from *V*. She grows more real and human as the book proceeds, trying to make connections but more impressive in her quiet despair and sexual *dis*connection, a mood that heightens gradually into a sense of apocalyptic foreboding. What really moves us in *Lot 49* is not the paranoid myth itself—we care almost as little about the Tristero System as about the impossibly elaborate plot of the Jacobean play Pynchon parodies—but rather the state of mind, the rhythm of perception it makes possible. The big novels of the early sixties really do belong to the expansive, world-projecting mood of that period. *The Crying of Lot 49*, published in 1966, already anticipates the more somber expectations of the late sixties, when paranoia gradually ceased to be an ecstatic enlargement of the possibilities of meaning and being, a positive subversion of ordinary reality, and instead darkened into an apocalyptic and pervasive anxiety. The paranoid became the victim of the plot or the helpless onlooker waiting to be engulfed, not the imaginative projector. If *Catch-22* foreshadows the soul-destroying madness of the Vietnam war, *The Crying of Lot 49* foreshadows the darkening green of the end of the sixties, when a government of lawless desperadoes and a half-crazed remnant of young radicals would pair off in an unequal contest of mutual paranoia, helping to destroy each other and confirming also Delmore Schwartz's much-quoted adage that "even paranoids have enemies."

The black humor novels of the sixties are not only deeply interested in history but create amazing parallels to the history of their own times, less in their actual subjects than in their whole mode of imagination. The sense of incongruity and absurdity, the mixture of farce, violence, and hysteria, that we find in these books we can also find in the wars, riots, movements, assassinations, conspiracies, as well as in much subtler and less spectacular manifestations of the spirit of the sixties. The black humor novel of the sixties, like the radicalism of the sixties, indeed like the American government and the architects of social policy in the sixties, began with elaborate efforts to assimilate history, to comprehend and shape it along the lines of private mythology, public planning, the enlightened will. By the end of the sixties—in both fiction and reality—this confidence was displaced by a sense that history was out of control, or that the Others had their hands on the wheel and were preparing to do us in completely. By the end of the sixties paranoia was the last fuel for direct action, the last gasp of a coherent world-view, which soon itself collapsed into fragments. "Fragments are the only forms I trust," wrote Donald Barthelme, as the influence of more titanic modernists like Joyce gave way to such inspired miniaturists as Kafka and Borges, negative visionaries whose work undercut all mythic inclusiveness. In late-sixties writers like Barthelme or Wurlitzer the sense of disconnection is complete, as it is in the Weatherman phase of sixties radicalism, where futility and frustration spawn random violence. Barthelme and Wurlitzer write as if they were surrounded by the curious artifacts of an extinct culture, which they plunder like collectors, or stroll past vacantly like sleepwalkers.

5

The Working Press, the Literary Culture, and the New Journalism

THE SOCIAL CATACLYSMS of the sixties resembled not a conventional war with large-scale battles so much as a hundred small guerrilla encounters in every corner of the country. In the United States as in Vietnam there was no "front," the enemy was everywhere, a Fifth Column within the gates. There were a few visible centers of conflict in the domestic struggle—the universities, the urban ghettos, the Supreme Court, the public flaunting of new sexual mores, the large demonstrations for civil rights and against the war—but despite the attention they got, and often deserved, they served to conceal more subtle and pervasive changes that were rocking and rending institutions, professions, and relationships. Fashions come and go, skimming across the surface of society, into an oblivion from which even history can scarcely rescue them. Much of what happened in the sixties was fashion in this sense. But within the vagaries of fashion were hints of profound alterations in sensibility, morals, and political feelings that would affect the most remote outposts of society.

Of all the professions that were shaken in the sixties, journalism was one of the stodgiest and most conservative, almost as rigid in its way as law and medicine. Yet reporters themselves, if no geniuses or heroes of nonconformity, were far from a conventional lot. The cynical, colorful, tumultuous world of Hecht and MacArthur's play *The Front Page* has always been a real part of newspaper life. Whatever sycophancy was required of him to keep the confidence of his editor and his sources, a good reporter was quick to acquire a healthy skepticism about men in power. More than anyone he knew all about the gaps between promise and performance, between fact and facade, between what was said and what really happened. Privately, in his bones, he knew at close quarters what made the wheels turn, and sometimes could even smuggle some of what he knew into print; more often the rigid conventions of newspaper journalism conspired with the facts of power and money within the organization to prevent it. Most reporters gave up trying and became even more cynical, knowing full well that they matched the credibility gap of men in public life with a yawning chasm of their own. In editorial columns, where opinion could be expressed, the influence of money, privilege, and small-town bigotry held full sway; so if journalists had a fractious streak, the product they published could not have been more conventional or less threatening to the status quo. No one could be surprised when more than 90 percent of America's newspapers supported Eisenhower over Stevenson in 1952 and 1956, including the august *New York Times,* then a pillar of conservatism in its own special way.

The conventionality of newspaper writing extended far beyond the limitations placed on political opinion. I spent eight years as a student journalist in high school and college—indeed, I had a deep and abiding attraction to the whole field—and in the course of this lively apprenticeship got dosed with all the well-worn nostrums handed down from city rooms and journalism schools. In the gospel according to the *New York Times,* the Columbia Journalism School, and the Scholastic Press Association—and confirmed by our high school history textbooks—the common coin of the realm was a Fact. The biggest story was the one that captured and displayed the biggest Fact and followed it in invariable order—the famous "inverted pyramid"—with the second-biggest, the third-biggest, and so on (so that whoever did the layout could always cut "from the bottom": those little facts bringing up the rear had no clout at all). The bad guys in this scenario were journalists called "Yellow," who started the Spanish-American War and put out the *Daily News* and *Daily Mirror*. Not only did such men have no proper respect for the facts but they also played on their readers' emotions by marketing the sensational. In retrospect we can see that this gospel was class-bound and rooted in a genteel image of human nature, in which emotion and sensation, all the nether impulses and those who could be reached through them, were sordid and inferior to the rational contemplation of the fact, which was how the cultivated person was assumed to conduct his citizenship.

But which facts? On the presumption that some facts were intrinsically more elevated than others, the *Times* could keep its eye on national and international politics while ignoring the metropolitan world that surrounded it at home. But while King Henry plays the mover and shaker, the Falstaffian life of the land and the street goes on—with the tabloids and the novelists left to cover it in their own ways. The journalistic gospel made yet another questionable assumption, an epistemological one: that facts were separable and self-explanatory, and hence could be sundered from interpretation. It takes no systematic Marxist to expose the fallacy of this positivist vision. In practice it meant that underlying causes would rarely be examined; that the news would be confined to the actions and statements, the public relations, of public men; that the journalist's invaluable private stock of hunch, skepticism, and worldly wisdom had to be censored out unless it took on the factual format. Even then there were certifiable facts that couldn't get printed, either because they offended the wrong man's sensitivities or because it just Wasn't Done. The rare analytical piece that got published in connection with a major story was hardly more than a reshuffling of the available facts: what passed for interpretation was simply a recapitulation of (and capitulation to) the given.

The arrival of television journalism and its gradual displacement of newspapers, photo magazines, and movie newsreels did not at first alter this situation, unless for the worse. If "serious" newspapers confined themselves to the bare skeleton of hard facts, and the tabloids put flesh and blood on mostly the wrong skeletons or missed the skeletons entirely, television reporting simply left room for fewer facts and remained stubbornly myopic in its attachment to surfaces. Television changed the American polity forever by bringing the look and feel of the news into every home. With Nixon's "Checkers" speech in 1952 and his debates with Kennedy in 1960, it altered the outcome of national elections. But the national power of networks and their dependence on government favor and on large advertisers made them far less willing to offend. The cult of "objectivity," which in practice meant adhering to official positions and avoiding controversial subjects, was carried to absurd extremes by television journalism. The result, though bland enough, helped saturate the country with the accepted line and contributed immensely to the narrow and repressive political climate of the fifties. Even a commentator like Edward R. Murrow, somewhat insulated from pressure by his great prestige, caused a sensation simply by dealing with certain subjects—McCarthy, migrant farm labor—albeit in an objective manner and outside the framework of "the news."

I've spoken of these conditions in the past tense, as if they had all vanished with the unlamented fifties, but most of them still exist, especially the cult of the discrete—and discreet—fact, and the continuing timidity and superficiality of television journalism, which the Nixon gang's war with the press managed to obscure. Starting with the escalation of the Vietnam war and culminating in Watergate, it required the most massive government deception and malfeasance to prod the news media into the mildly adversary role its enemies were quick to attack. During the Johnson and Nixon administrations, a fraction of the press went into opposition just by trying to keep in touch with reality. The "facts" themselves were so damning—and, in the case of the war, so suitable for televised coverage—that just reporting them seemed fraught with criticism, even tainted with radicalism. The almost messianic fervor with which the media welcomed and magnified Nixon's undistinguished successor in his first weeks in office was partly a sigh of relief at abandoning this unaccustomed role. It was a comforting leap into boosterism after the dark night of alienation. (Nor was the Watergate affair a triumph for the press, which largely failed to penetrate the cover-up during the 1972 election, when it would have mattered most, failed in most cases even to *cover* the story then, except as a minor "caper.")

The change in journalism in the sixties showed itself more spectacularly on the fringes than at the center of established institutions. The so-called New Journalism, or "para-journalism," as its critics labeled it, developed parallel to the chief organs of information, influencing them only subtly and gradually, in tandem with the influence of the age. By New Journalism I don't simply mean Tom Wolfe and his crowd of imitators, or even the larger group canonized by Wolfe in his 1973 anthology *The New Journalism*, but a wider range of defections from the journalistic gospel—aberrations that were responsive to the cultural tone of the sixties and even helped set that tone. This work included a broad spectrum of underground writing— political, countercultural, feminist, pornographic, and so on—that dealt with cultural developments ignored, distorted, or merely exploited by the established media. (The history of the sixties was written as much in the *Berkeley Barb* as in the *New York Times*.) Above ground, but still in newsprint, were publications that performed the same function, rather more respectably, for a somewhat different audience. In this category were the *Village Voice*, strongest in political and personal journalism and in its attention to life in New York City, and *Rolling Stone*, which found gold in servicing the rock and youth culture. Still further above ground, slick in format if not always in content, were magazines like *New York* and *Esquire*, which helped develop a special sort of essay/article that became identified with the New Journalism and that predominates in Wolfe's anthology. (These last magazines not only published and encouraged Wolfe's own work, but allowed it to influence their general tone.)

What these different strands of writing shared was the range of things traditional journalism left out: atmosphere, personal feeling, interpretation, advocacy and opinion, novelistic characterization and description, touches of obscenity, concern with fashion and cultural change, and political savvy. (Not all these features are found in any one writer.) Sometimes these writers developed a new voice *simply* by including the forbidden, not only the forbidden subject but more often the device or approach forbidden by the older journalistic code. Thus Hunter Thompson learned to approximate the effect of mind-blasting drugs in his prose style, especially in his book on Las Vegas. More successfully in 1972 he affronted the taboos of political writing, and recorded the nuts and bolts of a presidential campaign with all the contempt and incredulity that other reporters must feel but censor out. The result was the kind of straightforward, uninhibited intelligence that showed up the timidities and clichés that dominated the field. But in high gear Thompson paraded one of the few original prose styles of recent years, a style dependent almost deliriously on insult, vituperation, and stream-of-invective to a degree unparalleled since Céline. Similarly, but on a much lower level, Rex Reed turned the usually fawning celebrity interview inside out by sheer cattiness, a bitchy inquisitiveness, and downright hostility; he put in details and reactions that made his sketches seem more true-to-life than the usual public relations image.

Most New Journalists in the sixties did something more complicated than just naming the forbidden and interacted subtly with other cultural developments of the period. One dominant fact of the cultural life of the fifties, especially in the magazine world, was its stratification. Though distinctions like highbrow, middlebrow, and lowbrow, or masscult and midcult, may have originated in condescension or mere sociological convenience, in the fifties they really described separate audiences and wildly disparate intellectual styles. The lowbrow world stretched from *Saturday Evening Post* fiction and features to the wit of *Time* style, to the *Reader's Digest,* and even to lower depths unfit for the office of a respectable dentist. The cardinal rule: no traffic in ideas. (Even harmless platitudes were suspect if they slipped into ideational form.) In middlebrow periodicals, platitudes were OK, even ideas were OK, as long as they were the right ones: upbeat, cultivated, patriotic, vaguely anti-intellectual.

Magazines like *Harper's, The Atlantic,* the *New York Times Book Review,* and *Saturday Review* catered to an audience also serviced by the Book-of-the-Month Club and the Literary Guild. This segment of the literary life was the tattered remnant of the genteel tradition in American letters, going back to New England in the nineteenth century. By the fifties it had fought a hopeless rear-guard Thirty Years War against modernism and the New Criticism, against all manner of obscurity and experimentation in literature, against pessimism, alienation, and European influences among intellectuals. (Gloom and experiment were considered an alien graft on American letters, brought here by writers who had spent too much time in Paris, and nurtured by their highbrow epigones in the academy or in quarterlies like *Partisan* and *Kenyon Review*.) Robert Frost was a special hero to middlebrow critics because to them he was so obviously an adherent of nineteenth-century forms and values. When the quarterlies began to notice and claim him as a modern writer in the fifties, the self-appointed custodians of the culture reacted in fury. One of the first issues of *Partisan Review* I bought as an undergraduate reprinted a birthday tribute in which Lionel Trilling had called Frost a "terrifying" poet, much to the old man's delight, but less to the liking of J. Donald Adams, who had let loose a fierce barrage from his customary perch on page two of the *Times Book Review*. Not long afterward another issue of *PR* treated us to Dwight Macdonald's interminable attack on "Midcult," in which I found myself cast into outer darkness for taking pleasure in the Revised Standard Version of the Bible. My sympathies were already thoroughly highbrow, but I was offended by the snobbism and vacuity of Macdonald's polemic, its impulse merely to separate the In from the Out, the sheep from the goats. Most highbrow criticism in that age of the quarterly was a good deal more serious than that, but by the end of the fifties its stance and its self-confidence were dependent on cultural hierarchies that were already beginning to shift. The ground was moving under Dwight Macdonald and J. Donald Adams alike. The New Journalism and the magazines that published it would do much to alter the old terrain.

Periodicals rarely change the cultural climate on their own. More often they respond in a timely way to changes already taking place, which others have not yet perceived. The *New York Review of Books* moved into a long-standing vacuum of serious regular reviewing, then shifted into political controversy, from which it would one day quietly pull back when the climate had changed once again. The fifties were a great period for criticism and ideas, for irony, ambiguity, and the free play of brilliant if preening rhetoric. The middlebrow organs were moribund because they related only to an older literary culture that had already lost its vitality. But the sixties sealed the fate of the younger but already complacent highbrow culture as well; although the modernist classics would become the heart of the university curriculum and a renewed influence on younger writers, although the spirit of serious criticism would infiltrate and transform nearly all the former midcult bastions, the hierarchical basis of the old highbrow culture would be shattered. The academic tameness of its alienation and its modernism would fade before the more radical alienation and modernism that developed in the sixties.

The widespread diffusion of modernism in the new art and taste of the sixties, which purists lamented, worked to the detriment of the old elite culture with its emphasis on an enlightened vanguard. The quarterlies depended for their morale on the Philistinism and neglect of the general culture. When that abated the writers, who liked to eat regularly, understandably moved on to greener fields or, no longer young, ceased to produce the most interesting new work. With a whole culture geared up to ingest the New, the little magazines were no longer the main testing-ground for fresh talent.

More important still, with outlets for political action and practical change unavailable, the fifties had proved very congenial to reflection, to the long view of things. (In many ways this is true again today.) But the sixties began, as I said earlier, with demonstrations in San Francisco against the House Un-American Activities Committee, as well as freedom rides in the South, lunch-counter sit-ins, and civil rights demonstrations. For better or worse the inner space of reflection gave way to a field of confrontation. The humanist vision and the democratic creed were already finely honed; the time had come to push again for their practical enactment. Thus it happened that newsprint broadsheets like the *Village Voice,* in closer touch with the ongoing tumultuous flow of the new culture, displaced the once-preponderant quarterlies like *Partisan Review* as key voices of the sixties. For the same reason, the *New York Review,* which at first was labeled a *"Partisan Review* on newsprint,'' quickly took on a much more polemical and left-wing coloration; throughout our culture journalism and political controversy took on an energy and immediacy that had belonged in the fifties to the world of art and criticism.

There was quite another reason for this transition aside from the newly political tenor of the culture. Critical discourse in the fifties no less than journalism gained credence by its impersonality and objectivity. While the typical *Partisan Review* writer showed no lack of self-assertiveness or idiosyncrasy, he was expected to gain attention by brilliance and style alone, not by inserting himself too blatantly into his argument. (A comparable distance and reserve were even expected from the poet or novelist.) No matter how unique or unusual his views, the critic, still the Arnoldian cultural arbiter of old, felt free to don the robes of almost priestly intellectual authority; and when he examined a text it remained just that, a text, or a cultural document, not the evidence of a life lived or the product of sweat and blood.

The cultural mood of the sixties sharply challenged this premium on impersonal authority, which was cherished by journalists, critics, and social scientists alike. Starting with Beat poetry and fiction, subjectivity, self-display, the Romantic trust in the ego returned to the forefront of literary expression. Where the critic of the fifties would appeal to the cultural tradition, the critic of the sixties was more likely to seal an argument with personal testimony. Those two heinous Fallacies proscribed by the New Criticism, the Affective—what the work felt like—and the Intentional—what the artist himself had in mind, were resurrected with a vengeance, as both literature and criticism took on a more subjective cast. Young men began putting their experiences into precocious autobiographies rather than first novels. The line between fiction and autobiography grew blurry; a confessional rage took hold, as it did to a lesser degree in poetry after Lowell's *Life Studies*.

The trivial side of this tendency, the mere impulse toward self-display, had been evident from the first, when Beat poetry readings, moving and powerful as they could be, also lent themselves too readily to a carnival of publicity. (The culture of the sixties, because it was open and sometimes sensational, would always prove exploitable for those who approached it as a commodity.) But the serious side of this new subjectivity was far more important. A writer was now free to admit his fallibility; his biases and idiosyncrasies could be out on the table. In the fifties he was obliged to distance himself from his subject, distance it through form, through an effort of style, distance it by proving (if he were a discursive writer) that he was not an interested party. But the literature of the sixties—quite as much as the politics of the sixties—assumed that everyone was an interested party; it cherished immediacy, confrontation, personal witness. Experience became art and art became real only as they were proved upon the pulses, as they engaged the full man. More than at any time in recent decades, both art and politics became instruments of personal fulfillment, avenues to authentic selfhood. In this atmosphere of social confrontation and *self*-confrontation the New Journalism arrived to do battle with the bugbears of journalistic convention—with impersonality, with boredom (or "snoredom," as Tom Wolfe calls it), with the insider mentality that kept the reporter dependent on his sources and virtually a fixture in the institution he covered, with an ethical neutrality that turned hostile or exploitative whenever the new culture of the sixties came in for attention.

Though their role and their number were shrinking, the newspapers of America changed only grudgingly in the sixties. Perhaps they did more investigative reporting. They beefed up their cultural coverage with younger writers, sending a few old cows out to pasture. But none became outposts of the New Journalism. (The *Herald Tribune* did try briefly to become the American *Manchester Guard-*

ian before it merged and folded. *New York* magazine began life as its Sunday supplement.) Change came about from the arrival of a new generation of reporters, more highly educated and status-conscious, more iconoclastic, more liberal. The net effect of this shift was mild enough, though sharper television coverage did have a great impact, because the events and personalities it covered could not bear close scrutiny. Finally a national administration went to war with the press, which the vice-president (and *Commentary* magazine) now castigated as virtually a wing of the New Left.* Under attack, its every move vulnerable to powerful propaganda, the press recoiled and clung all the more rigidly to its cult of objectivity—until Watergate intervened to cripple the enemy and suspend the new reign of caution.

Outside the daily press, however, from magazines and Sunday supplements to ephemeral broadsheets, a new spirit took hold. It would be more accurate to call it "participatory" rather than subjective journalism, on the analogy of the New Left's cherished ideal of "participatory democracy." An excellent example of what this means can be found in Don McNeill's *Moving Through Here* (1970), a collection of fragile but finely tuned pieces by a *Village Voice* writer who was drowned in 1968. McNeill's reports on the hip, drug, and flower-child scene of New York's Lower East Side were the work of a sensitive insider, seamlessly attached to the world he describes yet still able to be lucid and critical.† They're "feel" pieces rather than topical accounts of events; slight as they are, they have the transparency of good history and an inobtrusive rightness that makes them more impressive between covers than they were in the noisier pages of the paper. Though subjective in the best sense, they hardly need the first person: a living subject informs every detail, shapes each perception.

* See Daniel P. Moynihan's article "The Presidency & the Press," *Commentary* (March 1971), reprinted with some apologies in his book *Coping* (1973).

† By comparison the *Times* has always discouraged identification by shifting reporters to far-off assignments whenever they get too comfortable or knowledgeable on their beat. Disguised as professionalism, this on-the-job training merely fosters the superficiality of the ignorant amateur.

The same cannot be said about most of the items in Tom Wolfe's anthology *The New Journalism*, many of which have an impersonal air which rivals conventional journalism. Wolfe's book is not only a bid for literary permanence and respectability; it has a strong polemical purpose. It's directed precisely against the subjective or Mailerian sort of journalism in which the writer appears as a central character, a personal reactor through whom the events are filtered. Mailer does make a brief appearance in the book, but Wolfe's comments about him are grudging, and he prints very little other work in that line—a vein he himself seems unable or unwilling to pursue. Even the more subtly infused subjectivity of Don McNeill's sort of piece gets excluded. Instead Wolfe, in his selections, headnotes, and fifty-page introduction, emphasizes a much more peripheral feature of the New Journalism: its novelistic quality (''Like a Novel''). Wolfe picks pieces that are shaped like old-style short stories; as editor, ever boastful of his academic credentials, he ponderously ticks off their narrative techniques. Unfortunately, few of his writers have strong novelistic gifts, and his own prefaces pose no threat to those of Henry James. Despite his proclamations of novelty, the real pedigree of Wolfe's selections is good old-fashioned feature-writing rather than fiction. Where the participatory journalist really gets involved, as an actual character or a responsive and observant narrator, Wolfe's boys simply latch onto an angle and play it for all it's worth. Though the whole collection reads well enough, Wolfe's pretentious literary claims make good magazine work seem disappointing, like failed literature. Only a few selections, including two by Hunter Thompson, survive the transition into literary showpieces.

The partiality of Wolfe's canon and the flaws in his conception of the New Journalism spring from the limitations of his own work, which some have unthinkingly taken as the prototype of this sort of writing. Wolfe pines for literary status and academic recognition, but his Yale Ph.D., however much he reminds us of it, really does point to what he can do well. Though no intellectual heavyweight—compare him, say, to another journalist with a doctorate, Garry Wills—he has a solid American Studies kind of analytical skill. Though much too fascinated by style and celebrity, too preoccupied by status rather than class or power, he knows the social map; he wields a smooth, digestible style and a lively curiosity about how people live and play—work I'm afraid is outside his ken—in the more picturesque corners of society. This comes out very clearly in the first piece in his first book, the article on Las Vegas in *The Kandy-Kolored Tangerine-Flake Streamline Baby* (1965), which manages to explain the city, not simply to evoke it. The freaky titles and lunatic typography by which Wolfe had gained attention were really quite marginal to this book; the manic highs were strictly for the torment of the printer. At heart, the early Wolfe was a genial observer of the byways of Americana and at moments a tolerable social analyst. But Wolfe seemed incapable of exposing or involving himself; for all his zeal to discover an invisible America in the subcultural muck of custom-car racing and demolition derbies, for all his contempt for the essayistic distance of the "Literary Gentleman in the Grandstand," Wolfe himself was too genteel to let go or to get involved, even in the harmless participatory manner of a George Plimpton. Hence he was attracted to the bizarre, to pure spectacle, where breathless excitement would obviate any taxing emotional claims and pump life into his prose.

But he couldn't be content with short pieces on demolition derbies and profiles of social butterflies. If Mailer could let a magazine assignment explode into a long book, if Mailer could "do" the sixties in *The Armies of the Night* and *Miami and the Siege of Chicago,* Wolfe could afford to be no less grandiose and ambitious. In *The Electric Kool-Aid Acid Test* (1968), his book on Ken Kesey and his Merry Pranksters, and "Radical Chic," his interminable account of Leonard Bernstein's fund-raising party for the Black Panthers, we confront Wolfe's larger claims as a social chronicler and literary stylist, and these claims don't hold up. The Kesey book is stupefyingly boring—I got through only half of it. Kesey himself is offensive and overrated as a writer and even less interesting as a sixties guru. Moreover, unlike Mailer, Wolfe seems to have nothing to say; hence he churns up all the typographical mannerisms he'd managed to keep down in his first book. Evidently they're meant to play a central role, to approximate the freaked-out sensations of the drug experience. How fully he fails can be gauged by a comparison with the incomparable style of Hunter Thompson, who's wildly erratic yet really gives the impression of having been there. And though Thompson can be glibly vituperative, he's also cuttingly savage and sharp where Wolfe is simply uncritical, inflating his subject like the old-style celebrity interviewer, passively letting the whole scene wash over him, desperately trying to write from ''inside'' characters whose subjective reality remains stubbornly uninteresting or inaccessible.

Somehow even in ''Radical Chic'' where Wolfe is far from uncritical, where he mobilizes an impressive irony yet tries to remain inward with his characters, the result is almost as monotonous. No good novelist would homogenize his characters into one inner voice, a single mentality, a collective embodiment of a social attitude, as Wolfe does. He creates what Alan Trachtenberg, in a shrewd critique, called the ''illusion of a group subjectivity, only and sheerly verbal, never completing itself in the reader's imagination except as display, as spectacle.'' And the point of view in ''Radical Chic'' is as limited as the technique. Wolfe later explained that to fill out to the collective stream-of-consciousness he ''depended heavily on details of status life to draw the reader inside the emotional life of his characters.'' This is a fancy way of describing the plenitude of brand names and In fashions that he uses to furnish out his characters' ''minds,'' so instead of having an emotional life they turn out to be mannikins of chic, butts of social satire. For all I know the contempt may be well-deserved, but it would take a Mary McCarthy to make it biting and convincing. McCarthy may be too cruel and condescending to her Vassar Group, but Wolfe never establishes a distinct point of view at all. For all the would-be satire, Wolfe himself is nothing if not a creature of fashion. His fastidious social knowingness puts him entirely at one with the mentality of his characters; their snobbishness and triviality mirror his own interests. The implication is, well, that chic is OK but *radical* chic, Black Panther chic, now, honey, that's going a little too far.

141

Compared to Mailer, compared to all the great realists he admires, Wolfe has no sense of what makes society work, what greases the wheels, what makes it run. Only the color and splash of fashion, the social surface, engages him. It's not that he's anti-radical: politics of any sort passes him by, except as spectacle.* Inevitably, Wolfe's distortion of the New Journalism is rooted in his misreading of the sixties, when politics truly came to the fore. To Wolfe the real history of the sixties had to do with changes in "manners and morals" rather than "the war in Vietnam or . . . space exploration or . . . political assassination." It was, he says, "the decade when manners and morals, styles of living, attitudes toward the world changed the country more crucially than any political events." I would be the last person to brand this utterly wrong or implausible—certainly not in a book devoted to shifts in sensibility and cultural style during the same period. It's simply a false dichotomy, built on a simplistic notion of both "manners and morals" and "political events." Wolfe undoubtedly borrows the first phrase from Lionel Trilling's seminal essay on the great nineteenth-century realist writers, "Manners, Morals, and the Novel," and he echoes Trilling's complaint that the novel today has abandoned its long-standing fascination with society. But for Trilling, as for the Marxist critic Georg Lukács, whose views of the novel complement his, society was intrinsic to the novel of realism not because society was so colorful and titillating, but because the period of bourgeois ascendancy witnessed a compelling interplay of money, desire, ambition, social mobility, historical occasion, and class structure. But when Tom Wolfe comes to New York in the early sixties, he sees "pandemonium with a big grin on . . . the wildest, looniest time since the 1920's . . . a hulking carnival . . . [an] amazing spectacle." He sees only a freakshow, a whirligig of fashion and social idiosyncrasy—another New Journalist actually called a collection of articles *Freakshow*—and Wolfe

---

* It's significant that almost nothing from the *Village Voice* gets into Wolfe's anthology. One has the impression that kind of writing would be too political *and* too subjective for him. But the *Voice* was the one above-ground paper that offered serious and deeply felt accounts of the great political manifestations of the 1960s.

wonders why the novelists are not there on the beat. It turns out that they have retreated into myth, "Neo-Fabulism," and alienation, so that "the—New Journalists—Parajournalists—had the whole crazed obscene uproarious Mammon-faced drug-soaked mau-mau lust-oozing Sixties in America all to themselves."

Even if we allow for the willed overheating of Wolfe's prose *— which faithfully mirrors the freakshow element that alone interests him—it becomes obvious that Wolfe has no notion of the kinds of social forces that impel both manners and morals *and* politics, no feel for what Trilling calls "a culture's hum and buzz of implication": "a dim mental region of intention" that underlies a culture and shapes its character at a given historical moment. This is the implicit unity of mood or moral temper that the cultural observer must seek out, by which, for instance, the style of confrontation in the politics of the sixties is closely related to the style of self-assertion in the poetry and sexuality of the period, which in turn is related to the unexpected impulse of the journalist, in covering these and other developments, to do *his* own thing in an authenticating subjective way. And to determine *why* the whole culture should be moving in this direction, and to make some distinctions and judgments about it, required someone with greater analytical acuity, with more political sensitivity and novelistic vision, than Tom Wolfe. It required perhaps a figure from the fifties, someone caught between that hinterland of irony, ambivalence, and reflection and the new culture. This is why it fell to Mailer rather than Wolfe to become the quintessential New Journalist, to report most deeply on what was happening, both inside and outside his own head.

As a relic of that earlier era, Mailer's impulse is toward performance rather than participation. For others, perhaps, but not for him were the egalitarian and communal fantasies of the hippie young. Like earlier would-be writer-adventurers—Byron, Hemingway,

---

* "Such writing," said Byron scurrilously of Keats, "is a sort of mental masturbation—he is always f--gg--g his *Imagination*. I don't mean he is *indecent*, but viciously soliciting his own ideas into a state, which is neither poetry nor any thing else but a Bedlam vision produced by raw pork and opium."

Malraux—he is attracted by the life of action and longs to live in the heroic mold.* He strains for an affinity with bullfighters, boxers, film directors, space explorers, romantic revolutionaries—all the street-fighters and drunken swaggerers of the world. Doomed by the accidents of talent and some inalterable wrinkle of character to be a writer instead, he places his work under the flag of adventure, sees it as an exploration of inner space, a struggle with death and dread. He repeatedly seizes opportunities to prove himself in the active life, but his incursions into politics, filmmaking, and public speaking prove disastrous, redeemed only by the torrent of printed words which transforms them into retrospective verbal triumphs. He revels in a protean variety of roles and occasions but is unable to bear "a last remaining speck of the one personality he found absolutely insupportable—the nice Jewish boy from Brooklyn. Something in his adenoids gave it away—he had the softness of a man early accustomed to mother-love." †

Yet it's this personality more than any other that helps make Mailer a better journalist than any of his contemporaries. Where the New Journalism in the hands of Wolfe and his imitators at *New York* magazine tends to be uncritical and frivolously atmospheric, Mailer really has ideas—he is *"our* genius," as Irving Howe said half-ruefully in his essay on the New York intellectuals. He complements a novelist's eye with an analytical power unparalleled among journalists and social observers. Like other adventurer-writers, who scorned inwardness but secretly nurtured a core of melancholy, anguish, or nihilism that kept them going and gave them their literary strength, Mailer's journalistic gift is rooted less in activism or reportorial skill than in a Montaigne-like affinity for every nuance of his inner life. In *Of a Fire on the Moon* he calls himself a "Nijinsky of am-

* "I do think the preference of *writers* to *agents*—the mighty stir made about scribbling and scribes, by themselves and others—a sign of effeminacy, degeneracy, and weakness. Who would write, who had any thing better to do?" (Byron, *Journal*)

† This brings to mind the dreadful caricatures of Goldstein and Roth in *The Naked and the Dead*. Mailer treats them throughout with a contempt (or self-contempt) that borders on anti-Semitism. Even his hostile acknowledgment of this part of his personality shows how Mailer had traveled in self-awareness.

bivalence," and it's the curse of "Jewish" self-consciousness rather than the bravado of gentile heroics that makes him a great writer. Condemned to intellectuality, softness, feeling, he secretly makes the most of his gift and of his resistance to it. He makes the dialectic of his own divided nature his special subject and writes journalism that's a running autobiographical dialogue with the world.

It was his inability to bring the full scope of this vision into fiction that first turned Mailer to other kinds of writing. *Advertisements for Myself* (1959) was built on the ruins of a great unwritten novel, of which it printed tantalizing fragments and sketched out a more-than-ambitious design. The novel was to include "The Man Who Studied Yoga" and "The Time of Her Time," indeed, was to be the dialectical interaction of those two contrary sensibilities: Sam Slovoda's eight-part dream of Sergius O'Shaugnessy, the failed bourgeois' vision of the fake Irishman (or Norman Mailer's escape from the Jewish novel). But he could not at that time bring together these ambiguities of self with his interest in society. In *Advertisements* he had made a signal advance in style, in complexity of vision, in a prophetic awareness of cultural change, all by stepping out from behind the impersonal mask of his fiction and directly confronting his labyrinthine character and violent ambition. But the metaphysics of sexuality and selfhood in *Advertisements* largely expelled the political elements that had made his three novels unusual for the fifties. Within a year, however, he made his first large foray into political journalism, covering Kennedy's nomination for *Esquire,* and it was journalism that would enable him to balance off self and world in a way that had largely eluded him. Kennedy was more than a political figure for Mailer; he was a creature of fantasy, identification, and envy who would galvanize his imagination for half the decade.

But there was always a touch of callow hero-worship in the way Mailer hectored and aggrandized Kennedy; Paul Goodman put his finger on it and earned Mailer's undying wrath, though he himself says as much in his preface to *The Presidential Papers* where he acknowledges a furtive wish to be a court-intellectual, some kind of hip Arthur Schlesinger. ("These are the Presidential papers of a court wit, an amateur advisor. They are papers written *to* the President, *for* him, they are his private sources of information. The President suffers from one intellectual malady—intellectual malnutrition.'') Left conservative or Tory radical, lush baroque stylist, hero-worshipper attracted to the strong leader, Mailer never sounded more like Carlyle than when writing about Kennedy, and surely the likeness was a mixed blessing. Thus when Mailer came to write about the Pentagon march for *Harper's* in 1968 he had not yet, as a journalist, found his perfect subject, and the big antiwar demonstration was such an unlikely candidate that he had hesitated even to attend. His days as a would-be revolutionary were over. ("He had lived for a dozen empty hopeless years after the second world war with the bitterness, rage, and potential militancy of a real revolutionary . . . but no revolution had arisen in the years when he was ready—the timing of his soul was apocalyptically maladroit.") His impulse to be a martyr, prophet, or "sexologue" had also waned; he had begun to enjoy society as it was, to accept his stake in the status quo. ("He was forty-four years old, and it had taken him most of those forty-four years to begin to be able to enjoy his pleasures where he found them, rather than worry about those pleasures which eluded him.") He had spoken out strongly and early against the war in Vietnam, but society had allowed him time for pleasure, reward for work, space for family and domesticity. At Chicago in 1968, as at the Pentagon, "he looked into his reluctance to lose even the America he had had, that insane warmongering technology land." This is the groundwork for the profound ambivalence that lurks behind *The Armies of the Night* and *Miami and the Siege of Chicago;* this is the knotty challenge that evokes the best in Mailer as a journalist.

The reactions to the sixties among established intellectuals compose a story in itself, some of which I've already narrated in Chapter 3. Suffice it to say here that Old Leftists generally were either radicalized or enraged; that the bitterest barbs came not from right-wing conservatives or unreconstructed cold warriors but from those who had been apostles of a new direction in the early sixties yet soon found themselves overtaken, outstripped; that others proved equally one-sided when they joined the youth brigade and suppressed their own historical experience. The sixties had to be a wringing experience for those who had gone through a drought of radicalism—who had learned to live with other expectations—only to see it reappear in a different and sometimes difficult guise. Those who wrote best about it were the ones who honestly faced up to their inevitable ambivalence, who matched its complexity with a complexity of response; so Mailer does in these two books, so Paul Goodman did in *New Reformation*, so Leslie Fiedler did in his essay ''The New Mutants'' (written before he became a one-sided booster of the new culture). By dethroning the *ex cathedra* essay of the old high culture, the New Journalism helped to make this sort of anguished self-examination possible, just as the sixties were making it socially meaningful.

It's not irrelevant to ask whether *The Armies of the Night* ought to be called journalism at all. Wolfe, with his penchant for academic distinctions, labels it autobiography (the one such specimen he admits into his canon). Mailer himself prefers the titles of novelist and historian, and bridles when Robert Lowell calls him ''the best journalist in America.'' These formal categories would be more to the point if Mailer's huge gamble had failed; but works that succeed create new configurations of form that make earlier pigeonholes obsolete. (In literary terms, the sixties were a ''romantic'' phase, when the intensities of individual vision melt down the traditional barriers between ''classical'' genres.) It's hard to recapture the audacity of Mailer's project, precisely because its success made us forget our previous expectations. The self-aggrandizement of Mailer's books, starting with *Advertisements*, was a frank bid for fame and recognition *outside* the accepted literary channels. In 1957 Mailer could still be described by one critic as ''confident but modest in manner,'' with ''a distaste for personal publicity.'' It was the blockage of his career as a novelist that drove him to beat his own drum, to come forward with the naked props and underpinnings of his ambition, with all the confessional razzle-dazzle of a public personality, at the risk of looking like a comedian, a juggler, a con-artist rather than an artist. Through it all Mailer demanded recognition as a *novelist:* hushed tones and an odor of incense descended on his prose as he talked of his Great Unwritten Work in Progress, and a cruel brilliance illuminated it as he cut up his literary contemporaries and rival claimants. Mailer remained stubbornly unaware of what he already instinctively knew: that the old literary hierarchies were under siege, that the novelist and the clown were no longer a world apart, that the action was shifting from the palace to the street.

If Mailer still lusted after the Great American Novel, he seems nonetheless to have come to like his brash, cocky new personality, so different from that of the "nice Jewish boy from Brooklyn." In *The Armies of the Night* he tells us of his gloom and distress at the onset of a chastening new modesty, the whiff of an earlier personality, for "he had been born to a modest family, had been a modest boy, a modest young man, and he hated that, he loved the pride and the arrogance and the confidence and the egocentricity he had acquired over the years, that was his force and his luxury and the iron in his greed, the richest sugar of his pleasure, the strength of his competitive force." But since the "intimation" of a "new psychical condition" is "never to be disregarded," he accepts the confrontation with the Pentagon, the "kids," the Movement, and his own ambivalence as a necessary turning point in his mental life.

Yet somehow there's a false note that runs through this pat little drama when we examine it closely: the not-quite-credible modesty, the stagy, rhetorical satanism, the handy peripeteia, the existentialist faith in a perpetual renewal of personality, a permanent emotional heroism. In each of Mailer's long books of reportage he claims to be chastened and humbled by the magnitude of events, but finally resigned to the necessary heroism of confronting them. Yet in each new book he comes back brash and bloated again, ready for new trials, new chastenings. The authentic self-revelation of Mailer's writing is but an inch this side of staginess and rhetoric. He constructs a *petit théâtre* of self and self, self and world, a novelistic microcosm of plot, character, tension, and dénouement that few journalists or autobiographers provide. Whenever Mailer aims at objective description or simply tries to supply information, especially in the moon book, his élan fails him. All assertions of modesty notwithstanding, Mailer's audacity always comes in his scene-stealing extravagance, his effort to project himself to the center of the event, to impose his outrageous metaphysical categories.

Mailer wrote *The Armies of the Night*, like *Advertisements*, at a crossroads of his literary career, after the mixed-to-violent reception of two more novels and a play. In it he grasps not only at celebrity and undisputed literary recognition—which the book in fact instantly brought him—but also at being born again, becoming the laureate of a new culture of which he had once—in "The White Negro" and the rest of *Advertisements*—been only the one-eyed prophet. In *Armies* he does something which, for all its rhetorical modesty, is more shocking than the frank self-promotion of the earlier book: he tries to steal history and harness it to his personal drama, to make his interior dialogue the scene of a whole new culture's ascent to self-knowledge. The opening pages of chitchat, the reply to *Time* magazine, the celebrity-talk about Lowell, Macdonald, Goodman, the fierce competitiveness—all this tells us from the beginning that this is Mailer's story. The shock is gone now, after years of consciousness-raising groups, personal confession, and subjective witness to just about everything. But Mailer helped show the way, helped show that the self could be tuned to respond at one time to its own promptings and to the most subtle cultural vibrations, that a novelist could provide both journalists and historians with a missing dimension of their subject.

The gradual decline of Mailer's journalism after *The Armies of the Night*, just when he acceded with surprising grace and dignity to a preeminent status among American writers, showed how easily the most novel strategy could harden into formula. Being human, Mailer could not go through a crisis of self-knowledge with every assignment.* The moon landing proved particularly distant and intrac-

---

* "Her work took on, gradually, a destructive cast, as it so often does with the greatly gifted who are doomed to repeat endlessly their own heights of inspiration." (Elizabeth Hardwick on Billie Holiday, *New York Review of Books*, March 4, 1976)

table—his imagination had always thrived on flesh-and-blood immediacy. In *Of a Fire on the Moon,* the strategies of self-examination
became more hollow, and Mailer's ambivalence toward technology,
which he had always freely detested, seemed worked up for the occasion, or at least less rich than his ruminations about politics, culture, and identity. By the time he wrote *The Prisoner of Sex* (1971),
Mailer was already parodying his novelistic devices and cloaking a
callow defense of his own work in a gallant homage to D. H.
Lawrence and Henry Miller. Through all this Mailer's prose sang
like a bird—success, status, fame, and money all obviously agreed
with him; they tapped an attractive reserve of personality at variance
with his bad-boy image—and the seven books from *Armies* to *Marilyn* provided some of the most solid pleasures of recent American literature, even as they lost their cultural and creative edge. The one
book Mailer pulled out of the fire was the second of them, *Miami and
the Siege of Chicago,* where the excesses of the Chicago convention,
which would prove one of the watershed points of the decade, enabled Mailer to repeat if not match the self-confrontation of *The
Armies of the Night.*

In a sense the real subject of the second book is the New Journalism, just as much as it's about politics, the "kids," and an apocalyptic new America. For most of the book Mailer is even more the
comic figure he claimed to be in *The Armies of the Night.* He's a
bumbler who, out of concern for missing his magazine deadline,
manages to miss all the action. In *Armies* he'd missed a great deal
because he'd been arrested, but in writing the book he scrupulously
tried to fill in the whole picture. At Chicago, however, he's kept
back by fear, laziness, an inability to acknowledge that the real action is in the streets. There's a bit of Teddy White and Walter Cron-
kite in Mailer—he really *likes* conventions (so do I!)—and he stays
inside and snug though he finds the proceedings a joke and a
charade, with the power brokers pulling the strings and another constituency barricaded outside the walls. Or else, like Hubert
Humphrey, he watches the street battles from a perch on the nineteenth floor of the Hilton, the epitome of the uninvolved journalist
above the fray.

Finally the "plot" unwinds. Mailer's distance and fear get to him as nothing else has. He goes out into the street and emerges as a character at the same time he emerges from the cocoon of the convention. In the last forty pages the book rises to distinction; it turns into "a novel about a week in this big city," a novel whose plot and power hinge on Mailer's emergence from observer to participant. He faces up to his own fear and hesitation, and to the drama of a nation in travail. He takes sides, and in a scene of pure comic exuberance he goes out to inspect "his" ragamuffin troops and take the measure of "theirs." The old war novelist goes to war, not in the ranks of the professionals he'd learned to respect but on the side of a youthful "army" whose prospects must have given him no great hopes, and even offended his winner's instincts. He steps forward and addresses them as their general ("extraordinary events deliver exceptional intuitions of oneself"): "They were fine troops, he declared, they were the sort of troops any general would be proud to have. They had had the courage to live at war for four days in a city which was run by a beast." Chicago becomes a microcosm for America, for its leadership, its interminable, soul-rending war, its generational conflict. Mailer could not know at the time that the "kids" were making their last stand and, with the abundant aid of Humphrey and the Democrats, were pulling Richard Nixon into office by a hair. But speaking to the crowd he discovers for himself "that they were a generation with an appetite for the heroic, and an air not without beauty had arisen from their presence."

I asked before whether what Mailer wrote should properly be called journalism. I can say now that he wrote a remarkable kind of journalism that shades off into fantasy and fiction. In the Miami part of the book he's just about taken in by the fiction of the "new" Nixon. In the marvelous scene I've described above he writes something that borders closely on fantasy. Yet who wrote better about the new forces in American life in the sixties? And who succeeded in confronting the confrontations of the period with his depth of personal witness? Himself no adventurer but powered by grandiose ambition, Mailer learned to live dangerously in his prose, and he encapsulated the sixties in many scenes of personal theater. But the sixties *were* a period of private theater—guerrilla theater, as I suggested at the beginning of this chapter, with an encounter in every head. The impulse to self-display, the gifts of a novelist thwarted in his creative course, enabled Mailer to impose his own psychodrama on his contemporaries and contributed to a whole age's self-understanding.

The subjectivity of the New Journalism did not fare as well in other hands as in Mailer's. Even his own later books adhere to the form of Mailer-as-character without the engagement or participation to justify his large personal presence. The best of the *Village Voice* writers, like Vivian Gornick and Paul Cowan, picked up where Mailer left off, and found in their own emotional tumult an exact gauge of changes in society and sensibility. But in many of the underground papers that sprouted in the sixties, kinky and amusing as they often were, *necessary* as they often were in a culture whose established organs of information remained distressingly blind and narrow, the "I" often nosed out the world entirely and sounded a hollow soliloquy in an echoing void. If Mailer sometimes borders on fantasy, the underground press bordered only occasionally on reality, which needless to say carried no great prestige in psychedelic circles.

Under pressure from both the New Journalism and the critical urgencies of the age, even above-ground reporters found circuitous ways of doing *their* own thing. Dan Rather became famous for the loathing he inspired in Richard Nixon as the CBS White House correspondent. As Timothy Crouse describes it in *The Boys in the Bus*, "Rather would go with an item even if he didn't have it completely nailed down with verifiable facts. If a rumor sounded solid to him, if he believed it in his gut or had gotten it from a man who struck him as honest, he would let it rip. The other White House reporters hated Rather for this." (For his troubles Rather was pulled from his beat, but not before Nixon resigned. Rocking the boat a little was all right, but we wouldn't want to keep it rocking. No doubt the suspension of Daniel Schorr in 1976 was another belated reprisal for troublesome persistence.) The press and media became more liberal, less uncritical, but were still basically bound by the formulas of objective journalism, which gave the clever reporter something challenging to circumvent. In the end I'm not sure I'd want to junk these formulas myself. We might get more of the shallow skepticism and mindless pseudocommentary that marred the banal coverage of the 1976 presidential campaign. Worse still, the press might become a party press, as it is in much of the world, and the tendentiousness of the right would be sure to get a wider hearing than the still, small voice of left-liberal conscience, however passionate and personal a voice that proved to be.

6

Black Writing and Black Nationalism: Four Generations

THE DOMINANT IMPULSE toward self-assertion in the sixties—
the quest for self-liberation, the therapeutic impulse toward self-fulfillment—did not confine itself to the lives of individuals, nor even to
novelists, poets, or journalists. It also showed itself in expressions of
group insurgency, outbursts of militant collective consciousness,
especially among ethnic groups. Despite the individualism and
pluralism of American life, we have always distrusted group subcul-
tures and fostered an ideology of assimilation that devalued ethnic
origins and worked to dissolve foreign influences. It was Tocqueville
who first observed how we pay for our political freedoms by subtle,
insidious exactions of social conformity, a tendency which reached
its apogee in the repressive climate of the 1950s.

The one exception, of course, was race, where assimilation was
anathema, where a separate-and-unequal ideology of Nordic suprem-
acy worked as long as black people were willing to stay in their
place. The integration movement of the fifties and early sixties aimed
to extend to blacks the same benefits of the melting pot that other
groups enjoyed. But once aroused, the liberation impulse could not
be contained by the struggle for civil and political rights. In any case
the visible reality of skin color made the assimilationist goals of

154

other groups unrealistic or unattainable for blacks without wholesale miscegenation, something desired by neither blacks nor whites. The result was a movement for full cultural autonomy, a push toward separatism and nationalism that had incalculably great effects on the whole life and mind of the sixties.

It was the Jews who first discovered how much of their identity and affective life they might have to surrender to the bland uniformity of the melting pot. If the growth of Jewish writing in the forties and fifties was connected to political quietism, the exhaustion of millennial hopes, as I argued earlier, it also had a more troublesome dimension. As the writer was thrown back upon the self, upon the private life, he knew at least that it had to be a genuinely personal self, not some hollow universal one. In the dark night of the soul the melting pot was irrelevant; the deep and tangled roots of identity, once glimpsed, did not encourage assimilation. Much as the Jewish novelists have recently complained about being typed as an ethnic grouping, their work in the fifties showed the way toward a healthy particularism and self-acceptance that would grow and flourish in the sixties.

The resurgence of black writing in the sixties was different from the Jewish flowering in that it ran parallel to a political and social movement, and had deep links to the ongoing social life of the mass of black people. If black leaders and black artists remained a highly self-conscious and sometimes neglected minority, they nevertheless reflected a shift of attitude that ran strong in the black community. The rage and frustration that showed itself in the urban riots of the sixties were the inchoate counterpart of the self-conscious new nationalism and militant separatism that emerged as a challenge to the old civil rights leadership. This new stance, which stressed cultural pride and autonomy over the old integrationist goals, spread quickly among artists, intellectuals, militants, and educated young blacks in general, as if their whole lives had prepared them for it. But America was not prepared for it, and reacted with something approaching panic to the inflammatory rhetoric of the new racial assertiveness. Who among us was not at times riveted, fascinated, perhaps even frightened by these resplendent and angry new blacks, by turns hard-edged and remorseless or smoothly self-delighting, all rage and assertion in public but sometimes twinkling with affability, even self-irony in private? It was this new spirit, rather than the more reflective self-consciousness of the Jews, that proved contagious to every other submerged minority, every group that had been maligned by prevailing Wasp values or had traded its birthright for a piece of the American dream.

In retrospect it's remarkable how much the spirit of change, the revaluation of values in America in the sixties, took its cue from the conflict over race. First, in the integration period of the early sixties, direct-action tactics like freedom rides, marches, and nonviolent sit-ins helped fire a new social consciousness, a spirit of protest and disenchantment that was quickly applied to both domestic issues and the Vietnam war. Thus the struggle for black rights can be said to have ignited the first phase of the politics of confrontation. Later, as the integration ideal gave way to nationalism, the group militance of blacks spread to students, women, and homosexuals, as well as to other ethnic groups including the Jews. Whatever his own sexual bias, it was the black man in an afro, proud of his skin and hair, who helped enable the gay person to "come out." The black challenge to American liberalism—the sixties' challenge, as it turned out—becomes in a different key the feminist or homosexual attack on Freud. The message at bottom was the same: your pluralism is a sham, a cover for assimilation and psychic aggression. "Come in," sang the siren, "and be like us. Park your identity at the door."

Today the college where I teach has programs not only in black studies and women's studies but in Jewish studies, Irish studies, and Italian-American studies, all interdisciplinary yet coexisting peaceably with the traditional academic departments. As in the culture at large, many of these programs are simply affirmative redress for a long-standing neglect. It's hard to know how well these offerings will survive institutional retrenchment, student job anxieties, and the abatement of the political pressures that brought them into being. From the vantage point of the mid-seventies, it's difficult to tell how long it will take for the new ethnicity to run its course. Among blacks its force has clearly diminished. The conservative politics and weak economics of the early seventies gave little scope even for social goals as far from radical as Lyndon Johnson's. The most militant black leadership, like the extreme offshoots of the New Left, was decimated, exiled, or driven underground. Blacks took the brunt of the economic downturn just as they'd previously borne so much of the actual combat in Vietnam, but even before the recession they recognized that they could not eat racial pride. Independent figures like Kenneth Clark rejected the surrender to "Black English" and segregated black studies, and insisted that black children learn English and acquire skills that would help them compete in the marketplace.

But this recent shift towards realistic and practical goals doesn't negate the immense revolution in consciousness that occurred among blacks in the sixties, which in turn contributed to the cultural revolution in America at large. This bold new attitude can best be traced in the upsurge of black writing, especially in fiction and autobiography, which reflected and fueled the ferment in the black community. Like all efforts in the arts, however, black writing has its own internal history, and to understand it we must go back before the gaudy flowering of the sixties, back at least to the looming figure of Richard Wright, still our most challenging American example of the writer as militant *and* artist—exile, spokesman, and personal voice.

I take it that the white critic no longer has to defend himself for discussing black literature, as he did at the height of the separatist wave in the late sixties, when even serious, well-meaning men insisted that it was a time to keep silent, to enable blacks to find their own voice. Richard Gilman, in two widely discussed essays in *The New Republic,* argued that black people were creating for themselves a set of new myths that were "not subject to being brought into the critical arena and there dispatched or pardoned," that our humanistic values were so corrupted by racist practice that they could not be applied to the new black experience, and hence the white critic should withdraw, should "stand back and listen, *without comment,* to these new and self-justifying voices." Many blacks made this argument more drastically and less rationally; it sometimes devolved into the absurdity that only blacks could write about blacks, only women could review women, and so on. Harold Cruse put the point a little more cogently when he suggested that the white critic "has a tendency to encourage the black writer not to be a black writer at all, but to be what he calls a universal writer."

These arguments made little sense to me at the time, for I never saw criticism as a defense of a static set of values, or a summary court to dispatch or pardon books and ideas, or a eulogy of an empty universality over lived experience. It seemed self-evident that criticism, like literature itself, demanded the gift of empathy as well as the faculty of judgment, self-evident too that only a critic's knowledge and skill, his actual performance of his task, provided any index of his competence. I could understand it when Cruse told us that black people had to develop indigenous cultural institutions, such as theaters and periodicals, and could only do so without direct white participation or support. I could understand why he urged black artists to deal with black themes. But who were the white critics who suggested otherwise, who directed them instead to some nonexistent man-in-general? Especially in the sixties white observers were more likely to flagellate themselves in public, to love being called honkies and perverts. For the sake of atonement, works by and about blacks in the sixties were ritually praised as if no standards at all were applicable. All authors want critics to become their boosters and advance men, but if criticism has any independent value to a writer or his audience, this kind of receptivity does no service to literature, black or white.

Today the moratorium on criticism that Cruse and Gilman proposed would be unthinkable, yet in fact it exists. Black writing has been given over to the same benign neglect that the President's counselor recommended for blacks in general, and this is likely to continue until they begin to make trouble again. Meanwhile several promising writers of the sixties, including a few I'll discuss later on, have yet to publish a second book. Yet the cultural revolution among blacks and its tremendous impact on our whole society can scarcely be undone. Instead, we've learned to live with the anger and pride and cool hip arrogance of many younger blacks, just as they've learned to make practical accommodations, to survive the frustration of utopian hopes, and to settle for the consolations of personal style. As the cultural pendulum has shifted to and fro, as the rage and frustration of many blacks has gone underground but hardly gone away, as the country has veered its attention to the sensibilities of white ethnics, there's some point in recalling that scarcely a generation ago, while black men died in a Jim Crow army under a liberal President, Richard Wright had to mobilize his own large resources of anger to tell the world that, whatever the appearances to the contrary, Negroes were not really very happy with their lot. This was the message of *Native Son* in 1940 and *Black Boy,* his 1945 autobiography, and, despite his quarrel with Wright, it remained the burden of James Baldwin's early essays as they began to appear in the late forties. Irving Howe has written that "the day *Native Son* appeared American culture was changed forever. . . . It made impossible a repetition of the old lies. . . . Richard Wright's novel brought out into the open, as no one ever had before, the hatred, fear, and violence that have crippled and may yet destroy our culture."

Well, American culture is an elephantine thing, hard to change with a novel. But with *Native Son* the consciousness of blacks themselves was indeed altered, and surely no black writer could ever tell himself the old lies. Whatever the later attacks on Wright, his work became an effective north star of Negro writing, which helped his successors to find their own directions. Attacked, abandoned as a literary example by Baldwin and Ellison, whose early work he had typically encouraged, he became, after a long eclipse and after his death in 1960, the favored ancestor of a great many new black writers, who rejected his successors and felt more akin to his militant spirit. Parricide, after all, is one of the quicker methods of succession, and nothing can more conveniently legitimate the bloody deed than an appeal to the authority of the grandfather, himself the previous victim. Thus, the rapid evolution of black awareness these past decades has repeatedly crystallized in moments of sharp generational conflict that, to a curious outsider, cast much light on the origins of the present phase of black writing and black culture.

Despite the inevitable metaphor of parricide, it would be superficial to think that Baldwin alone killed Richard Wright until the angry sixties came along to resurrect him. In some sense Wright's kind of novel was already dead or dying by the time he found it. In *Black Boy* Wright describes the impact of reading Dreiser for the first time: "I was overwhelmed. . . . It would have been impossible for me to have told anyone what I derived from these novels, for it was nothing less than a sense of life itself. All my life had shaped me for the realism, the naturalism of the modern novel." How quaint the last phrase must have seemed in the late forties and fifties, when the modern novel meant the modernist novel, when everyone knew without reading him that Dreiser was crude and vulgar compared to Henry James, when, increasingly, the only modern American classics in fiction were Hemingway, Faulkner, and (perhaps) Fitzgerald, when every writer was summoned to the bar of style and the test of inwardness and self-consciousness, of the private life in general, where both Dreiser and Wright were found wanting.*

Nothing so clearly dates Baldwin's early essays, especially the attacks on Wright, as the assurance that the novel has intrinsically little to do with society but rather involves "something more than that, something resolutely indefinable, unpredictable. . . . The disquieting complexity of ourselves . . . this web of ambiguity, paradox, this hunger, danger, darkness. . . . This power of revelation which is the business of the novelist, this journey toward a more vast reality which must take precedence over all other claims." I excerpt these phrases from "Everybody's Protest Novel," Baldwin's famous attack on *Uncle Tom's Cabin* and *Native Son,* which still seemed per-

---

* "Dreiser came of the kind of people who copulate in the dark and live out their lives without seeing their sexual partners nude; and he was brought up on the kind of book which made it impossible for him to write convincingly about the act of love." Thus Leslie Fiedler in *Love and Death in the American Novel,* where he also alludes casually to "the passionate, incoherent books of Richard Wright."

suasive in 1960 but soon, with its upper-case mockery of "Causes" and a writer's "Responsibility," seemed fatally marred by the end-of-ideology mood that produced it. It is a nice question how a purely formalist conception of the novel came to be articulated not so much through Jamesian notions of craft—though there was much of that—but through a pseudo-metaphysical rhetoric, a kitsch existentialism, bordering less on mysticism than on gibberish. Yet writers spoke of the novel that way all the time, as a mysterious inward quest toward some ineffable region of personality. Mailer spoke of the novel that way, still does perhaps, and became the only one of the band to make something of such hash. What chance had Richard Wright in that climate of critical "thinking"?

Native Son is an untidy novel, many novels. It looks backward to *An American Tragedy,* sideways to a lurid potboiler, forward, strikingly, to *L'Etranger* and the ideas of Sartre. Two-thirds of the way through it changes horses and devolves into a curious but inert ideological essay on a novel that has essentially ended, but that had until then been remarkably free of the clichés of proletarian fiction and the party line. This immensely long and disappointing coda has served to obscure the book and date it. The hidden strength of *Native Son*—hidden from formalist and Communist alike—is in essence Dostoevskian rather than Mike Goldian: a harrowing mastery of extreme situations, of the mind *in extremis,* a medium not so much naturalistic as hallucinatory, dreamlike, and poetic. The following lines describe the hunger of Bigger Thomas, in flight, trapped, hungry, cold: "He wanted to pull off his clothes and roll in the snow until something nourishing seeped into his body through the pores of his skin. He wanted to grip something in his hands so hard it would turn to food." Psychologically this is vivid, almost surreal, but it is also socially emblematic, a fierce heightening of the whole condition of the ghetto where he is trapped, within a police cordon that only makes more literal the color line that divides it from the rest of the city.

To Wright hunger is not an absence of food but a form of violence. "Hunger came to his stomach," the same paragraph begins; "an icy hand reached down his throat and clutched his intestines and tied them into a cold, tight knot that ached.'' If this sentence is not as good as the two later ones it's because the violence of society is less palpable than the counter-violence that Bigger Thomas represents. In convicting society, Wright thus slips toward luridness and cheap symbolism (as when Bigger is later ''crucified'' in the same white omnipresence of the snow) and, finally, endless theorizing: Wright is forcing his theme. But in depicting Bigger from the inside and giving his fantasies and feelings a more-than-private shape, Wright truly approximates Lukács' description of classical realism as the union of the personal and the general, the fully rendered type, Hegel's concrete universal.

It was just this dimension, which Dreiser and other American realists shared, that dropped out of serious American fiction toward the end of the forties. ''Social affairs,'' Baldwin announced in the preface to his first book of essays, *Notes of a Native Son* (1955), ''are not generally speaking the writer's prime concern, whether they ought to be or not.'' Baldwin's novels illustrate this lame conviction all too painfully. As Eldridge Cleaver said of *Another Country* (1962), ''his characters all seem to be fucking and sucking in a vacuum.'' On the other hand, that same preface is titled ''Autobiographical Notes,'' and we ought not to underestimate the boldness and healthy egotism of Baldwin's thrusting his private case forward as a significant public example. Baldwin had before him, as he later acknowledged, the precedent of *Black Boy,* but there was little else to encourage him to break the then-prevalent mold of the impersonal artist who peers at the public through the coy mask of his ''works''—a mold to which he generally adhered in his novels, as Mailer did. Later the precedent of Baldwin himself would make Mailer's own breakthrough more thinkable. *Advertisements for Myself,* with its rich, bloody life mostly in the italics of its autobiographical transitions, appeared four years after *Notes of a Native Son.* And *The Armies of the Night* was quite deliberately Mailer's *Fire Next Time,* the essay that would explode into a book, the journalistic occasion that transforms itself into a crucial act of self-definition (and, not by chance, a literary sensation).

But where Baldwin and even Mailer—despite his fascination with power—must *reach out* to their public subjects (the Black Muslims, the march on the Pentagon) in order to make that distance, that ambivalence, their true subjects, Wright's *Black Boy*, though more purely autobiographical, sits in effortless mastery over *its* social theme, the condition of the black man in the South. Yet Wright's book is also more convincingly personal, even in incidents he may have invented. Neither Baldwin nor Mailer, immense egos both, has as yet written a true autobiography; their revelations are obsessive but selective. Genuine sons of the forties and fifties, they remain essentially private persons despite their fame. Wright, however, a disaffected son of the thirties, did write an autobiography at age thirty-seven, but honed and sorted his memories into a coherent fable, aiming, like all great autobiographers, to fashion a myth— typically a myth of conversion or election—rather than to convey information about the past.

In scene after scene Wright presents his younger self as a rebellious misfit, incapable of adapting to the modes of deference that obtain in his coarse and brutal family and in Southern life as a whole. On the very first page, as a four-year-old boy, he sets fire to the curtains, nearly incinerates his ailing grandmother, and almost ends his own life by taking refuge under the burning house. When his desperate parents finally rescue him they show their relief by beating him into unconsciousness, nearly killing him themselves. This pattern of instinctive rebellion and savage counter-violence recurs repeatedly though more subtly throughout the book. When Wright goes out at last among whites, he makes an intense effort of self-restraint, but try as he will there is always a provocative hint of pride and self-respect, a touch of the uppity nigger about him. A latecomer to the white world, he is unable to quite master the shuffling, degraded, but apparently contented manner that will tell whites he not only knows his place but loves it. He is the perennial loser, always half-willingly skirting an abyss, awaiting the fatal misstep that might reveal his true feelings and get him killed.

The turning point of *Black Boy* comes in an incident that reverses this pattern and shows him (and us) the true nature of his situation.

He goes to work for a benevolent Yankee but soon is typically hounded and threatened by two white co-workers. They warn him to leave the job. He wilts briefly but returns the next day to see the boss, who quickly invites him to tell his story. It would seem that a great moment has come. For the first time a quantum of power is on his side. Instead, his sassiness and pride, irrepressible before, completely desert him. "An impulse to speak rose in me and died with the realization that I was facing a wall that I would never breach. . . . What would I accomplish by telling him? I was black; I lived in the South. . . . I looked at the white faces of Pease and Reynolds; I imagined their waylaying me, killing me. I remembered what had happened to Ned's brother."

The writer, with characteristic economy, does not belabor the lesson of this most humiliating of all moments, but to the reader it is clear enough: there can be no separate peace, no private accommodation. Neither the well-meaning Yankee, archetype of the ineffectual liberal paternalist, nor the defeated but unbroken black boy can buck the whole Southern way of life. Wright will break the mold by escaping to the North, becoming a writer and radical who will turn his rebelliousness from an ineluctable fatality to a fighting virtue. With word and deed he will try to change society rather than nest in the shelter of its exceptions.

I go on at this length about Wright not only because of the important connections and differences between his work and that of the new black writers, but also because his books enunciate a fundamental pattern of black writing, that of the *Bildungsroman,* or "How I got my consciousness raised." The black writer is almost by definition someone who has made it, struggled out of the cave not only of oppression but illusion—a mental bondage that issues in impotence and self-hatred—and has come to deliver an account of his journey. Just as Wright in *Black Boy* develops from terrified deference to rebellion and flight, *Native Son* moves from a crime-and-punishment plot to an account of how Bigger Thomas, by accepting his crime, achieves a measure of freedom and awareness. But the theme and its material increasingly clash; the crime is finally *not* acceptable, nor is it reducible to symbolism. Pursuing the matter, Wright's own liberated consciousness becomes too heavy, too subtle for Bigger, yet remains too entangled in the remnants of the murder plot to evade moral confusion.

Ralph Ellison complains that "Bigger Thomas had none of the finer qualities of Richard Wright, none of the imagination, none of the sense of poetry, none of the gaiety," and in his own novel, *Invisible Man,* he transformed the *Bildungsroman* into a freewheeling, episodic, surreal mode in which the hero could contain and express the most diverse kinds of consciousness. In prose, black writers generally tend toward an urgent but impure mixture of fiction, autobiography, and discursiveness, and the most original thing about *Invisible Man* is its eclecticism and discontinuity, which foreshadows the style of the black humorists of the sixties, in whose work we have observed how technical, verbal, and structural inventiveness takes the place of realistic setting and psychology. Yet Ellison's book, which is finally too serious to be pinned down as black humor, essentially follows the pattern of *Black Boy* and *Native Son,* as do Malcolm X's autobiography, Cleaver's *Soul on Ice,* and George Cain's impressive novel *Blueschild Baby*—whose hero is named George Cain—in which the distinction between fiction and autobiography has disappeared entirely. In this last book only the scene and subject change, not the basic pattern: for Cain the journey goes not from South to North but from heroin addiction, prison, and self-hatred to self-respect, to writing, and above all, as with Cleaver, back to the arms of the black woman. Malcolm X's autobiography even more classically reenacts the fundamental pattern of spiritual autobiography since Augustine; it is built around not one but two deep conversions—first to the Nation of Islam, then from black racism to a brand of humane radicalism that might have made him one of the crucial American leaders. (Malcolm even parallels Augustine in richly conveying the pleasures of the unconverted life.)

James Baldwin is a distinctive figure here; his spiritual style is rooted in the Negro church, but his essays follow the Augustinian pattern far more than his novels do, and this helps account for their superiority. Baldwin's problem as a novelist is not simply his difficulty in fully imagining other people, or his inability to take the form in hand, as Ellison did, and mold it to his own vision. (Ellison himself, accepting the National Book Award, aptly stressed the importance of the novel's "experimental attitude.") It has been Baldwin's misfortune to move from one false notion of the novel—the New Critical one, that of a highly crafted, distanced object—to the exact opposite fallacy, by which an aimless assortment of characters serve as threadbare masks for a purely personal set of obsessions and intensities. If his third novel, *Another Country,* was shapeless, at least the feelings were still vigorous and sharp, but by the time he published his next novel, a long, dismal failure called *Tell Me How Long the Train's Been Gone* (1968), Baldwin the novelist seemed to have lost all ability to command belief. If anything he was more rather than less obsessed by the formative incidents of his childhood, but they became more distant and abstract even as they extended their hold on him; and to dramatize the later experiences of fame and success he could bring no spirit at all. (These impressions have been confirmed by his later books, such as *A Rap on Race,* his book of conversations with Margaret Mead, a typical publisher's brainchild.)

By all accounts Baldwin's life has been much entwined with white people and white books; he deeply resisted having his consciousness raised in the direction of separatism; *The Fire Next Time* summarizes his ambivalence even as it burns with the intensity of his anger. By the late sixties he was nowhere, an expatriate again, *all* anger—though the lengthening chain of corpses from Malcolm X to George Jackson served to make his feelings plausible. It is ironic that the man who was partly responsible for the new black mood, or at least prophetic of it, should also fall victim to it. Baldwin's later essays become very harsh, and powerfully anticipate the anti-integrationist militance that developed in the mid-sixties. "Do I really *want* to be integrated into a burning house?" he asked in *The Fire Next Time.* Earlier, in 1961, he summed up his message by saying that "to be a Negro in this country and to be relatively conscious, is to be in a rage all the time." But for Baldwin that rage was a torment and an anguish; he quickly added that "the first problem is how to control that rage so it won't destroy you." For the angry young blacks of the sixties, who perhaps avoided the worst scars that Baldwin and Wright received so early, rage was their pride and their power, not a poison at the wellspring. Thus, paradoxically, while Baldwin re-hashed and flattened what was once a richly complicated, ironic view of the race problem in America, partly out of a desperate attempt to keep abreast of the new mood, younger black writers regularly de-fined their own positions by attacking him, much as he once attacked Richard Wright.

Two of the most severe and damaging assaults, both by writers not simply envious of his fame but deeply involved with his work, came from Eldridge Cleaver in *Soul on Ice* and Calvin C. Hernton in the first issue of *Amistad* (a black periodical launched with much fanfare and dropped with typical unseemly haste by Random House). They were a good index to the sensibility that, for better or worse, dis-placed him as a representative figure. Significantly, both coupled their attacks on Baldwin with extravagant praise of Richard Wright. Cleaver's simpler charge, already mentioned, is that his work, espe-cially as compared with Wright's, is "void of a political, economic, or even a social reference." Paul Goodman said something similar in his unfavorable review of *Another Country*. This criticism is much more true of the novels than the essays, and least true of *Nobody Knows My Name* (1961), the more public and journalistic collection, which once seemed a paler echo of *Notes of a Native Son* but later came to feel impressively direct and referential.

It might be noted in passing that Ralph Ellison was hardly vulnera-ble to Cleaver's charge, though his conservative political views were undoubtedly more repugnant to Cleaver and Hernton than Bald-win's. Though Ellison shares some of the fifties mystique of identity and personality—as evident in the "invisibility" theme of his novel, which particularly mars the prologue and the very tedious epilogue—he was in truth almost as much a child of the thirties as was Wright. Because he has written so deliberately, we forget that Ellison was born in 1914, that he is ten years older than Baldwin and closer in age to Wright, that he came of age during the Depression under the aegis of Wright and the Party, writing for the *New Masses*. Though he has attacked naturalism and said, "I despise concreteness in writing," he himself is a great realist of the Dickensian rather than naturalistic sort. His novel captures both South and North, Uncle Tom and street-rebel, Communist and nationalist; it is a human comedy of the whole scene, the only one yet written. If *Invisible Man* begins in ripe Southern Gothic on the order of, say, Flannery O'Connor's *Wise Blood*, it matures unexpectedly in the Brotherhood sections into a first-rate political novel. Irving Howe, in one of the few missteps in his commendable essay "Black Boys and Native Sons," complains that this part of the book "does not quite ring true." I find it a brilliant success, done with something like a Dickensian freedom and accuracy of caricature. Howe stumbles, I think, on Ellison's method. One can't of course "refute" the CP by inventing a leader with a slippery glass eye—unless you are Dickens, or Ellison, and are dealing with an organization that was evidently more Kafkaesque than functional. In any case, Ellison's refutation is more convincing than all the labored anti-Communist polemics that run through Harold Cruse's idiosyncratic but indispensable book *The Crisis of the Negro Intellectual*. The two books together should be enough to convince anyone too young to remember that the Party was probably the worst thing that ever happened to American radicalism.

The crucial charge against Baldwin had little to do with his politics, or his literary craftsmanship, or even, for that matter, his precise position on the race question. The argument was that Baldwin's homosexuality, his unconfident masculinity, is the hidden root of all his writing and completely disqualifies him as a representative spokesman. Cleaver and Hernton spoke for an aggressive new generation, bursting with phallic pride and masculine assertiveness, contemptuous of fags (and women?), certain of its identity however much that may threaten the white world. But white America loved Baldwin because he was spineless and effeminate, claims Hernton, and "does not symbolize the historic fear of the great, black phallus which lurks to rape and pillage," while Wright "was perceived as a powerful, black phallus, threatening their guilt-ridden, lily-white world.'' According to Cleaver, ''Baldwin's essay on Richard Wright reveals that he despised—not Richard Wright, but his masculinity. He cannot confront the stud in others—except that he must either submit to it or destroy it. And he was not about to bow to a *black* man.''

By quoting these passages—there are others even more extreme— I risk making the argument seem like absurd fantasy-projection and chest-pounding (cock-waving?), which it partly is. But whatever their violence of language and attitude, however rigid their defini- tions of masculine and feminine and their feelings about homosex- among younger blacks in the six- 's work contains more than a grain me responsibility for their hostile alicious and ridiculous, but they Baldwin's strengths, the *mauvaise* eloquence. Baldwin's great theme, ocial oppression involved in being den. Indebted perhaps to the Sar- ionable during his years in France, color, especially in this country, ns of the self.'' He told how he, a usly to internalize the white man's skin and people, and hence to feel y and masculinity. He wrote of the the face of The Man, and of his and model. How unbearably poi- gnant, then, that he, the black man, so cruelly undermined, should ironically remain the mythical phallus, the object of the deepest sex- ual fantasies and expectations of white people. How cruelly misguided were white writers like Mailer and Kerouac who continue to play upon those myths.

* When homosexual students at Columbia requested a separate lounge, a privilege that had already been accorded to blacks, the Student Afro-American Society chafed at the implied parallel, and gratuitously proclaimed its refusal ''to wallow in the mud with people who cannot decide if they are men or women.''

I say "he, the black man," because this is just where Baldwin gets into trouble; he never makes the necessary distinction. Everywhere in the essays he presents himself, with little qualification, not as a case history but as a representative figure, almost a generalized historical consciousness, spokesman for a mutely suffering mass. Out of reticence or ambitiousness, he hesitated to damage his standing by dealing as candidly with his sexuality as he does with his racial feelings, despite the intrinsic connections. Even in an essay on Gide, which deals directly with the subject of homosexuality, he skirts his own relation to the problem; the subject is suspended in a void. It was inevitable that those blacks who did not (or would not) feel their masculinity undermined in the generalized way he describes would see their image distorted in his mirror. Eventually the most articulate part of the next generation, formed by different experiences, began trying to disentangle itself from his powerful, at times almost incantatory formulations.

Even if history should somehow corroborate Baldwin's view of the Negro psyche, even if his critics proved wishful thinkers decreeing mental liberation by fiat, Baldwin's early essays would still be distortions—disfigured by their 1950-ish politics, or apolitics, but also by something indeed rooted in his sexuality. There is a distinct but masked sexual animus in Baldwin, especially in the essays on Wright, where Baldwin repeatedly describes Bigger Thomas as "a monster created by the American republic," a ghetto rat, a doomed figure of pity and terror. This account, echoed by other critics, is false to the tone and substance of the book. Wright portrays Bigger as a sort of symbolic time bomb that goes off, and finally something of an existential hero, never the sort of repulsive figure Baldwin describes. One blatantly wrong sentence especially stunned me as I reread Baldwin; it misses a good deal more than Wright's tone or intention. "All of Bigger's life," says Baldwin, "is controlled, is defined by his hatred and his fear. And later, his fear drives him to murder and his hatred to rape." The fact is that Bigger, though briefly tempted, never commits rape in the novel, certainly not the rape for which he's pilloried and condemned. By accident, though

I say "he, the black man," because this is just where Baldwin gets into trouble; he never makes the necessary distinction. Everywhere in the essays he presents himself, with little qualification, not as a case history but as a representative figure, almost a generalized historical consciousness, spokesman for a mutely suffering mass. Out of reticence or ambitiousness, he hesitated to damage his standing by dealing as candidly with his sexuality as he does with his racial feelings, despite the intrinsic connections. Even in an essay on Gide, which deals directly with the subject of homosexuality, he skirts his own relation to the problem; the subject is suspended in a void. It was inevitable that those blacks who did not (or would not) feel their masculinity undermined in the generalized way he describes would see their image distorted in his mirror. Eventually the most articulate part of the next generation, formed by different experiences, began trying to disentangle itself from his powerful, at times almost incantatory formulations.

Even if history should somehow corroborate Baldwin's view of the Negro psyche, even if his critics proved wishful thinkers decreeing mental liberation by fiat, Baldwin's early essays would still be distortions—disfigured by their 1950-ish politics, or apolitics, but also by something indeed rooted in his sexuality. There is a distinct but masked sexual animus in Baldwin, especially in the essays on Wright, where Baldwin repeatedly describes Bigger Thomas as "a monster created by the American republic," a ghetto rat, a doomed figure of pity and terror. This account, echoed by other critics, is false to the tone and substance of the book. Wright portrays Bigger as a sort of symbolic time bomb that goes off, and finally something of an existential hero, never the sort of repulsive figure Baldwin describes. One blatantly wrong sentence especially stunned me as I reread Baldwin; it misses a good deal more than Wright's tone or intention. "All of Bigger's life," says Baldwin, "is controlled, is defined by his hatred and his fear. And later, his fear drives him to murder and his hatred to rape." The fact is that Bigger, though briefly tempted, never commits rape in the novel, certainly not the rape for which he's pilloried and condemned. By accident, though powerful, black phallus, threatening their guilt-ridden, lily-white world.'' According to Cleaver, ''Baldwin's essay on Richard Wright reveals that he despised—not Richard Wright, but his masculinity. He cannot confront the stud in others—except that he must either submit to it or destroy it. And he was not about to bow to a *black* man.''

By quoting these passages—there are others even more extreme— I risk making the argument seem like absurd fantasy-projection and chest-pounding (cock-waving?), which it partly is. But whatever their violence of language and attitude, however rigid their defini- tions of masculine and feminine and their feelings about homosex- uals—attitudes all too common among younger blacks in the six- ties *—their analysis of Baldwin's work contains more than a grain of truth, and he himself bears some responsibility for their hostile reading. Their charges were malicious and ridiculous, but they hit home to reveal the defects of Baldwin's strengths, the *mauvaise foi* near the heart of his abstract eloquence. Baldwin's great theme, after all, was not the physical or social oppression involved in being black, but the psychological burden. Indebted perhaps to the Sar- trean psychology that was so fashionable during his years in France, he insisted that ''the question of color, especially in this country, operates to hide the graver questions of the self.'' He told how he, a black man, had been taught insidiously to internalize the white man's view of himself, to hate his own skin and people, and hence to feel precarious, uprooted, in his identity and masculinity. He wrote of the powerlessness of black fathers in the face of The Man, and of his own confused search for father and model. How unbearably poi- gnant, then, that he, the black man, so cruelly undermined, should ironically remain the mythical phallus, the object of the deepest sex- ual fantasies and expectations of white people. How cruelly misguided were white writers like Mailer and Kerouac who continue to play upon those myths.

* When homosexual students at Columbia requested a separate lounge, a privilege that had already been accorded to blacks, the Student Afro-American Society chafed at the implied parallel, and gratuitously proclaimed its refusal ''to wallow in the mud with people who cannot decide if they are men or women.''

anguish; he quickly added that "the first problem is how to control that rage so it won't destroy you." For the angry young blacks of the sixties, who perhaps avoided the worst scars that Baldwin and Wright received so early, rage was their pride and their power, not a poison at the wellspring. Thus, paradoxically, while Baldwin re-hashed and flattened what was once a richly complicated, ironic view of the race problem in America, partly out of a desperate attempt to keep abreast of the new mood, younger black writers regularly de-fined their own positions by attacking him, much as he once attacked Richard Wright.

Two of the most severe and damaging assaults, both by writers not simply envious of his fame but deeply involved with his work, came from Eldridge Cleaver in *Soul on Ice* and Calvin C. Hernton in the first issue of *Amistad* (a black periodical launched with much fanfare and dropped with typical unseemly haste by Random House). They were a good index to the sensibility that, for better or worse, dis-placed him as a representative figure. Significantly, both coupled their attacks on Baldwin with extravagant praise of Richard Wright. Cleaver's simpler charge, already mentioned, is that his work, espe-cially as compared with Wright's, is "void of a political, economic, or even a social reference." Paul Goodman said something similar in his unfavorable review of *Another Country*. This criticism is much more true of the novels than the essays, and least true of *Nobody Knows My Name* (1961), the more public and journalistic collection, which once seemed a paler echo of *Notes of a Native Son* but later came to feel impressively direct and referential.

It might be noted in passing that Ralph Ellison was hardly vulnera-ble to Cleaver's charge, though his conservative political views were undoubtedly more repugnant to Cleaver and Hernton than Bald-win's. Though Ellison shares some of the fifties mystique of identity and personality—as evident in the "invisibility" theme of his novel, which particularly mars the prologue and the very tedious epilogue—he was in truth almost as much a child of the thirties as was Wright. Because he has written so deliberately, we forget that Ellison was born in 1914, that he is ten years older than Baldwin and closer in age to Wright, that he came of age during the Depression under the aegis of Wright and the Party, writing for the *New Masses*. Though he has attacked naturalism and said, "I despise concreteness in writing," he himself is a great realist of the Dickensian rather than naturalistic sort. His novel captures both South and North, Uncle Tom and street-rebel, Communist and nationalist; it is a human comedy of the whole scene, the only one yet written. If *Invisible Man* begins in ripe Southern Gothic on the order of, say, Flannery O'Connor's *Wise Blood*, it matures unexpectedly in the Brotherhood sections into a first-rate political novel. Irving Howe, in one of the few missteps in his commendable essay "Black Boys and Native Sons," complains that this part of the book "does not quite ring true." I find it a brilliant success, done with something like a Dickensian freedom and accuracy of caricature. Howe stumbles, I think, on Ellison's method. One can't of course "refute" the CP by inventing a leader with a slippery glass eye—unless you are Dickens, or Ellison, and are dealing with an organization that was evidently more Kafkaesque than functional. In any case, Ellison's refutation is more convincing than all the labored anti-Communist polemics that run through Harold Cruse's idiosyncratic but indispensable book *The Crisis of the Negro Intellectual*. The two books together should be enough to convince anyone too young to remember that the Party was probably the worst thing that ever happened to American radicalism.

The crucial charge against Baldwin had little to do with his politics, or his literary craftsmanship, or even, for that matter, his precise position on the race question. The argument was that Baldwin's homosexuality, his unconfident masculinity, is the hidden root of all his writing and completely disqualifies him as a representative spokesman. Cleaver and Hernton spoke for an aggressive new generation, bursting with phallic pride and masculine assertiveness, contemptuous of fags (and women?), certain of its identity however much that may threaten the white world. But white America loved Baldwin because he was spineless and effeminate, claims Hernton, and "does not symbolize the historic fear of the great, black phallus which lurks to rape and pillage," while Wright "was perceived as a not without sexual overtones, he has killed the girl instead. It is only the white world—press, prosecutors, and public—that universally assumes both rape and deliberate murder, and since Bigger in his panic has destroyed the body, he never manages to prove otherwise. Bigger does force himself on his own girlfriend, Bessie, after they have run off together. But to use this to explain Baldwin's allusion would make no sense: no "hatred" is involved, only confusion, violence, and irrationality. When Bigger kills her, it's his most gratuitous and senseless act, though typically ignored by everyone else in the book, who attend only to the white victim. Baldwin's hostility to Bigger, his horror at the violent street-nigger, causes him unconsciously to take over the white man's perspective, to project the same sexual fantasies that he debunks so brilliantly when they are applied to himself. Cleaver, for his part, was even more eager to sexualize Wright's characters than Baldwin, for the same reason that he defends Mailer and Kerouac: he and his contemporaries were determined to reclaim the very myths that Baldwin did much to question. To Cleaver the Negro homosexual was a historical interlude, an aberration, a disease. Cleaver came forward as the proud black stud, the verification of the myth, the fantasy made real. There is an unresolved aura of sexual suggestion about both of Bigger's killings, but then, by making the rape a white fabrication, Wright withdrew onto the easier ground of protest and injustice. Wright withdrew, Baldwin recoiled, but Cleaver. . . . With a jolt we remember that Cleaver began his career as an actual rapist—"an insurrectionary act," he calls it in *Soul on Ice,* the book that at its best enacts his conversion to other, more humane forms of insurrection.

It was Cleaver's book that occasioned Richard Gilman's controversial essays, which discerned—in Cleaver, in Malcolm, in Fanon—a new mode of writing not simply by blacks but of them and for them, standing outside the white tradition and its audience. The aim of these books, as he saw it, was not the production of literature but the creation of new myths, the production of new modes of consciousness. But Gilman's refusal to judge, his stance of silent wonderment, caused him somewhat to patronize what Cleaver was actually saying, a luxury that blacks themselves, especially black writers, could scarcely afford. All were marked in some way by the new consciousness. The wheel of black culture was turning rapidly, however, and in the late sixties a whole new generation of writers emerged, a fourth generation, so to speak, that was almost as distinct from Cleaver and Malcolm as *they* were from Baldwin, as he was from Wright. These writers, to whom I'll devote the remainder of this chapter, returned for the most part to traditional genres, especially fiction; they were private persons rather than would-be ideologues, and had to grapple with an assortment of problems, both human and technical, that were not central for Cleaver, Malcolm, or Fanon.

It would be too sweeping to say that these writers returned, by the grandfather principle, to the example of Baldwin. A various group, the young fiction writers range broadly from conventional to experimental, but all show a renewed attention to art and craft, an unwillingness to fall back solely on the raw data of experience to make their impact. All were baptized in the issues raised by the tension between Baldwin's work, still very vivid, and Cleaver's or Malcolm's; all responded to the increasing predominance of black nationalist ideas among Negro intellectuals, and to the general cultural ferment of the sixties, which in fiction opened the door to a diversity of technique and a freedom of expression unparalleled since the early modernist period. What these writers share is a sense of historical and personal grievance, and a willingness to take their blackness as the starting point of their writing; there is no Eliotic escape into form. Chosen by circumstance to bear privileged witness, they exhibit the scars of survival, the honors and burdens of election, the thrill of newly articulate speech. Toward whites they are invariably hostile or pitying, not at the behest of ideology but as if released by it, reveling in a long-suppressed passion of execration. But they show little impulse to sentimentalize blacks, and they heap satirical venom on the life style of the black middle class. They pay for their one-dimensional anger, as Richard Wright did, by being unable to represent white characters convincingly; they are cut off from the residual humanity of the oppressor, from the whole shape of his malevolence, even his very ordinariness.

Among older writers Baldwin was exceptional in his feel for the reality of the other side—the important Baldwin, I mean, not the later hysterical one—and it is James Alan McPherson, the most Baldwinesque of the newcomers, who is a partial exception in the younger generation. His excellent book of stories *Hue and Cry* (1969) and Toni Morrison's novels *The Bluest Eye* (1970) and *Sula* (1974) bring to mind strengths of Baldwin that my criticism has so far obscured. Relatively conventional in form, straightforward in style, both McPherson and Morrison are anatomists of the nuance and feel of personal relationship. Their characters are children, or grownups as vulnerable and complex as children, who grow and learn, or fail to, who experience love and unhappiness, brutality and special grace, all without disturbing the cosmos or the body politic. These writers resume the fifties' concern with identity in a new and fresher tone. I'm reminded that if Baldwin's "we" sometimes wobbles in the early essays, acting out his predicament by assuming now a white, now a black face, yet the brilliance of his introspection is directly indebted to that fluid and infirm sense of himself, and to a literary tradition and prose style that nurtured psychological complexity. His tormented, ambiguous sexuality made for further complications of awareness and feeling, though it would be invidious to call his emotional sensitivity "feminine." But later groups of blacks, proclaiming their masculinity, would aim to turn identity from a personal problem into a function of group solidarity. Such a project has some truth for blacks, or for women, who suffer disabilities in common, but it tends to confuse identity with power, or absolution, or pride, all of which groups can more readily bestow.

The continuing relevance of Baldwin's books in the late sixties, then, especially the first three volumes of essays, lay not only in their eloquence, which no other black writer has yet equaled, but in their vigorous dissent from a cultural mood that excessively devalued inwardness. So too, McPherson's stories were a bold evasion of the stereotypes of black militance and "black writing." His central characters are plagued by personal and sexual uncertainties similar to those we find in Baldwin. They are heterosexual, but just barely; intellectual, but not very assuredly; black, but not convinced of their superiority or their exemption from ordinary human needs. They are set off against other figures who are more firmly, if not more happily, implanted: half-demented black racists, assured cocksmen, confirmed homosexuals. The stories usually end unhappily. Either the hero is weak and falls under the domination of one of these predators, or he arms himself and casts them out until, eschewing all relationship, all human risk, he becomes an empty shell.

McPherson's stories are the opposite of protest literature. They are built on a principle of reversal by which the victim, the apparent object of aggression, turns out to be most deeply victimizing himself. Often these reversals do not quite come off, and the stories become a little arbitrary as they freeze into their final tableaux, but three or four of the stories are first-rate, especially "Of Cabbages and Kings" and "All the Lonely People," in which McPherson shows his facility at choreographing his characters almost diagrammatically around the uncertain figure at the center. Best of all is "Hue and Cry," a 45-page *tour de force* and surely one of the best stories of the sixties. There the main character is a woman, sensitive, intelligent, full of possibility. She is dragged down in a terrible round-robin of mistakes and misfortunes in love, described in tones of sardonic understatement and controlled irony or pathos that are virtually unique in black writing.

Toni Morrison shares McPherson's emotional intelligence, and some of his irony as well, particularly when she writes of the black middle class. The first third of *The Bluest Eye* is shaky, but when she undertakes, quite tangentially, a sketch of a certain type of Negro woman, destructive, respectable, unfunky, self-hating—a "plain brown girl" who "will build her nest stick by stick, make it her own inviolable world"—the whole novel comes alive and stays that way. Morrison values all the "funkiness" that this girl tries to extirpate, using the word to signify not only physicality but feeling, "the dreadful funkiness of passion, the funkiness of nature, the funkiness of the wide range of human emotions.'' Clearly black anger is not the province of the black man alone; and, like Cleaver, Morrison is as much distressed by a sexual model as a racial one. But finally as a novelist it is a human model that she satirizes or embraces, all in rich if not loving detail.

Besides irony, Morrison's other tone is a lyrical one, though her rhetorical cadences are sometimes heavy-handed. She is a poet of the open horizons that children can still experience even in sordid surroundings, and of the first joys of even a doomed marriage; as the noose tightens, sometimes by trivial stages, her sense of fatality and pathos are inexorable. But *The Bluest Eye* is finally too small a book, too conventional in form, too much of a horrific anecdote gotten up with great skill into a Novel.

In this respect *Sula,* though equally small in compass, represents a great advance for Morrison. (Its quiet, serious reception by reviewers of every stripe—it was nominated for a National Book Award—may signal the end of ''black writing'' and the recognition of blacks as writers, period, without allowances, fanfare, or special attention.) Gone are the stiffness and ''fine writing'' of the earlier book. Gone too are the poetic lyricism and the direct, angry satire. What we have instead is a truer, more muted eloquence, which helps develop a beautiful interplay between two young women, one funky and impossible, the other fragile, respectable, and a little self-deceived. Though the book is marred by casual catastrophes and arbitrary turns of plot, Morrison never lets us rest in a fixed and simple view of these two girls; neither is wholly good or evil, and the meanings that shift and reverberate between them contain something of the enigma of all personality and relationship. Like the good fifties novelists, like Baldwin at his best, Morrison is an artist of personal histories, and even of social life as it flows through the vagaries of personal relationship.

At the other end of this spectrum are writers whose deepest commitment is not to art or experience but to ideology, even as they insist that they are thereby creating a new black aesthetic. This is the position of Larry Neal, a protegé of LeRoi Jones (Imamu Amiri

Baraka), in a 1968 manifesto called "The Black Arts Movement." According to Neal, "the Western aesthetic has run its course: it is impossible to create anything meaningful within its decaying structure." Going one up on the Baldwin-Wright controversy, he condemns all black literature that is not essentially ethnic, that uses established forms and techniques, that does not speak exclusively to black people, as " 'protest' literature. . . . an appeal to white morality." Poetry must be the handmaiden of Black Power, a missile in the hand of the Revolution, "a concrete function, an action." Jones himself sums it up best in lines Neal explicates approvingly:

> We want poems
> like fists beating niggers out of jocks
> or dagger-poems in the slimy bellies
> of the owner-jews . . . .

(There's no end to the delicate uses to which these "poems" can be put: "Another bad poem cracking/ steel knuckles in a jewlady's mouth.") Since such poems do not even marginally belong to literature, they need not concern us here except as a point on the compass. The novelist Cecil Brown does belong to literature, but since, like other members of his generation, he is attracted to that point, his work brings into focus the crucial conflict between art and ideological commitment.

The Life and Loves of Mr. Jiveass Nigger, published in 1969, is not a very good novel by conventional standards. The plot is loose and perfunctory; no character is quite as real as the hero, who seems to be a somewhat fantasized version of the author, and the occasional leaps into big thinking fall flat. By the same standards, Ishmael Reed's first two books of fiction, *The Free-Lance Pallbearers* (1967) and *Yellow Back Radio Broke-Down* (1969), which are far freer in form, don't qualify as anything at all; they are really anti-novels, and probably wouldn't have gotten published ten years earlier. In the interim the sixties did much to undermine conventional standards, and fostered some wild and inventive alternatives to the well-made artnovel, some merely self-indulgent, others genuinely rich in new modes of perception and behavior. Reed's third and best novel,

Mumbo Jumbo (1972), a wildly imaginative sketch of the Harlem
Renaissance of the 1920s, complete with footnotes and bibliography,
is just the sort of mythmaking appropriation of history that I've attributed to the structural black humor of the early sixties. In that
sense both Brown and Reed owed more to the sixties than they did
to other black writers, just as Baldwin belonged intrinsically to the
postwar period and Wright to the thirties. Whatever they share of
Wright's aggressive militance has little to do with his politics or his
defining sensibility. In a reminiscence, Saunders Redding described
how Wright always burned with "zeal for a cause. . . . He never
seemed to believe that an attitude toward life that was lighted by the
faintest ray of hedonism could be quite real and legitimate. . . . He
could only just tolerate . . . the people to whom life is a joke, and
not an ironic joke."

Here is the nub of uniqueness in the emerging generation of black
writers, for Brown and Reed combine the self-assertive militance of
the sixties with the hedonism and jokery of the same period—with
surreal effect in Reed's case, with *Portnoy*-like lubricity in Brown's.
Reed's work is a cross between the satirical lunacy of a Terry Southern and the free-swinging verbal exuberance of an Ellison. His basic
medium is the sick joke, through which he strings together a phantas-
magoric pastiche of American culture that is so intent on being outrageous it finally becomes incoherent. Reed himself calls his books
"circuses" and in his second book he includes a mock dialogue with
a "neo-social realist" who calls him a "crazy dada nigger," dismisses his work as "far out esoteric bullshit," and tells him that "all
art must be for the end of liberating the masses." Reed, for his part,
insists on an anarchic pluralism of artistic ends and styles; his own
Marxism is of the Groucho and Harpo variety. Similarly, Brown
wrote a piece for the short-lived *Black Review* on pop singer James
Brown, whose politics were anathema to the militants. The message
was D. H. Lawrence's—trust the tale, not the teller. It was a sharp
rebuff to the would-be cultural commissars who apply a political test
to artists and art—ideologues, he says, who could not themselves
create a single poem, story, or song.

Gates of Eden

Such an unexpected defense of the autonomy and worth of art was more than a straw in the wind; it was closer to a manifesto. So was Brown's freewheeling attack on *Native Son* early in his own novel, where his hero inverts Baldwin's complaint by blaming Bigger Thomas for *not* screwing Mary Dalton, dismissing "all those stupid ass Biggers who think violence is sex, who don't have enough cool to seduce a 'white' woman but who end up *stealing* a kiss from a 'white' girl when he should have fucked her, fucked her so good she would have gotten a glimpse into the immortal soul of the universe and come away from it all a changed woman, fucked her so beautifully that she would come away feeling he was a man, that his fucking (his humanity) had brought out that core of goodness which is in the worst of thieves." This may be bullshit, but it's significant bullshit. There are echoes of both Cleaver and, surprisingly, Baldwin here, but the presiding genius is none other than Norman Mailer. The white Negro comes home to roost; the stud-redemptor of "The Time of Her Time" and *An American Dream* comes strutting out in black face. If Cleaver and Hernton sexualized Bigger Thomas into a walking phallus, for Brown he is limp and inadequate. He says of his own hero that "he could relate to Julien Sorel, to Tom Jones; he could relate to the nigger in Malcolm X, LeRoi Jones, James Baldwin, and Eldridge Cleaver. . . . But he could not relate to Bigger. He could not relate to stupidity, fear, and demoralization."

Who is Mr. Jiveass Nigger that he is so far beyond the demoralization of the ghetto, so exempt from human weakness? The book worries that question, taking us back circuitously to the problems of identity that plague other black writers. Brown's hero is an American expatriate in Copenhagen with the mock-patriotic name of George Washington, which is as good as having no name at all. He rarely uses the name though, for he lies compulsively and assumes a variety of spontaneous identities through which he puts on and cons almost everyone he meets, especially white women. This is his "jive," about which he theorizes endlessly, insisting that "there was nothing under the sun that was really phony if it was functional." George is a Portnoy in reverse, burdened not by excessive moral feelings but by their absence, not by sexual inhibition but by utter sexual facility. He is the Julien Sorel of the color line, a Tom Jones who exploits his anonymity. His solution to the problem of identity is to live without one, or with many, which turns out to be the same thing. George is another version of a figure that has long flourished in black writing, in Jewish writing, in the folklore of many beleaguered cultures: the trickster-hero, confidence man, king of schnorrers, the virtuoso of survival. He is the anti-type of Bigger Thomas, the victim-aggressor of protest literature, the alienated hero who confronts society head on and either conquers or is destroyed. The trickster is everywhere at home, always able to land on his feet, as different from Bigger as Falstaff is from Hotspur. Probably the best such figure is Rinehart, the man of many roles, whose brilliant non-appearance all over Harlem clinches the argument of *Invisible Man*. But Ellison finally judges against Rinehart, and would later call him "the personification of chaos . . . who has lived so long with chaos he knows how to manipulate it." Manipulate it but not change it, or himself. And Brown's hero finally judges against himself and renounces his game, discovering at the end that "everybody in this town, every black person, seems to be living off someone or something else. Everything but their insides. Black men fancy themselves potent when they can flatter themselves to be gigolos." He goes home to America, to try to live off his own insides, and by doing so he sharply delimits the wisdom of his early attack on Bigger, with its brash equation of the black man's "fucking" and his "humanity."

In the process both book and character become perhaps more serious than the author intended, for Brown has yet to produce the sequel that might confirm his talent. One imagines that Brown's own "jive" was to write a sex novel, to put on public and publishers as well. This is all they want, says George, "and if you say something about sex and being a nigger then you got a bestseller." I don't know how well the book sold, but Brown happens to write very well about sex. Steeped as much in Miller as in Mailer, not only for sex but for the whole expatriate ambiance, he can be very funny about it. But in the end the jive and exploitation catch up with Brown, as with

George, and the novel becomes serious in spite of itself. Of course it's possible that this reversal is also a put-on—of critics like me who are hot for meaning. Brown jokes bitterly about this in an epilogue. So what. That too is part of the meaning and, like the sex part, it works. Brown is a deeply conflicted writer, despite the surface brashness, and he has George imagining various books he'd rather have written than this one. Such as a book with a real stick of dynamite in it, to be acclaimed by the *Saturday Review* as "a searing blast from the depths . . . slashing . . . dynamite," and then actually to blow up in the reader's face. Or else a 700-page book, every page empty but for the words KISS MY BLACK ASS, with a footnote reading MY BLACK BALLS TOO, and a preface by Marshall McLuhan saying, "White America: I ask you to kiss this black ass." Brown never wrote those books, but they are part of the knife-edged comedy, part of the meaning, of the one he actually did write. "I won't mind writing a book," says George, summing up his quandary, "but I'd hate to be a black author in America."

I am not sure why Brown's fantasies evoke in me little of the disgust and aversion I feel for those of LeRoi Jones. Probably the word "jew" is crucial, the literal threat, the humorless viciousness of Jones' impulses, which lean consciously on a pogrom psychology and reveal a truly sadistic, kamikaze mentality. Brown by comparison is coining dada jokes, doing a verbal turn, not making a statement of intent. He remains an artist, flailing himself for the limitations of his role, enacting his own inner conflict. Jones and Neal scorn inwardness as a sterile remnant of bourgeois individualism; they envision an artist who will be an impersonal emanation of the *Volk*. Brown's novel, or Cain's *Blueschild Baby*, both of which are drenched in militant anger, also fulfill Whitman's boast that if you touch this book you touch a man. Both are full of human density and human contradiction—both are works of art, in other words—and much as they may finally preach what Cruse calls "black-skin chauvinism," they do so only as an end-point in a process of self-discovery, only rarely bending their immediate perceptions to fit the frame of their finally raised consciousness.

Let me illustrate this point briefly. Both writers follow Cleaver in depicting the black man as stud and sexual athlete, as the avenger at once exploiting and redeeming white flesh. Cain says of his white activist girlfriend, "She lived in the dead yesterday of news reports or the tomorrow of reform. The pressing moment never intruded till I came and drove her into life." Two pages later he adds, "I was amazed that she could have opinions and attitudes about everything and still hadn't fulfilled her primary function. I made her into a woman to meet my needs." This is silly enough, more sexist than racist, but it is not where these writers are going: it's just the sort of relationship that Brown and Cain show their characters growing away from, as they discover that being used and using others are interchangeable, that they must learn to live off their own insides. "Everyone but me had a piece of George Cain. Was no longer me, but a composite of all their needs and desires." The healthiest side of black separatism was the return not just to group solidarity but to that typical sixties destination, one's own head. When Cain discovers that whites, all whites, are as ugly as he had once thought them attractive, he is simply inverting a racist stereotype. But doing so helps convince him that "The Man can't free me. I must free myself." Like Brown, he finds that the sexual myths he had exploited had also exploited and devalued him. When he finally comes back to the black girl who had waited patiently during his *Wanderjahre* in the white world, in prison, on dope, he makes contact without a touch of bravado, with affecting anxiety and humility: "Am afraid to sleep with Nandy, make love to her. . . . Have been with only white women where I enjoyed the advantage of the myths each of us brought to bed. . . . Have never come to a woman naked and defenseless, just a man. Am shamed knowing I know nothing of black women."

One can see that Cain, like Wright in *Black Boy*, meant to shape his life into parable—a sermon to the ghetto kids against junk, a preachment against interracial sex. For a long time we were told that such didacticism was impure, an artistic flaw. Baldwin spoke for what later became a vast critical consensus when he insisted that ideological purpose was inconsistent with art, that it was hostile to the representation of full human realities. But here is Cain breaking the rules, acknowledging no line between fiction and autobiography, preaching and teaching, but finally proving himself neither myth nor stereotype but "just a man."

Toward the end of the sixties Ralph Ellison lashed out at "talented but misguided writers of Negro American cultural background . . . who regard their social predicament as Negroes as exempting them from the necessity of mastering the craft and forms of fiction." But surely the author of *Invisible Man,* that wildly eclectic, impure, and rambunctious work, knew that blackness was more than a "cultural background" or a "social predicament," knew that the rules of fiction can hardly be enumerated let alone rigidly applied, that form does not dwell majestically alone, like Shelley's Mont Blanc, apart from immediate experience. In the sixties, literary form renewed itself under the pressures of new experience, of fantasy, of verbal experiment, of politics, and in the process became boldly impure. This new impurity, which some saw as a liberating openness and others considered formlessness and decadence, is still with us, and it apparently meshed well with the contradictions of being a black person in contemporary America. It fostered an exceptionally interesting range of writers, who began to find a new solution to the problem of literature and ideology, a solution in which literature is by no means abolished, and ideology is humanized.

7

The Age of Rock Revisited

I

WHEN did the sixties begin to come to an end? Was it in the bloody streets of Chicago in August 1968, when the young and antiwar movement were robbed of their victory over Lyndon Johnson and his war policy? Or was it the following year when their illusions of peaceful change and of the effects of moral witness on the tide of history gave way to Weatherman fantasies of violence and revolutionary suicide? Or was it the year after, during the invasion of Cambodia, when the campuses mounted their last great surge of resistance against the war?

What I'm groping for is not a date but a symbol, a turning point, a coded moment in the garbled flow of our moral history. Perhaps the war was too numbing to the spirit and too lacerating to its victims to be symbolic of anything but its monstrous self. Perhaps I ought to accept the hackneyed notation of Woodstock and Altamont, the love-trip and the death-trip, as emblematic of how the bright hopes of the sixties—among them the Edenic, utopian dream (in Ginsberg's words) "that a new kind of man has come to his bliss/ to end the cold war he has borne/ against his own kind flesh"—had foundered in bitterness, frustration, destruction. There are no real beginnings and endings in history, certainly not in the histories of sensibility and consciousness, only irruptions that alter the flow and shift the continuities. But after a while one phrase kept coming back, provoked by anything from an item in the paper to a major decision altering one's life: "Boy, the sixties are really over." The meaning had very little to do with the calendar.

Of course the sixties kept happening; every phase of life adds something permanent to our stock of options, desires, strategies for coping. Even sixties *events* kept on happening: rock concerts, peace demonstrations, local pockets of activism and community; but even the warmest of these moments had something hollow at the core, a Wordsworthian sense of the irretrievable, "of something that is gone." Never were the sixties more over than on those illusory occasions when it seemed that nothing had changed. Such a moment for me was the concert by Bob Dylan and The Band in Madison Square Garden on the last day of January 1974. Dylan had been hiding from his public for almost eight years, polishing his mystique, and no one knew why he'd been chosen to reemerge for a grueling national tour; but twenty thousand well-behaved young men and women were there to welcome him, were there, like him, to recapture (or at least revisit) an era in their own lives, to put some flesh and blood on something that had atrophied into myth.

Dylan didn't let them down. Whatever his private horror of performing in public—his face was utterly impassive as he sang, but he grimaced painfully between numbers—he proved a much better showman than when I'd seen him last. He gave the audience its money's worth, threw himself into the performance as he'd thrown himself into the tour, ferociously, and delivered up an anthology of work from every phase of his career. Except that artists who are still great, who are still at the cutting edge of their creative powers, don't do anthologies, don't recapitulate earlier styles that they've abandoned or outgrown: they leave that to the professional anthologists or to their own imitators. But here everyone was content to watch Dylan imitating himself, cannibalizing his earlier work. They knew what they wanted, *he* knew what they wanted, and not much of it was what he'd been doing lately. It was still a bit early for sixties nostalgia, but an epidemic of it had broken out in the Garden; as Dylan chanted not only the old favorites but one of the best of the recent songs, "Forever Young," time was suspended. Toward the end of the concert, matches and lighters flared up all over the house—everyone was lighting a candle to his own immortality—and as Dylan sang "Like a Rolling Stone" the decorous crowd began to surge forward in a spirit of generational solidarity. Since I was a little bit older and even more correct than they, I had no desire to join them and, since the luck of the draw had put me in the second row, practically under Dylan's nose, I had no place to surge to. But my wife, surrounded, obstructed by a mass of palpitating humanity, surged upward onto her seat, clapping rhythmically to the beat of the music. She seemed to catch Dylan's eye, and he flashed a momentary smile, his first and last of the evening. Amid all that fervor it was a rare moment of spontaneous warmth. Perhaps there was a spark of life in the sixties yet, something to be salvaged from these awkward but gratifying rituals of recollection.

It's certainly appropriate that above all a rock concert should symbolize and recapture that whole cultural period. Though changes in the other arts *reveal* the sixties and expose its sensibility, rock *was* the culture of the sixties in a unique and special way. Those who dislike rock probably dislike other developments in the arts of the period, from Pop Art and black-humor fiction to open-form poetry and off-off-Broadway theater. Richard Goldstein once gave the simplest possible description of rock: "It makes you want to move." The arts of the sixties, even the poetry of the sixties, were kinetic— they tended toward dance. (A Tom O'Horgan production was not so much staged as choreographed, like the early René Clair movies.) The hallmarks were energy and intensity. On the other hand, the arts of the fifties tended mainly toward speech: their hallmarks were irony and control, the sublimation of energy into form. The spirit of the fifties was neo-classical, formal; the sixties were expressive, romantic, free-form. Rock was the organized religion of the sixties—the nexus not only of music and language but also of dance, sex, and dope, which all came together into a single ritual of self-expression and spiritual tripping.

Was rock music great art? The question is hard to answer, perhaps even meaningless. If literature is "news that STAYS news" (as one description goes) and popular culture is by nature ephemeral, then rock music has begun to pass the test of time. Though much of the seventies rock scene has fallen into decadence and imitation, or simply lacks inspiration, or has turned back deliberately to a less significant sound and message, the best rock albums from the mid-sixties are as fresh and exciting as they were ten years ago. What many highbrow critics are still unable to acknowledge is that the line between high culture and popular culture gave way in the sixties and on some fronts was erased entirely. Serious artists in all fields were attracted to the simplicity and emotional directness of popular culture *and* the complexities of modernist experimentation. As Ginsberg turned from the acerbic irony and disgust of Eliot to the bardic intensities of Whitman and Blake, Bob Dylan and John Lennon wrote song lyrics that seemed as surreal as any modernist text. In *Popular Culture and High Culture* Herbert Gans argued that every segment of society was entitled to its taste and deserved whatever level of culture it demanded, and that highbrow judgments were therefore snobbish and irrelevant. But to me this easy pluralism devalues the seriousness of some popular culture and eliminates the critic's necessary role, which is to make distinctions and judgments. What infuriated some conservative critics in the sixties, what they were always at such pains to deny, was that a good deal of popular culture was successful even in terms of their own most stringent aesthetic, made it *by their own standards,* which they were unable to apply to the new art. Even critics committed to experiment sometimes cling to what was New in their own youth. Thus, some of them felt impelled to defend "true" modernism against sixties barbarism, just as their predecessors had found only barbarism and incoherence in the early works of modernism itself. When I first heard Dylan sing it seemed, if not ugly, then artless and inept. That was close to a decade before Madison Square Garden, at a smaller and tackier version of the Garden called the New Haven Arena. But that concert was so much the symmetrical opposite of the one I've described that it deserves a brief digression of its own.

That earlier concert was not a rock concert at all but a folk concert, whose chief attraction to us was not Dylan but our longtime idol Joan Baez. Folk meant a performer and his guitar, an acoustic guitar, usually with no backup instruments. The hallmarks of folk music were purity, simplicity, and sincerity, which seemed fully incarnated in the melliflouous voice and the decent, humane politics of Joan Baez. We were hardly prepared for Bobby, her waiflike sidekick, who was then still riding her reputation and whom she affectionately patted on the ass now and then to show encouragement or approval. Dylan's singing had none of her simple unaffected beauty. Already it seemed raucous and mannered, like the sound of the harmonica suspended near his lips. With his talky drawl he seemed determined to throw songs away, or hadn't the talent to do otherwise. No surprise, then, that other singers began to make hits of his songs while his own performances met with resistance and derision. Not until the Pennebaker documentary film *Don't Look Back* was I fully gripped by the beauty and power of Dylan's singing. Only then did I realize how expressive that snarl and whine and drawl could be. It was a perfect example of the aesthetics of ugliness that's one key to every modern avant-garde since Wordsworth and Coleridge (—who were also condemned by critics for artlessness and banality, according to eighteenth-century standards of poetic "beauty"). Every modern movement at first looks ugly and inartistic to the extent that it dislocates existing norms. Only later does it create its own norm, which gets established but eventually succumbs to imitation, self-caricature, a certain devolution of energy (which readies the scene for the next avant-garde). Dylan's songs not only looked like modernist works but had set in motion another twist in the modernist spiral of innovation and decay.

This would matter less if Dylan's work alone were the issue. Dylan's career has a protean character—no two albums are alike; even the worst of them, *Nashville Skyline* and *Self Portrait,* show

Allen Ginsberg in the sixties: *upper left,* Allen Ginsberg visiting
Columbia during the student uprising in 1968 (*Columbia Daily
Spectator*); *lower right,* Allen Ginsberg walking with Peter Orlovsky
on East 10th Street on New York City's Lower East Side, 1966
(UPI).

The Rosenberg case: *upper left*, Julius and Ethel Rosenberg en route to jail after their conviction on spy charges in March, 1951 (Wide World); *upper right*, thousands of Parisians rally, under communist auspices, shortly before their execution, June, 1953 (Wide World); *lower right*, counter-demonstration picketing against clemency in front of the White House, June, 1953 (UPI).

Writers whose work became central to the culture of the sixties: *upper left,* Kurt Vonnegut, Jr. (M. Ginsburg, Magnum); *upper right,* Norman Mailer (Wide World); *lower left,* Joseph Heller (Wide World); *lower right,* Herbert Marcuse (Wide World).

The range of black writers over the generations: *upper left,* Richard Wright (1908-1960), the effective North Star of black literature (Gisele Freund, Magnum); *upper right,* Ralph Ellison (Bob Adelman, Magnum) and *lower left,* James Baldwin (Wide World) were protégés of Wright who attacked his work and developed in contrary directions; *lower right,* Eldridge Cleaver: convict, writer, militant, and 1968 presidential candidate. In *Soul on Ice* he attacked Baldwin and defended the example of Richard Wright (Wide World).

The three greatest sounds of the Age of Rock:
upper left, Mick Jagger of the Rolling Stones
(UPI); *upper right,* Bob Dylan (Wide World);
below center, the Beatles when they were still
cute ragamuffins from Liverpool (Magnum).

Scenes from the most famous counterculture gathering of the sixties, the Woodstock Rock Festival, which brought 400,000 people to White Lake, N.Y. in August, 1969: *above center,* Charles Gatewood, Magnum; *lower left,* Burk Uzzle, Magnum; *lower right,* Wide World.

Playful and solemn scenes of antiwar protest: *above center*, the demonstrators at the Chicago Democratic Convention in 1968 (Magnum); *lower right*, picketers in New York City (H. Kubota, Magnum); *lower left*, demonstrators in Washington, D.C. (Burk Uzzle, Magnum).

Campus in turmoil: *upper left,* black students with guns leave building at Cornell University after thirty-six-hour siege in April, 1969 (Wide World); *upper right,* Mark Rudd, head of Columbia's SDS chapter and leader of student revolt, addresses rally in front of Low Library (*Columbia Daily Spectator*); *below center,* two of New York City's Finest on Columbia University's campus during the occupation of five university buildings (*Columbia Daily Spectator*).

their own distinctive direction and purpose—and on that score alone his career is fascinating. But Dylan's odyssey was also central to the changing cultural scene: like only a few of the most interesting artists, his shifts reveal those of the age, as if the Hegelian *Zeitgeist* had for a space of time come to rest on his shoulders. (Hegel himself saw Napoleon in 1806 as the world-spirit on horseback. Dylan had his own way of trying to conquer the world.) It's hard to say how much a figure like Dylan simply is attuned to the winds of change and how much he himself stirs them up, simply by marching to his own beat and following his inner needs. But when Dylan plugged in to an electric guitar at the Newport Folk Festival in 1965, to the anger of much of his audience, in effect the folk era ended and the rock era began.

Even that large resonance has a still larger one, for folk music was the perfect expression of the green years of the early sixties, the years of integration, interracial solidarity, "I have a dream," and "We shall overcome"; the years of the Port Huron statement and the early New Left; the years of lunch-counter sit-ins and ban-the-Bomb demonstrations. Folk music was a living bridge between the protest culture of the New Left and the genuinely populist elements of the Old Left of the 1930s and after. Its carriers and most creative spirits, like Dylan's idol Woody Guthrie, had been through the Depression and lived and worked among the people; they incarnated the Americanism rather than the Bolshevism of the Popular Front, which the early New Left shared. For their pains they had been hounded and blacklisted in the fifties (when Woody's heir, Pete Seeger, and his group, the Weavers, were hauled before congressional committees and banned from television). In an age of protest and moral witness like the early sixties, folk music was a staple of every demonstration, the pulsing chorus of a new moral solidarity. (Songs like "Joe Hill" played the same role in the early years of the labor movement.) The movement even helped create a whole "folk culture" of young minstrels and renegades—centered in Greenwich Village, with pockets in many other cities and university towns—which, along with the Beat scene, was the closest thing to Bohemia that the late fifties and early sixties could produce.

In my own case, since I never mastered the guitar and never attached myself to the folk culture, but went off to graduate school instead, it was the music itself rather than the politics or the "scene" that exerted the main appeal. Like my friends I had grown up on the aesthetic perverseness and moral ambiguities of modern art and literature. The primitive satisfactions of narrative in fiction, representation in painting, and melody or harmony in music—like clear-cut positions in politics—were highly suspect. We learned to think of the world as a tragic and complex place, just as we learned to look at art as a subversive and disquieting assault on our senses and certitudes. And in good measure we were right. We were the children of modernism, existentialism, and the New Criticism, ready for paradox and ambiguity of every sort but unprepared for a world that was turning more black-and-white every day. In our sophistication we were suspicious of simple pleasures and values, and hence we were suspicious of ourselves, of our native roots and loyalties. Folk music legitimized the primary satisfactions that modern art and the modern consciousness had taken away from us. For me in particular Zionist folk culture helped restore some of the ethnic identity and joy that I had checked at the door of the House of Intellect. For all the hostility of the folk culture toward pop music, the folk craze was the first wave of a tide of populist taste that would sweep broadly over the culture of the sixties—that would in literature see Dickens displace James and the influence of Whitman dislodge that of Eliot, that would cause similar stirrings in each of the other arts.

The subsequent evolution of folk into rock showed that the complication of awareness and technique that we call modernism couldn't really be abandoned after all. Instead the new music kept developing the complexity and subtlety of its resources. The elite religion of modernism went through its most unexpected phase: it was assimilated and—horrors!—popularized. A mass audience was created that was as tolerant of obscurity—as mystically addicted to it—as the audience of the early part of the century was indignant at it. Surrealism lost its shock-value—though not its hostility to the audience—and became another ordinary language of verbal discourse, the royal road to the unconscious and the irrational. The very names of rock groups became acts of imagination, vying with one another in gaudy grandeur. The plainness and understatement of the communal folk-sing became the gorgeous overstatement of the rock concert. At Bill Graham's Fillmore East, the high temple of rock in New York, an amazing light show above the stage accompanied every undulation of the music. For the typical stoned customer, the psychedelic colors and the deafening volume of the music created a total environment, a complete imaginary space that compensated for the cramped quarters and the lack of a dance floor.

The volume of the music was something that older people universally objected to; they found it literally painful, even in the farthest reaches of the theater. One effect of the blasting level of noise was that the music seemed to come from within rather than without, to be emanating from one's own guts and vitals. Gradually the eardrums became calloused and hardened, and the sound was muffled into reverie and fantasy.

Like its forebears in the heyday of modernism and surrealism, rock music was partly an assault on the audience, just as rock lyrics are full of jeers and sexist insults. As the first auditors of *The Rite of Spring* accurately responded to Stravinsky's violence by rioting, the audience at a rock concert sometimes longed to assault or devour the performers. The terror one glimpsed on Dylan's face at moments in the Garden was exaggerated but hardly inappropriate: there was a touch of *The Bacchae* in every successful rock performance. There was a sense of sexual interchange, surely, but also a whiff of possession, loss of control, a hint of destructiveness in the air. (Antonioni catches some of this in *Blow-Up*.) Like ill-trained shamans, rock singers manipulated energies they could scarcely keep in tow. This was closely akin to their self-destructive streak; they loved putting their heads in the lion's mouth, and several were dead before the sixties ended. Janis Joplin was particularly naked in her vulnerability to the audience, in her visible need of them. Once I saw her really *give* herself to an audience at the Fillmore East; she would throw herself into a performance and let the crowd devour her like vampires, until she looked utterly drained and limp with fatigue.

The frightening quality of these rituals was an all-too-faithful reflection of the changes in America since the comparative innocence and hopefulness of the folk period. Dylan went electric at almost the very moment that Lyndon Johnson began bombing North Vietnam and escalating the war in the south. The increasing violence and intensity of Dylan's work mirrored the expanding violence in the country. The shift from folk to rock also reflected a shift in values from "sincerity" to "authenticity" (as Marshall Berman and Lionel Trilling, in two books provoked by the experience of the sixties, have analyzed those terms).* The illusion of the folk period was that we need only a good community for our natural goodness to shine through. Hence the idealization of rural life and a pre-mechanized society of small artisans.

Rock music, on the other hand, is aggressively urban. It not only exploits technology and accepts modernity as an irreversible given but it also grooves on the demonic energies and role-playing liberties of urban life. If the ideal of sincerity accepts the self but treats society as an artifice, as a given, the quest for authenticity takes the self as problematic and yet as a vast field of possibility. The authentic person aims to become himself, not simply to be himself: the self must be created and won, not simply excavated. Authenticity is related to both modernism and psychoanalysis in its affinity for the irrational and the unconscious, for masks, roles, and fantasies, for all the complications and byways of selfhood rather than its broader, more sweeping simplicities.

The twang of a phony country drawl mars even the loveliest of Dylan's early folk albums, *The Freewheelin' Bob Dylan* (1963), just as a false pathos and lugubrious humanity mars what is otherwise the best of his late-sixties albums, *John Wesley Harding* (1968), which marked Dylan's return to music and to a more quiet folk sound after his near-fatal 1966 motorcycle accident. In truth, Dylan never really abandoned folk music; he never let the backup music or the sound engineer overwhelm the basically simple pattern of stanzas and re-

* Berman, *The Politics of Authenticity* (1970); Trilling, *Sincerity and Authenticity* (1972). In what follows I depart rather drastically from their fine discussions of these two key concepts.

frains, music and lyrics. Even *Blonde on Blonde*, his rock masterpiece, has as many lilting, wispy, liquid love songs as hard-driving, intensely rhythmic rock numbers. Dylan is as deeply rooted in folk music as the Rolling Stones are in Negro blues and the Beatles in American rock'n'roll of the 1950s. But within a short period in 1965 and 1966, just before and after he plugged in electrically, Dylan brought out three remarkable albums that epitomize the rock music of the sixties: *Bringing It All Back Home, Highway 61 Revisited,* and *Blonde on Blonde.* These albums drop the mask of the country minstrel, the itinerant hobo, and the protest-poet. (One of the paradoxes of "sincerity" in folksinging is how often it involves the assumption of other people's roots, or imaginary ones, rather than a search for one's own.) But these discs exhibit far more complicated masks, which enable Dylan to ventilate the hostility and aggression that's screened out of folk music but is obviously central to his character and his talent. In his useful biography Anthony Scaduto shows, without debunking, how ruthlessly Dylan used and discarded people on his way to the top, and some of the songs he wrote after his accident contain oblique apologies for his earlier life style. But the later Dylan's message that "love is all there is, it makes the world go 'round" (which comes as "a tip from one who's tried" to "do without it") doesn't carry as much conviction and genius as his former fury. Like earlier modernists, being an appealing human being is not Dylan's forte, and it damages his art. The very style of delivery in his raucous middle period is utterly different from the bland crooning of some of his later albums: it's a hard-edged enunciation, full of bite, snarl, and insinuation. The highly mannered phrasing and emphasis torture each syllable as much as the surreal lyrics torture the language; it's all highly charged, freighted with abysses of feeling and suggestion.

We can detect the origins of this distinctive style in the more straightforward numbers of *The Freewheelin' Bob Dylan.* On the first cut, "Blowin' in the Wind," a song that a more pop-style group (Peter, Paul and Mary) turned into a great hit, Dylan sounds like a withered old man, the archetypal folk-spirit, with the opaque sybilline wisdom of one who's seen generations come and go. It's hard to believe that this is the same writer who would soon compose such fierce generational battle anthems as "The Times They Are A-Changin' " and "Ballad of a Thin Man" ("something is happening here/ But you don't know what it is/ Do you, Mister Jones?"). Not too many other pieces have quite the same doleful minstrel sound—the album is too various for that—but most of the songs remain well within the typical folk spectrum, whatever Dylan's peculiar nuances of manner. One song that does begin to break out, one of the best things on the album, is "Don't Think Twice, It's All Right." Significantly, it's not a love song but an end-of-love song, full of muffled resentment and self-justification and spiced with mock-humility. The delivery is marked by what would later become Dylan's characteristic style of over-precise and odd emphasis, which helps him to convey a volatile mixture of love and hostility, of irony, disdain, and ruefulness.

All this makes for a new sort of dramatic complexity quite different for the simple, heightened emotions of most folk songs. In retrospect we can see that Dylan already was exhibiting a brilliant though not always pleasant gift for self-dramatization, which was readily kindled by hostility and a sense of being used or manipulated. Like many other creative artists of the sixties, Dylan's genius is closely bound up with paranoia. Scaduto also documents Dylan's compulsion to invent identities for himself—the aged minstrel is only one of them: when he first came to New York Dylan invented a whole range of past lives which he embroidered differently for everyone he met. Whether he dodged the world or came out to meet it, Dylan has usually been able to satisfy deep personal needs in a way that also contributed to his mystique. There's reason to believe that the obscurity of Dylan's later lyrics arose more from personal evasiveness (and a need for self-dramatization) than from any conscious surrealist aesthetic. Dylan has always been drunk with language, the more purple the better, and this enabled him to transmute the stuff of personal experience into riddles and images.

How he did this can be seen in the three big antiwar songs on the

Gates of Eden

Freewheelin' album. "Masters of War" is a typical stark protest song, finger-pointing, artificial, highly rigid in tone and musical structure. It knows who the villains are and it denounces them. On the other hand, "A Hard Rain's A-Gonna Fall," written during the Cuban missile crisis, points toward the kaleidoscopic imagery and terrible spiritual intensity of the later Dylan. The song is an ingenious adaptation of the traditional "Lord Randal," but every line has an obliqueness and poetic suggestiveness that's alien to the popular aura of folk music or protest poetry, that marks the presence of an individual imagination rather than a collective mentality.

> I'm a-goin' back out 'fore the rain starts a-fallin',
> I'll walk to the depths of the deepest black forest,
> Where the people are many and their hands are all empty,
> Where the pellets of poison are flooding their waters,
> Where the home in the valley meets the damp dirty prison,
> Where the executioner's face is always well hidden,
> Where hunger is ugly, where souls are forgotten,
> Where black is the color, where none is the number. . . .

While other protest material didn't really suit Dylan's temperament, World War III played nicely into his paranoia, his fear of being overwhelmed and misused. Some have maintained that the resulting lyrics are great poetry, that Dylan was one of the important poets of the sixties. Robert Christgau, one of the best of the rock critics, has argued more accurately that most of Dylan's writing is marred by "awkwardness and overstatement," equivocation and cliché. While "hackneyed on the page," he says, Dylan's " 'poetic' language" is "effective in the musical and emotive context." Christgau is writing about "Blowin' in the Wind" but his point can be extended to the spectacular songs of the 1964–66 period, when Dylan's lyrics and music took on a fire they hadn't had before but which produced nothing that could be anthologized in any first-class collection of verse. Verbally, whatever Dylan did well during that period had already been done better by a whole line of *poètes maudits* from Blake, Rimbaud, and Lautréamont to his friend Allen Ginsberg (who exerted a direct influence on Dylan's new style).

The effectiveness of these songs in the musical and emotive context is quite a different story. First of all the lyrics, which have a verbose, run-on quality on the page, take on far more variety in performance. The third of the anti-Bomb songs on the *Freewheelin'* album, for example, "Talkin' World War III Blues," has a puckishness and improvisational wit that puts it at an even more oblique angle to its subject than "A Hard Rain's A-Gonna Fall." It's one of the many "dream" songs of the early Dylan, a form he then needed to legitimize his flights of imagination. (He jokingly called a later song "Bob Dylan's 115th Dream.") According to Nat Hentoff's jacket note, the song "was about half formulated beforehand and half improvised at the recording session itself," and it rings some very funny changes on the whole civil defense/fallout shelter scene of the early sixties. "I Shall Be Free," the final cut on the album, is in a similar vein of improvised tongue-in-cheek hilarity. The fluidity of the "talking blues" was important for Dylan, even when he ceased to improvise: it helped to accommodate the eruptive run-on flow of his verbal imagination, since any number of stanzas would fit, and the strumming, understated accompaniment enabled him to put an emphasis on the lyrics that was unusual in popular music. Dylan was as restless and protean a performer as he was a composer: there is no definitive version of these early songs (the recorded version of "I Shall Be Free" is quite different from the one printed in Dylan's *Writings and Drawings* in 1973), and even when the music and lyrics do get more or less finalized Dylan alters their effect drastically in performance. It was a little unfair of me to say earlier that Dylan had simply anthologized himself in his 1974 tour with The Band. Even a cursory examination of *Before the Flood*, the recorded version of the tour, confirms what was already obvious at the concerts; that while The Band was simply replicating the splendid songs on its first two albums, Dylan had rethought and recreated every number. For better or worse—in my view, worse—every song was different from what it once had been.

The overriding reason why Dylan's songs are capable of so many changes, including the more drastic alterations of other performers, comes through even in his weakest albums and most perverse performances: Dylan is a great melodist. During his manic, hyperactive middle period, he let loose a flow of continuous melodic invention rivaled only by Paul McCartney of the Beatles, whose numbers also adapted well to quite different singers. Insofar as the arts of the sixties were kinetic and fluid (rather than oriented toward the creation of beautiful objects) they tended toward performance anyway, much as the poetry of the period tended toward reading aloud. But it's worth recalling how much prior creative invention in pop music made the later improvisions of performance possible. And where poetry has no intrinsic need to be read aloud, music or choreography scarcely exists except as fulfilled in performance. This is what makes so many of the more literary analyses of Dylan's songs beside the point. What one actually hears in performance (or while dancing) is not the words as they lie on the page, but snatches and intonations of those words as they couple with the music and with the inflections of the singer's voice. It just happens that Dylan has a real genius for the suggestive phrase and for the buildup of a mood, but a much lesser gift for overall coherence. Analyzing the words is like analyzing the shooting script rather than the finished movie. Take a favorite song of mine, "I Want You" (on *Blonde on Blonde*), which combines a terribly simple, hard-driving refrain, consisting mainly of the words in the title, with the most surreal and inaccessible stanzas, some of whose lyrics can't even be made out, let alone understood. With its overpowering rhythm it's a great song for dancing, as well as a riveting expression of intense sexual need. But the tune, the rhythm, and the refrain would be hollow without the suggestive, bizarre poetic fragments of story and metaphor that create the mood, build up feeling, and intimate deeper meanings. It's as if Dylan needed esoteric mysteries to support the pop refrain, needed a private history to set off the universal ache. Dylan has a penchant for settling private scores in his songs, and, like most modern artists, his own experience comes into his work with a strange mixture of evasiveness and exhibitionism (which parallels his love-hate relation to his celebrity and his audience). Moreover, some of these songs were almost surely written on drugs, possibly "speed," which may keep their meaning private even from Dylan himself. But in that especially creative middle period they break through to an intense expressiveness to which the words greatly contribute, but in a fragmentary way that varies too much to be pinned down.

I won't try to go through all of the three albums I've singled out as Dylan's best, the tip of his creative powers. The greatest songs range from the deeply moving "Sad Eyed Lady of the Lowlands" (which takes up one whole side of the four sides of *Blonde on Blonde*), to the incredible side two of *Bringing It All Back Home*, four dazzling songs on acoustic guitar, just before Dylan went electric ("Mr. Tambourine Man," "Gates of Eden," "It's Alright, Ma [I'm Only Bleeding]," and "It's All Over Now, Baby Blue"), to "Like a Rolling Stone," an intriguing but obscure case history, set to great music, that Dylan twisted into the concluding anthem of his 1974 tour concerts. The albums include several lovely, quiet numbers that are much less famous because less assertive, and others that quite rightly became the battle cries of a whole generation in rebellion against the styles and values of its elders, but which had enough art and style to appeal to many people a good deal older, who had no special investment in the youth revolution and who were even likely to be its victims if it succeeded. It's no small matter that the young of the sixties had a serious culture created largely by people not far from their own age, which could give expression to those universal post-adolescent longings, joys, and traumas that once were the province of fatally precocious romantic poets. But it's even more astonishing that out of the absurd and embarrassing rituals of growing up could come creative work that could speak to others not especially nostalgic for their own adolescence.

It was perhaps when Dylan lost touch with this subject that he lost his sharpest creative edge. A great rock composer over thirty is something of an anomaly, but Dylan's decline set in at twenty-five, after his accident, when his frantic life style changed and he settled into what seemed by all appearances a happy and very private marriage. Perhaps the general qualities of his middle period can best be described in contrast to what followed in the late sixties, in such albums as *John Wesley Harding, Nashville Skyline, Self Portrait,* and *New Morning.* The first thing one notices on these discs is a great loss of energy and nuance. Happiness may agree with Dylan as a person but it doesn't suit him as an artist; that's why the doleful *John Wesley Harding* is easily the most poignant and unified of these albums, a recording that's grown rather than faded with time. There's certainly something mannered about the assortment of drifters, gamblers, immigrants, tenants, and hoboes who people this album and infuse it with all its not-quite-credible spirituality. It would seem that the brush with death and the isolation that followed had fostered a rush of human sympathy in Dylan, perhaps even some kind of religious conversion, which brought him back from the psychedelic excesses of the middle period to the simpler vein of folk and country styles. Undoubtedly too, Dylan, who didn't need a weatherman to know which way the wind was blowing, was reacting against the new vogue of sequined, spangled, over-decorated rock that had been set off the year before by *Sgt. Pepper's Lonely Hearts Club Band* and its inferior imitations (including the Rolling Stones' lamentable *Their Satanic Majesties Request*). Dylan knew decadence and artiness when he saw it, and he tried to ride the pendulum back to simpler pop, folk, and country sources, not in their naive form but in his own highly artful and self-conscious versions. Most of *John Wesley Harding* is an effective series of laments, fables, and even prayers to his maker (''Dear Landlord''), but the last two cuts presage the pop music clichés of *Nashville Skyline* and *Self Portrait,* with their moon/June lyrics, bland crooning style, and insipidly optimistic message about life and love, straight out of Tin Pan Alley. On the first cut of *Nashville Skyline* we hear a perverse duet, with Johnny Cash trying to sing soulfully, like the old Dylan, and Dylan trying to sing blandly, like Cash—two ships passing in the night. By comparison, *New Morning* represented something of a recovery, with three or four numbers (''If Not for You,'' ''Day of the Locusts,'' about the day he got his honorary degree at Princeton, ''New Morning,'' and ''The Man in Me'') showing something of the energy and charge of the earlier Dylan.

Perhaps it's as impossible for us to account for the violent, inexhaustible creativity of Dylan's middle period as it is for Dylan to recapture it fully. The energy of these great songs seems to come out of a maniacally driven life style, a tangle of tense but neurotic relationships, and an oppositional fury that Dylan could hardly maintain once he was king of the hill. As a well-rewarded young millionaire, Dylan was too honest to go on telling society that he was dropping out, that he wasn't "gonna work on Maggie's farm no more." It seemed anachronistic enough at the Garden concert when Dylan sang of his fear of being stoned, assaulted, and his simple faith in *getting* stoned. By 1974 that song, "Rainy-Day Woman # 12 & 35," was already a period piece, since Dylan and his aging fans were now neither society's victims nor pot's novitiates. Here was nostalgia pure and simple, and Dylan could not help but be embarrassed that an aura of make-believe had descended over the arena, good as it may have felt.

Here we come close to unraveling the mystery of Dylan's 1974 tour, with which I began this short history. The style Dylan adopted in these performances was one that seemed designed to answer just the sort of criticism I've leveled at his albums of the late sixties. It was the approach of his newest album, *Planet Waves,* and a more driving, hard-edged, rhythmically intense manner couldn't be asked for. When Dylan reinterprets his earlier songs, he does so with all the jeering fury he could muster. The dulcet pop tones of the love era have vanished—one heard soon afterward that his marriage was breaking up—and a new kind of assertiveness takes its place. Also it's a highly musical style, for after his accident Dylan had shifted much of his interest from the words to the music; he had become a better musician and was supported by the extremely versatile musicians of The Band. But there at the Garden a pulsing rhythm and a shouting manner seemed designed to rescue and slur songs whose words had dated, or which had gone stale for him, by turning them into percussive riffs and rhythmical noises. The results can be heard on *Before the Flood* where Dylan's new versions, stripped of the excitement of the live performance, stand out in clear relief in all their ugly barbarity.

In "Ballad of a Thin Man" (the Mister Jones song), for example, which belongs so much to the insurgent phase of the counterculture, Dylan simply slurs and garbles most of the words, letting the musical "background" overwhelm them and turn them into pure pounding rhythm and sound. Thus Dylan "updates" the song by emptying it out. Quite the opposite thing happens with the opening and closing numbers of the concert, "Most Likely You Go Your Way (And I'll Go Mine)" and "Like a Rolling Stone". ("Blowin' in the Wind," which comes last on the album, was only an encore.) Both are brilliant put-down songs, in the most sarcastic and ingenious battle-of-the-sexes vein of Dylan's great period. But they are put-downs of real people, individuals, while at the concert Dylan appropriates them to express his love-hate relation to his audience, again by blurring and smothering the precise content of the songs and heightening a few details into one sweeping statement. Some of the first song is general enough to accommodate this change, and the pulsing music and opening lines serve as an ingenious prologue to the concert. ("You say you love me/ And you're thinking of me,/ But you know you could be wrong./ You say you told me/ That you wanna hold me,/ But you know you're not that strong./ I just can't do what I done before,/ I just can't beg you any more.") Dylan is telling his audience that though they have him again he's not really theirs. He's back in their clutches but remains his own man, and can never again be the person or performer he was before. It's nasty, but probably necessary for him to say, and probably true. The original song is violated and the statement is offensive, but the new version works.

The same can't be said for "Like a Rolling Stone," which was a great hit at the concert and really turned the audience on, but which Dylan had reinterpreted in the most vulgar style imaginable. The song is not only about a complicated and fascinating individual relationship but also has a complex poetic fabric, all of which is washed out in the raucous version we hear on *Before the Flood*. The song is basically a Rolling Stones sort of anti-female statement, one that comes close to the heart of Dylan's psyche and sensibility; it's also a good story, though misty in its details. But Dylan buries the song in shrieking and shouting, and heightens the chorus into an uplifting anthem to get his audience charged up and excited. Much as I enjoyed the concert this latest turn in Dylan's work depressed me, especially in the recorded version, where the electricity of the live event gives way to the ugliness and fraudulence of Dylan's self-cannibalization. Dylan had recaptured much of the force and fire of his great period, more than I anticipated he ever could, but very little of its spirit and inner glow. The 1974 concert illustrated one of the terrible paradoxes of the avant-garde: work that's daring and new may at first seem ugly, but art that aims to be ugly isn't necessarily daring and new. Dylan remains a fascinating and unpredictable figure who may yet surprise us all. In 1975 Dylan recorded some haunting songs on an album called *Blood on the Tracks,* his best since *John Wesley Harding,* in which he wrests poignant sounds and affecting fables out of the ruins of his shattered marriage. (Again, unhappiness and rueful, bitter retrospection provide him with the keenest inspiration.) A year later there's another lovely and uneven album, *Desire,* less personal, more in a ballad-and-storytelling vein. It's good to have Dylan back again, but it's hard to believe that he'll ever equal his best work, which came from a unique conjunction of the man and the moment. We're grateful that he survived the sixties and goes on making music. But his not-quite-comeback with The Band in 1974 went far to reconfirm Fitzgerald's adage that there are no second acts in American lives.

I I

There were many other important sounds on the rock scene of the sixties besides Dylan's, but only two others imposed themselves with the uniqueness and authority that his did. Of course these belonged to the two English groups that stormed young America in the mid-sixties, the Beatles and the Rolling Stones, the yin and yang of rock music. A writer for the *New Left Review* once praised the Stones for their rebelliousness and unpleasantness—which he felt society could not co-opt—compared to the amiable irreverence and whimsy of the Beatles. But he might just as easily have praised (on Marcusean grounds) the irrepressibly childlike qualities of the Beatles, their incurable addiction to the pleasure principle, over the rather theatrical satanism of Mick Jagger and the Stones. Where Dylan was ignited by anger and hostility, everything about the Beatles bespeaks exuberance and effervescence, which may be why the group couldn't survive growing up. ("I was the walrus/ But now I'm John/ And so dear friends/ You just have to carry on/ The dream is over"—John Lennon, 1970.) In the hands of a puckish and talented movie director, Richard Lester, they made two films that were the perfect expression of their own high spirits. Later their lyrics became more serious and their music more subtle. They peaked around the same time as Dylan, in three glorious albums that came out between 1965 and 1967, *Rubber Soul, Revolver,* and *Sgt. Pepper's Lonely Hearts Club Band,* then began to disintegrate as a group with a scattering of songs that were as melodically liquid and fluent as anything they'd ever done. Finally each went his separate way, without recapturing on his own the magic they'd had as a group.

It's much harder to trace the career of the Rolling Stones along a simple curve, though some of their later albums show an even more disastrous falling-off than Dylan's or the Beatles'. But they've always been more up-and-down, and lately they've been up: their 1974 album *It's Only Rock 'n Roll* breaks no new ground, but it's a lovely and modest sample of the kind of blues and rock they do so well. The Stones have survived drug busts, the death of guitarist Brian Jones, the unpredictable antics of Mick Jagger, and the negative apocalypse of the Altamont concert. Simply as a rock *band,* the Stones were probably the best the sixties produced—the Beatles achieved their greatest feats only in the recording studios. The Stones were best when they didn't stray too far from the pop format, worst when (under some heady influence or other) they reached out for "art." Their 1974 album seems to say that they'll now settle for being a good band, settle for survival: "It's Only Rock 'n Roll (But I Like It)."

Yet the Stones, who were younger than the Beatles, were serious artists quite early in their career, certainly by 1965, when both their words and music already had a raw, harsh, negative quality that the pop music of the fifties had tried to strain out. At a stage when the Beatles were scarcely beyond "I wanna hold your hand" and "She loves you, yeh, yeh, yeh" the Stones were memorably exploiting adolescent *Angst* with "I can't get no satisfaction," "19th Nervous Breakdown," and the haunting "Heart of Stone." When they got to "Let's Spend the Night Together," disc jockeys in the provinces began having their own nervous breakdowns. The bad-boy image was by then established—perhaps to distinguish them from the Beatles—and it worked, not only as publicity but as music. In their brilliant use of negative material they greatly expanded the pop spectrum, just as Dylan did. In fact the songs of Jagger and Richard are closer to Dylan than to the Beatles in their vocabulary of scorn and contempt, and their best work is full of sardonic put-downs of women, which many women seem to like. But in Dylan's case, as Paul Cowan has observed in a review of *Blood on the Tracks*, "pain is the flip side of his legendary cruelty": pain, shyness, defensiveness, disconnection, and even self-hatred. In other words Dylan's work is rooted in the famous insecurity we find in the heroes of Jewish novels or in self-denigrating Jewish comics like Woody Allen. Perhaps this was the pain we saw on his face between numbers at Madison Square Garden, and in *Blood on the Tracks* Dylan gets back in touch with his vulnerability, after years of playing it super cool. But the narcissism and aggression of the Rolling Stones suggests not defensiveness and raw insecurity but the careless violence of street kids and young toughs. (Jagger himself was a middle-class boy who went on to the London School of Economics.) The Beatles, M.B.E., were street-kids from Liverpool who loved to dress up as gentlemen; they first made their mark as insouciant prole upstarts, but their later songs are nothing if not elegant, even when they reminisce about "Penny Lane." Meanwhile the Rolling Stones, in their twenties, chose to become the street-kids the Beatles had left behind.

For my part I prefer the jeering, sneering monologues of the early

Gates of Eden

Stones to their later, more self-conscious and stagy diabolism, just as I prefer the natural magic of the early Beatles to their later conjuring tricks, like *Magical Mystery Tour* and their songs about the nirvana of dope ("Turn off your mind relax and float downstream,/ It is not dying . . ."). Even the Beatles explore the dark side of love at times, usually with satirical good humor rather than contempt, but both Lennon-McCartney and Jagger-Richard are best when they stay close to real men and women. The sarcastic lyrics for Beatles songs like "Norwegian Wood" and "I'm Looking Through You" (on *Rubber Soul*) even read well on the page. They have a wit and style, a simplicity and immediacy, that usually evaded Dylan. ("I'm looking through you, where did you go?/ I thought I knew you, but what did I know?/ You don't look different, but you have changed,/ I'm looking through you, you're not the same.") Lennon's lyrics are sometimes so simple they look like children's nonsense verse, which he also writes very well. But the Beatles were growing up, and finding that "Love has a nasty habit of disappearing overnight." In *Rubber Soul* the Beatles don't as yet have the musical and dramatic gift to deal with these more troubling experiences. "Norwegian Wood," like many other sophisticated rock songs, finds very little musical and vocal equivalent for its ironic lyrics, so that much of the effect is lost. The song blends in smoothly with the delicious (but somewhat too uniform) melodic flow of the whole album.

By their next album, *Revolver*, however, the Beatles had made great strides. Though less unified and more uneven, the album contains songs that are like little dramatic poems, in which Lennon's and McCartney's writing and the group's always excellent singing are supported by musical effects very different from the simple, lively beat that had made the group famous. I don't have the musical vocabulary to describe these effects, but they're easy enough to hear. "Eleanor Rigby" is like a short documentary about "all the lonely people," whose lives would have had no place in the more ebullient vision of the earlier Beatles. Its fragments of dramatic narration look forward to their more surreal and eerie masterpiece, "A Day in the Life"; both are haunting little tragedies that enable the rock performers, for a change, to get out of their own skins and into someone else's; they evoke a little world as a novelist or filmmaker might. The other stunning song on *Revolver* is called "For No One," a brilliantly complex love scene that rewrites "I'm Looking Through You" in an even more serious vein. It may be the best end-of-love song in the whole rock repertoire, more so because it's written not in accusation or defensiveness but out of despair and confusion and muddled sympathy. It's what happens when you're still in love with someone who suddenly, definitively, inexplicably, falls out of love with you. The lyrics have a poetic compression and razorlike unexpectedness, from the opening lines ("The day breaks, your mind aches, you find that all her words of kindness linger on when she no longer needs you"), to the refrain ("and in her eyes you see nothing, no sign of love beyond the tears, cried for no one"), to later crushing lines that drive the nail into the coffin ("she says that long ago she knew someone but now he's gone, she doesn't need him"). All this gets sung with brilliant phrasing and emphasis, urgent, rapid, pulsating—the whole song takes hardly more than two minutes—and the words are backed up by a driving, clanging piano and, of all things, a horn solo of the most wistful beauty and desolation, which looks forward to the astonishing musical resources of their next album, *Sgt. Pepper*.

In a sense the Beatles were sowing in bleak territory that had already been plowed by the Rolling Stones, though Jagger was not one to sympathize with anyone's unhappiness but his own. Yet Jagger from the beginning was an amazingly expressive vocalist, full of nuance and insinuation, just as the Stones were highly versatile and expressive musicians. Songs like "Heart of Stone" and "Satisfaction" don't depend on personal charisma; they use voice and instruments in an advanced and subtle way, which rivals Dylan in intonation if not in "soul." These early numbers hold up very well where later and more ambitious pieces have already dated. Yet the Stones' music can't be partitioned into phases; it would be easier to divide their work into *pièces roses* and *pièces noires*. After the early songs their best albums are probably *Between the Buttons, After-*

math, *Flowers* (an anthology album), and *Let It Bleed,* which cover a span of time that also includes weaker and more derivative material. *Flowers* was a showcase thrown together at the height of the hippie period, a gift to the flower-children of the "love" generation. Though it contains its quota of sarcasm and put-down, it seems on the whole designed to show that these boys too have positive and appealing personalities. The album is like the *Hard Day's Night* the Stones never made and never could have made, and it's a lovely collection. But to go from *Flowers* to an uncensored "black" album like *Aftermath* is to enter a strange and disturbing world, surreal and druggy, full of pain and conflict, bad vibes and driving sexuality, along with visions of death.

Even the sound of Mick Jagger's voice is different on this album—jeering, screechy, cutting—compared to most of the songs collected on *Flowers,* where even the most cynical numbers get sung in a mellifluous way. On *Aftermath,* Jagger is not so much a singer as a dramatic performer, full of unexpected changes and outrageous effects, and the whole album has a thread of narrative that loosely pieces the scenes together. The title seems to refer to the aftereffects of a disastrous love affair or series of affairs. The album begins with death and separation and proceeds to songs that dramatize the tensions of a Strindbergian battle of the sexes (such as "Under My Thumb" and "Think"), while side two is all about escape, flight, aloneness, waiting. It ends finally with "Going Home," the return, a powerful song about reunion and sexual consummation that lasts eleven and a half minutes and displays an extraordinary dramatic virtuosity and suggestiveness. Like the overture to the album, "Paint It Black," it's a song in a class by itself, with a tremendous buildup and release of tension and sexual energy. "Paint It Black" is an even more dramatic fantasy of death and apocalypse, a duet between Keith Richard, the bereaved, and an eerie Jagger, who may or may not be the voice of the beloved from beyond the grave. (This last suggestion fits well with the famous androgynous quality of Jagger's sexuality: the bullying *macho* exploitativeness, the thick, ambiguous, sensual lips and the teasing camp stage mannerisms.) The apocalyptic power and atmosphere of the song looks forward to the later "Sympathy for the Devil," in which Jagger plays a modern camp Lucifer and redeems kitsch lyrics by sheer brilliance of performance.

The more virile side of Jagger's persona comes out in brutally sexist songs like "Under My Thumb" ("Under my thumb the girl who once had me down,/ Under my thumb the girl who once pushed me around . . ."), which also ends in simulated fucking, like "Going Home." (Jagger not only has a special repertoire of breathy humping sounds but like any fine actor knows how to give an insinuating aura to the most simple phrases: it's hard to describe the mocking sexist intonation of his fake Southern drawl in "unduh maaaaaah thummm . . .") Now that the woman is docile and under control—"Siamese cat of a girl,/ sweetest pet in the world"—they can finally make it together. One of the virtues of rock songs is their frank sexuality, with lyrics and performance that complement the physicality and energy that's there in the music. Even when the sex verges on the sophomoric, as it does in "Going Home," it's far more honest than the disembodied romantic clichés of the pop music of the fifties, which reflect the repressiveness and fraudulence of the whole period.

But the rock scene gave rise to its own sexual distortions, especially in the way sex gets expressed so heavily in terms of power games. This arises, I suspect, not only out of the temperament and talent of the Rolling Stones but from the character of the rock world, whose total sexual ambiance turned rock stars into powerful idols and teenage fans into adoring groupies, all hungry for a piece of the action. Too much rock material obviously comes out of a world of strange cities and exhausting travels, casual sex encounters between all too unequal participants. These experiences only confirm the rock star in his contempt for women—see the invective of a song like "Ride On, Baby" on *Flowers*—or make him long sentimentally for something utterly different, as in "Going Home."

What he longs for comes out in the more benign side of the Rolling Stones' vision, the sheer adolescent hunger and beauty of "Let's Spend the Night Together" or "Ruby Tuesday," or the more complex bluesy humanity of *Let It Bleed* and *It's Only Rock 'n Roll*.

Gates of Eden

Like Janis Joplin but more so, Jagger has no right to imitate blues singing as well as he does, to appropriate it toward a style distinctly his own: "Love in Vain" is a terrific blues performance that should simply be out of the range of a sassy young middle-class Englishman but isn't. In "Gimmie Shelter," "Let It Bleed," and "Midnight Rambler" the Stones add a special touch of menace to basically quiet performances: these songs are a perfect combination of the darker and rosier sides of their sensibility. A similar synthesis is achieved by the Beatles in their rock masterpiece, *Sgt. Pepper's Lonely Hearts Club Band,* the most unified and carefully conceived album of the sixties, which touches a central nerve of the whole rock scene by focusing on the metaphor of performance itself. The Beatles try to escape from the narcissism and subjectivity of many rock songs, including much of Jagger's music, by telling us that they're not the Beatles at all but old-time music hall entertainers, not the serious musicians of *Revolver* but just another act, designed only to amuse and pass the time; with Billy Shears singing and Mr. Kite "topping the bill," "A splendid time is guaranteed for all." With this dramatic distance they can populate the album with circuslike characters and make room for little narrative vignettes like "She's Leaving Home" and "A Day in the Life." These last two songs follow from the serious storytelling side of the preceding album; if they need an excuse, they're legitimized by the fiction that they're only "acts," only performances.

Musically, the album is also a leap forward from the most advanced elements in *Revolver*. Recorded in several tracks over a four-month period, the album achieves a more lush and complex sound than rock music ever had before. The Beatles use the recording studio to achieve effects that would be impossible for a live rock band. In "Tomorrow Never Knows," the last track of *Revolver,* they had begun in earnest to explore the unique potentialities of the recording medium. This is the song that invites the listener to turn off his mind, relax, and float downstream; the garish, gaudy musical effects seem designed to create in music the equivalent of—or complement to—an LSD trip, while the boys tell you to "listen to the color of your dreams." Several trippy numbers on *Sgt. Pepper* mix musical and verbal effects for a similar purpose; two of them, "Lucy in the Sky with Diamonds" and "A Day in the Life," might be described as complementary, the good trip and the bad trip, the one with "tangerine trees and marmalade skies" and "a girl with kaleidoscope eyes," the other depicting a man "who blew his mind out in a car" but ending, "I'd love to turn you on." Thus the album is full of contradictions. The disguise of light entertainers enables the Beatles to be more serious than ever, but the pose of self-distance enables them to be more self-indulgent: not only to play with expensive electronic toys but to use both music and drugs to gratify every infantile wish; in short, to let go. The road from "Tomorrow Never Knows" and LSD led through *Sgt. Pepper* to the Maharishi and the message of "Strawberry Fields": "Nothing is real." In a sense, starting with *Magical Mystery Tour*, the Beatles declined the gambit of their own seriousness and moved on instead to the more lightweight music of their final albums, especially the "white" album, a nice collection of tunes. The circus and the trips and the dressing-up and the Maharishi were ways of remaining children to the end. *Sgt. Pepper* was both the culmination of their achievement and the beginning of the end. The gimmicky side of the album has dated more rapidly than their simpler, cleaner efforts, and though half a dozen of the songs remain ravishing, the frame they're put in isn't very convincing anymore. *Sgt. Pepper* was the album people appealed to when they thought of rock as art or a rock album as a unified conception, but if the sound of the album has already aged and become a little quaint, this suggests that it depended too much on ingenious ideas and too little on art. Time is harsh on ingenious ideas, though the Beatles easily outlive their gaudy imitators.

The Beatles could afford not to grow up because a certain childlike magic had always been central to their appeal. After *Sgt. Pepper* they pulled back from their own excess and, like Dylan and the Stones, came full circle to their earlier work: they sang "All You Need Is Love" and at the end of it quoted from their early hit "She Loves You," an allusion that was typically both primitive and self-conscious, nostalgic and modernist. "There's nothing you can do that can't be done," the song insisted, "nothing you can sing that can't be sung." It was their perpetual message, a belief in their (our) own magical omnipotence but delivered in a form that bordered on simplistic gibberish and therefore suggested self-irony. In that song, as in all their final albums in the waning days of the sixties the Beatles both were and were not (just like the sixties), while everyone speculated on their probable demise. No longer a working group or a performing one, they merely came together to do one another's stuff. They were bound up with the decade in more ways than one, for the sixties were a period that believed in magic and innocence, that had a touching faith in the omnipotence of individual desire. If one strand of the sixties was Edenic and utopian, the Beatles were its most playful incarnation. Irving Howe labeled this a "psychology of un-obstructed need" and insisted that it threatened the values of the culture. But in the end the believers threatened only themselves; the Beatles sang that "nothing is real," but night-sticks and bad trips were a dose of reality designed to counteract excessive faith in the perfectibility of man and his institutions. Nixon was another serious downer, and when hard times came to pinch and squeeze the economy—and to contract our psychic space as well—we could see how much of the rainbow colors of the culture of the sixties were painted on the fragile bubble of a despised affluence, an economic boom that was simply taken for granted.

III

BREAKING DOWN,

OR HOW IT ALL CAME OUT

"Since everyone strives toward the Law," says the man, "how does it happen that in all these years no one but me has come seeking admission." The doorkeeper realizes the man is near his end and, since his hearing is failing, he bellows at him: "No one but you could seek admission here, for this door was intended just for you. I am now going to shut it."

Franz Kafka,
"Before the Law"

8

Fiction at the Cross-roads: Dilemmas of the Experimental Writer

SOMETIMES we only discover what we have to say in the course of saying it; in that sense we're all modernists today, artists and critics alike. In the sixties, when politics itself became modernist, we went even further and invented the existential radical, the spontaneous revolutionary who invents his goals and tactics as he goes along. I would hardly call this book spontaneous, and I leave it for others to say whether it is radical, but I'd like to take a page or two to specify what I think I've been saying—or discovering as I've been writing it.

I began not with a fully formed theory but simply a fascination with the whole cultural phenomenon of the sixties, which had already reached into so many corners of our lives and brought drastic changes. The sixties are over, but they remain the watershed of our recent cultural history; they continue to affect the ambiance of our lives in innumerable ways. Having grown up in the fifties I'm still astonished that pornography can be freely circulated in this country, that abortion and birth control are publicly accepted rights even for the poor, that politicians and entertainers can espouse mildly radical causes without instantly destroying their careers, that the Burger Court has not reversed even more of the liberal decisions of its predecessors, that the President of the United States has visited Moscow and Peking, and so on. Perhaps this merely reveals a conservative temperament that doesn't adjust readily to change.

In any case, I found that I couldn't write about these changes without exploring the frame of life, the tissue of assumptions, that had been overthrown. Thus the book turned into an examination of the polarity between the fifties and the sixties, a study in transformation. At the root perhaps was my own private confusion and wonder, but I was ready to wager that the feelings were shared by many others, who could not help but be affected by the changing sensibility of the culture at large. For evidence I've gone to the work of writers and artists who are the most sensitive reflectors of alterations in consciousness, both in themselves and in the world around them. In their work, in its shifts in form as well as content, we perceive the deepest conjunction of private and public, the personal and the general. The artist can be idiosyncratic, yes, but his idiosyncrasy is also significant—as a harbinger, or as a symptom.

Along the way I discovered that terms like "the fifties" and "the sixties," though indispensable as shorthand, scarcely denote unified cultural phases, even if they do represent what social scientists call "ideal types." But I wasn't content with a typological study abstracted from the actual flow of cultural history. (I dislike it when terms like "classicism" and "romanticism" are employed as permanent polarities, apart from the messy movements that take place in historical time.) It became clear that though there was a striking shift around the turn of the decade—and around the end of the next one as well—the roots of much of what broke out in the sixties were already there in the latter half of the fifties, mostly unnoticed and unheralded. Moreover it became obvious that most of the cultural developments of the sixties, apart from momentary flights of fashion, went through at least three different phases, sometimes at different periods of time. (Thus the early stages of the new feminism coincided with the declining phase of the New Left.) Furthermore, there was a tangle of vertical and horizontal influences on each of the artists who interested me. Thus the Jewish writers of the fifties and the black writers of the sixties were not only responding to the spirit of their own cultural moment but also were reacting to earlier Jewish and black writers within a special culture that had its own set of concerns. A similar vertical pattern exists within the world of rock, or journalism, or poetry, or fiction, and I tried hard to respect it. But within this welter of conflicting lines of force I could make out three roughly separate phases of the sixties as a whole: a nascent, hopeful period during the Kennedy and early Johnson years, that saw the birth of the New Left and the growth of experimentation in the arts but preceded the escalation of the Vietnam war; a high phase lasting from 1965 to 1968 that witnessed the growth of the antiwar movement, the gradual shift "from dissent to resistance," the arrival of direct-action tactics in the universities, the surge of drugs and communalism among youthful dropouts, and the growth of a reform constituency in many stable and conservative social institutions; and finally, what I have called the Weatherman phase, when the frustration of the often unrealistic hopes of the second stage and the need for continual radicalization led to a state of guerrilla warfare not only in politics and the universities but also in the arts. This last phase is the subject of the present chapter, which deals with the radicalization of art; a final chapter will deal with the radicalization of ourselves and raise the question of where we are now. This discussion has all along been founded on the parallel between art and experience, and the need for a criticism of the arts in terms of experience. But one of the characteristics of the Weatherman phase is a certain detachment from experience, sometimes to the point of a disintegration of the sense of reality, both in art and politics. Where the high sixties had brought the subjective participant to the forefront, as an individual, with all his contradictory needs and perceptions—the New Journalism is a perfect example of this, or the anarchist politics of the New Left—the Weatherman phase tended to be Leninist rather than anarchist, impersonal and abstract rather than existential, language-oriented rather than people-oriented. This is the cultural situation that developed between 1968 and 1970, and though the violent, activist phase passed quickly—and led to retrenchment and conservative backlash—it's substantially the situation we inherit today, within the limits of a straitened economy. It's a mixed picture, and I examine it with hopelessly mixed feelings. I hope my criticism does something to illuminate our present alternatives.

Since I've so often in this book examined the world of fiction to illustrate the stages of cultural change, I'd like to use it once more to represent this third phase. This is not an arbitrary choice, for though the innovative impulse that surged in fiction in the early sixties palled by the middle of the decade, when other kinds of art like rock and poetry and drama took the leading edge, it came back unexpectedly toward the end of the sixties. With noticeable ups and downs it has been with us ever since. By now the arrival of modernism, especially in short fiction, has proved to be one of the sixties' most durable cultural developments. I'd like to trace the history of this trend in its own terms, concentrating on a few positive and negative examples and what they portend for the health of the arts. If I stress too much the disintegrative aspect, the Weatherman aspect, it's mainly because my implicit subject is a melancholy one: how the sixties ended. If we face up to the betrayal of certain bright hopes, we may soon learn to be hopeful about new realities.

I

When two publishers in 1962 brought out overlapping collections of the work of the Argentine writer Jorge Luis Borges it was an important event for American readers, but few could have anticipated the impact it would have on our fiction. His work hardly fit into any traditional niche. The short story, even in the hands of Chekhov and Joyce, had always been the most conservative of all literary genres, the most tied to nineteenth-century conventions of incident and character, the least given to formal or technical innovation. Borges' stories hardly seemed to be stories at all; some of the best masqueraded as essays, laborious researches about nonexistent countries, ingenious commentaries on nonexistent books, mingled fantastically with the most out-of-the-way knowledge of real countries and real books. Where the traditional story took for granted the difference between the solid world out there and the imaginary world that tried to imitate it, Borges willfully confounded them. His stories were "fictions," original creations, less reflections than subversive interrogations of reality. They were also "labyrinths" which, like Kafka's writing, dressed out their mystery in a guise of earnest lucidity and matter-of-factness.

Today there is not much life in the old kind of story, though some good ones and many bad ones continue to be written. This sort of well-crafted object, which used to be the staple of dozens of now-defunct magazines, became so moribund in the sixties that it will now probably experience a mild resurgence, since changes in culture often proceed like swings of the pendulum. But the publication in 1975 of anthologies like *Superfiction* by Joe David Bellamy and *Statements* by members of the Fiction Collective confirms that our younger and more talented fiction writers have by no means abandoned the experimental impulse, though it may sometimes take them in wayward and even fruitless directions. Like so much of what emerged from the sixties, fiction today is a lesson in the uses of liberation. Whatever the results (and I intend to stress their current limitations), they remain inherently superior to a return to the old stringent molds, which conservative pundits are always ready to reimpose.

The progress of American fiction in the 1960s conjoined two different but related insurgencies against the constraints of traditional form, and against the cautious realism and psychological inwardness that had been dominant since the second world war. The first rebellion gave rise to big, eclectic books like John Barth's *The Sot-Weed Factor,* Heller's *Catch-22,* and Pynchon's *V.*, as well as ribald free-form tirades like Mailer's *Why Are We In Vietnam?* and Roth's *Portnoy's Complaint.* In all these books the grand raw materials of history, politics, literary tradition, and personal identity were transposed into fantasy, black or obscene humor, and apocalyptic personal expression. (I've already discussed many of these books in detail in my fourth chapter, especially for the light they shed on the sensibility of the early and middle sixties.)

217

These writers did not so much cease to be realists as seek grotesque or hilarious (but accurate) equivalents for realities that were themselves fantastic. *Catch-22* not only did not lie about war, it scarcely even exaggerated. Portnoy is not fair to his mother but he is true to her, even as he caricatures and mythicizes her. These writers took advantage of the decline of censorship and of the constricting demands of formal neatness and realistic verisimilitude to broaden the range of fictional possibility, to discover new literary ancestors—Céline, Henry Miller, Nabokov, Genet—and to claim their legacy.

In the last three years of the sixties, however, culminating in the publication of Donald Barthelme's *City Life* (1970), but to some extent continuing right to the present day, a second insurgency came to the fore. Between 1967 and 1970 American fiction, following its Latin American counterpart, entered a new and more unexpected phase, which was also a more deliberately experimental one. For convenience we can call this the Borgesian phase, though Borges has not been the only model for the short, sometimes dazzlingly short, and multi-layered fiction that is involved. (Interestingly, Borges' example served to release the influence of others, including his own master, Kafka, and even such different writers as Beckett and Robbe-Grillet.)

In just these three years there were many significant collections of this new short fiction, including Barthelme's *Unspeakable Practices, Unnatural Acts* (the mock melodrama of the title is typical of him). Barth's *Lost in the Funhouse* (Barth's funhouse is the genial American equivalent of Borges' labyrinth), William H. Gass's *In the Heart of the Heart of the Country*, Robert Coover's *Pricksongs & Descants* (subtitled "Fictions"), plus many of the impacted, truncated melodramas in Leonard Michaels' *Going Places* and some of the stories in Vonnegut's *Welcome to the Monkey House* (his novels were even more to the point). But the last of them, Barthelme's *City Life*, was more audacious and more successful than any of the other volumes, a book that went beyond experimental ingenuity to find new ways of connecting fiction with feeling. I'd like to use it as my positive pole in examing the uses of liberation in fiction, and I'll play it off against a larger number of other works, including some by Barthelme, which (to my mind) take experiment and liberation down less rewarding paths.

The collections I've listed all had a great deal in common, yet no two were alike. All tended to eliminate (or use ironically) the realistic matrix in which most works of fiction are embedded—the lifelike quality that gives them credibility and coherence, the thematic explicitness that gives them the gratifying feel of significance. "We like books," Barthelme once wrote, "that have a lot of *dreck* in them, matter which presents itself as not wholly relevant (or indeed, at all relevant) but which, carefully attended to, can supply a kind of 'sense' of what is going on." But these writers sometimes pay a heavy price for excising or satirizing this dross, which is rarely dross in good fiction anyway. They fall into inaccessibility, abstraction, or mere cleverness, substituting the *dreck* of literary self-consciousness for that of popular realism.

Coover and Barth, for example, seem overwhelmed by their own freedom, by the writer's power to invent a scene, a character, a world, to choose which word and which sentence he will set down next. Take Coover's maniacally brilliant and finally oppressive story "The Babysitter" (in *Pricksongs & Descants*), an elaborate set of variations on a few deliberately banal and melodramatic characters and plot possibilities, all merging into one another, all going off at once—a fiction-making machine run amok with its own powers, threatening to blow up in our faces, or blow our minds.

Several of Barth's stories in *Lost in the Funhouse* do comparable things in a more playful and self-ironical way. The title piece, for example, interweaves a sharp-minded yet pedantic commentary on fictional technique between the lines of a story that can't quite get itself written. In "Title" and "Life-Story," Barth can already subject this very manner of formal self-consciousness to a weary and ambivalent parody, which in turn gives the stories another layer of the same self-consciousness they criticize. Barth's fictions make the case against themselves neatly: "Another story about writing a story! Another regressus in infinitum! Who doesn't prefer art that at least overtly imitates something other than its own processes? That doesn't continually proclaim 'Don't forget I'm an artifice!'?'' At times the formalism and literary preciosity that were routed from the novel during the sixties seem to have returned with a vengeance in the new short fiction.

Self-consciousness has always been a key element in modern art, however, and in fiction (as Robert Alter has demonstrated anew in *Partial Magic*) it has a long ancestry that goes back beyond modernism to Diderot, Sterne, and Cervantes, a tradition that sometimes makes nineteenth-century realism look like a mere episode. (Fortunately we also have Erich Auerbach's book *Mimesis* to demonstrate the long and complex history of the realist method.) E. M. Forster once said that it's intrinsic to the artist to experiment with his medium, but in the twentieth century we've often seen how the spiral of self-consciousness can reach a point of diminishing returns. This happens when artists mimic other artists without fully appropriating them, or when they make their concerns as artists their exclusive subject. We need to hold fast to the distinction, often hard to apply, between experiment for its own sake, out of touch with any lived reality, and experiments that create genuinely new ways of seeing. The fiction of the sixties shows how the once-subversive gestures of modernism can themselves become tiresome conventions (as Barth suggests but can't seem to evade); but it also indicates, quite to the contrary, that only now that the towering first generation of modernists has been safely interred in literary history have our young writers been willing to resume the risks of the modernist program, which is nothing if not experimental and avant-garde.

I'd like to examine Barthelme's achievement in *City Life* and elsewhere to show what experimental writing has only recently been able to do without becoming self-indulgent or imitative. From there I'll go on to other texts of the early seventies to show what pitfalls and dilemmas await the experimental writer as he tries to develop upon these initial breakthroughs. Barthelme's earlier books, which were as intransigently original as *City Life*, were mostly notable for what they did *not* do, for the kinds of coherence they refused to supply, for their discontinuities and even incongruities, which mixed abstract ideas with pop allusions, political figures with fairy-tale characters, pedantically precise facts with wild generalities and exaggerations, and so on. They aimed to cut the reader off, to keep him guessing and thinking, to make him angry. His novel *Snow White* (1967) was a book that adamantly refused to go anywhere at all. Without benefit of plot, characters, or even much of the sober-zany humor of the stories in his first book, *Come Back, Dr. Caligari* (1964), the novel mainly limited itself to fragmentary take-offs on a huge variety of rhetorical styles and verbal trash. It was a minor-league version of what Ezra Pound saw in *Ulysses,* a species of encyclopedic satire; the book was all language, and at least on first acquaintance it seemed certain that the language was just not good enough to carry it.

Subsequent readings of *Snow White* have given me much more pleasure; though the book doesn't work as a whole, it has grown with time. It's still too detached, too satirical and fragmentary, but the author's really dry and wicked wit has worn surprisingly well. But it's finally too much of a book about itself and crippled by the absence of a subject. Its detachment is deliberate, but it leaves a void that language and satire can't entirely fill. By the book's whimsical discontinuities, by a certain deadpan mechanical quality, by a whole range of Brechtian alienation devices, Barthelme was deliberately blocking the debased and facile kinds of identification that we readers make in traditional fiction, yet he found little to substitute. (As Barth writes, "Plot and theme: notations vitiated by this hour of the world but as yet not successfully succeeded.") Taking a cue, I suspect, from Godard's films, Barthelme eliminated most of the dross of primitive storytelling so that the *dreck* of contemporary culture could more devastatingly display itself. He tried to remain, as he said, "on the leading edge of this trash phenomenon," but the project was too plainly negative, and despite his wit he nearly foundered in the swill.

In his next book, *Unspeakable Practices, Unnatural Acts,* Barthelme still proclaimed that "fragments are the only forms I trust," but the fragments began insidiously to cohere, into pointed fables like

"The Balloon" and "The Police Band," into surreal and indirect political commentary, such as "The President" and "Robert Kennedy Saved from Drowning." Like Vonnegut and Pynchon, whom he somewhat resembles—indeed, like Dickens and Kafka—Barthelme discovered that fantasy and caricature could serve maliciously to heighten reality as well to block it out, that fiction could, by symbolism and indirection, recover the world that it had long since abandoned to the journalists and historians.

"The President" is part Swift, part Kafka, part surrealist playlet; its hero is "only forty-eight inches high at the shoulder," a graduate of City College, a "tiny, strange, and brilliant man." He is like no president we've ever had, but his spooky presence tells us something about all of them. (In a similar way, when Pynchon and Vonnegut take on the Southern California scene, or the Eichmann case, or the Dresden bombings, they refract these topical subjects through a very personal imaginative medium, but without losing touch.)

In the Kennedy story Barthelme tried neither to explain Kennedy nor to give a credible portrait of him, but rather to thicken him into an enigma—he is called K. throughout—to find symbolic equivalents for his image, and for our fascination. Authentic facts—how he frequently changed shirts each day—mingle with astonishing inventions, such as Kennedy's capable discourse as the literary criticism of Georges Poulet. The result is neither "about" Kennedy nor an exercise in Barthelme's technique, but a weird mélange of the two. The example of Borges may have made such an interrogation of reality possible, but Barthelme's handling of it is wholly original.

In *City Life* Barthelme for better or worse abjured topical occasions for literary and personal ones. The public immediacies of politics and war give way to Borgesian meditation on books, writers, and ideas. Barthelme was exploring his loyalties as an artist, and even his stylistic virtuosity, though toned down, served him well. There were few stretches of mere verbal display or experiment for experiment's sake (an unreadable piece of Joycean gobbledygook called "Bone Bubbles" was the main offender).

Most of the stories move in an entirely different direction. At a time when some of Barthelme's contemporaries were trying hard to leave personal experience behind in hot pursuit of technical innovation, the pleasure of *City Life* came from seeing Barthelme break through to new areas of feeling with no loss of rhetorical verve. Without falling back to direct emotional statement or personal psychology, he learned to write fables whose ironies, far from blocking our emotions, make more complex demands upon them.

"Views of My Father Weeping" at once mimics a style of personal narrative, pays tribute to a whole body of literature in which such narrative abounds—it's written in the style of 1910 translations from the Russian—and interweaves two strands of action more successfully than Barthelme had ever done before. The speaker's father has been run down and killed by an aristocrat, but it is his father whom he repeatedly sees weeping: these alternating actions create between them a field of significance, an atmosphere rich in implicit emotion, while the author himself remains cool, detached, tantalizingly elusive. (The story concludes, staggeringly, on the word "etc.," as if to say, you've heard all this before, fill in the blanks. The text of *Snow White* included an actual questionnaire addressed to the reader.)

Following Borges (and Cervantes, for that matter), Barthelme discovered anew how crucially books mediate our access to our deepest experience, and he brings to his "discussions" of literature his own large reserves of fervor and ambiguity. Few passages in the book are more vivid than the retelling of a Tolstoy story in "At the Tolstoy Museum" or the paraphrase of Kierkegaard's theory of irony in "Kierkegaard Unfair to Schlegel." In each story the narrator, who may or may not be Barthelme, feels fascinated and alarmed by the strange, imposing figure he is confronting, by the book he is bringing to life. Tolstoy's story, he says, "is written in a very simple style. It is said to originate in a folk tale. There is a version of it in St. Augustine. I was incredibly depressed by reading this story. Its beauty. Distance."

Most of Barthelme's story, however, is not about Tolstoy's work but about a museum full of huge pictures, clothing, and other supposed effects of Tolstoy—the book provides large illustrations of them—all of which are the absurdly displaced objects of the speaker's ambivalence toward Tolstoy, his nostalgia for Tolstoy's kind of writing. (The story begins with an echo of Psalm 137, a poem of exile and loss.) Tolstoy is after all the greatest of the realists, and his work is the immense anti-type to Barthelme's own mode of fantasy and irony. Yet the story that Barthelme chooses to retell, "The Three Holy Men," is a small religious parable about three hermits and the strange but authentic way that they too pray. Moreover, his account of its atmosphere is eerily exact: "Its beauty. Distance." Though mostly realistic in detail, the parable as a whole is cool in tone, integral, moving but untouchable—in short, very much like Barthelme's own tone. Tolstoy and Barthelme, opposites, rearrange themselves, and our conventional expectations are disoriented. Traditional parable and contemporary fable meet, as if to arrange a joint subversion of realism in the cause of reality.

One could give a comparable account of the Kierkegaard story, which raises different issues, or of "The Phantom of the Opera's Friend," which, besides being wonderfully funny, further develops Barthelme's rich involvement with melodrama, conventional realism, and kitsch, his longing, like Barth's, to be a more traditional kind of writer. (The book's illustrations, half absurdly old-fashioned, half surreal, betray the same secret wish.)

Should the Phantom of the Opera leave his sumptuous underground quarters to take up a respectable life in the "real" world? Will the "hot meat of romance" be "cooled by the dull gravy of common sense"? Does the narrator deserve a more conventional friend, from the world of Henry James perhaps, "with whom one could be seen abroad. With whom one could exchange country weekends, on our respective estates!"? Will the angels in "On Angels" recover from the death of God and find new employment to replace their lapsed duties of adoration? Tuning in next week will not answer any of these questions, but Barthelme raises them in a way that gives a new wrinkle to the possible uses of pop material for serious purposes in fiction (mingled, in his case, with flotsam and jetsam of the most arcane intellectuality). Along with so many other of our new writers, Barthelme relegates the cultural hierarchies of the fifties to a memory. Learning to appreciate his best stories, we also learn to read in a new way, savoring them for their mock-serious humor, their imaginative weight, and their profound urbanity.

I've hardly done justice to the great variousness of *City Life,* or to the design of the book, which beautifully complements its substance. One story that must be mentioned is ''Brain Damage,'' which has no story at all but is a superb justification of Barthelme's fragmentary and surrealist method—he brings to mind the painter Magritte as much as he does any writer. It is one of the best pieces of non-sequential fictional prose I've ever read, a series of brilliant but unrelated narrative fragments—Barthelme could have been a fine conventional novelist—that finally cohere around the single inspired metaphor of the title.

The quality and character of Barthelme's work in the late sixties, and its frequent appearance in a glossy, above-ground periodical like *The New Yorker,* helped experimental fiction come of age in this country and released a flood that has continued to swell, though aside from *Gravity's Rainbow* it has yet to roar. In this, his best book, there's very little about city life but much that adds to our imaginative life and the life of our feelings (a domain where experimental fiction has been notably weak, as I'll soon try to show in more detail). *Snow White* and a later collection called *Sadness* have shown that Barthelme is not always strong in this way. More than fiction must have been involved when a character in *Snow White* made the following speech:

> After a life rich in emotional defeats, I have looked around for other modes of misery, other roads to destruction. Now I limit myself to listening to what people say, and thinking what pamby it is, what they say. My nourishment is refined from the ongoing circus of the mind in motion. Give me the odd linguistic trip, stutter and fall, and I will be content.

Barthelme comes out of all his books as a complex and enigmatic person, one who has seen many things, but *Snow White* was a book of personal withdrawal, dour satire, ''the odd linguistic trip.'' I hope

I've been able to indicate how *City Life,* with its new risks and new emotional defeats, represents a quite different sort of fictional victory. Before returning to look at some of the later work of Barthelme and Barth, to see how well they fare in sustaining the experimental impulse into the seventies, I'd like to examine the work of another talented young novelist who emerged in the seventies, Rudolph Wurlitzer, whose books are extreme cases of the temptation to emotional withdrawal that *City Life* eschews but which haunts so much other experimental fiction.

I I

In a four-year period Wurlitzer published three short but substantial novels, all startlingly different in everything but length, *Nog* (1969), *Flats* (1970), and *Quake* (1972). Although hardly candidates for the best-seller list, they were widely read and praised by serious students of fiction, and achieved a cult status among some of the young, especially on the West Coast. This is a difficult body of work informed by a distinct view of experience, and it deserves to be treated seriously, whatever judgment we finally make.

Nog and *Flats* were typical of the experimental fiction of the late sixties in largely eliminating plot, causality, milieu, psychology—indeed, any sort of significant action. But where other writers then invested their energy in style and self-conscious verbal ingenuity, Wurlitzer avoided such precious gamesmanship. No serious writer in recent memory has cultivated a style so clipped and flat, so pristine in its subject-verb-object matter-of-factness (even when there are no recognizable "facts"). In *Nog,* a comparatively ingratiating book, a rare metaphor or rhetorical cadence slips through. In *Flats* all eloquence is ruthlessly censored: "That's too poetic, too fragmented. I'm not in touch with any of that."

"Not in touch": Wurlitzer's main subject is the loss of affect or connection of any sort, a perception that's at the core of his abandonment of the traditional novel. The structured narrative, the adventure, the measured unfolding of man and motive—these do not speak to his sense of reality, much as he might wish they did. "If I could remember a story I would tell it. That always helps to hold ground, to pass the time. . . . Stories in the dead of night are always fabricated, pointing to relief, to a way out, to a cozy direction. . . . I am unable to bring it all together, to say something clear, that I can remember."

At the center of each of Wurlitzer's three novels is a nameless narrator who can scarcely express an emotion more complex than a twitch, or have a memory more shaped than a list or a log. Heavily indebted to Beckett and Burroughs, the books have a drab, poignant, dead-end quality, a cultural and personal amnesia that vaunts its freedom from all traditional "shucks" and cozy directions—indeed, from all direction, period.

Wurlitzer never makes clear whether the catatonic types who people his world are sad cases, the expectable debris of a culture without meaning or satisfaction, or modest heroes who have seen through the sham of personal relations and purposeful actions. They are undoubtedly both, but the author mainly identifies with them, which helps explain the attraction his books had for alienated counterculture kids and California types not usually interested in arcane literary experiment. In Wurlitzer's world there are no families, jobs, or traditional relationships. His people are always floating loose, rubbing up against one another, or getting into binds that may destroy them but at least will free them from the remnants of personal identity.

What really engages his imagination is not the individual and his problems but a ruder stratum of behavior and sensation, a kind of primal slime that precedes individuation. The most brilliant chapter in *Nog* is dominated by a fantasy of the self as a "dark wet hole," an empty swamp of undifferentiated sensations, where the lines are blurred between self and other, between acting and being acted upon: "I am a repository, I suppose. The dark wet hole where everything finds its way sooner or later. I remain near the entrance, handling goods as they are shoved in, listening and nodding. I have been slowly dissolving into this cavity.'' At another point he imagines himself merging with the vegetable world: ''The vegetables will become an envelope, an extension of my skin. I will grow avocado plants. Fungus will appear between my toes.''

All this is a fascinating variant on that strain in American literature that Quentin Anderson calls ''the imperial self,'' the self which, in Whitman, Emerson, and many other American writers, dilates to ingest the whole world. In Wurlitzer's book, on the other hand, the self shrinks back toward a passive and primeval state in which the world remains uncreated, unformed (monosyllabic, one might say, thinking of Wurlitzer's titles). He rarely lets the fantasy go this far, but the magnetic pull of such a wish explains much in his work that is otherwise puzzling. In *Nog,* for example, characters who seem at first to have separate identities soon begin to merge and overlap. Nog himself, at first a distinct creature (''apparently of Finnish extraction''), also becomes an aspect of the narrator's identity, the primitive anti-type toward which he tends. In *Flats* the very idea of character is abandoned, or rather broken down into rudimentary traits. The figures in the book all bear the names of American cities and the oddly mingled attributes of both persons and cities (something Blake did in his prophetic books). In an almost random sequence of dialogues and paragraphs, Wurlitzer atomizes all experience into a succession of minimal gestures, incanted in a numbingly limp, abstracted, and hypnotic prose.

Flats is Wurlitzer's most uncompromising work, a true American *nouveau roman,* but it's more a stew of quasi-novelistic ingredients than a novel. Even as we yield to the distinct shape of Wurlitzer's imagination, the impulse to go on reading ebbs. Once we've gotten any of it, we have all of it. Any 20 pages will do. The book is boring, repetitive, shapeless; its language (to quote Wurlitzer himself) is ''self-involved, whispering, frozen.'' What life it contains is disembodied, a drifting series of voices, a late-night radio band from somewhere beyond the fringe. Drifting in fact is the key image of the book, as it is of all three novels, which is why, we are told, there are no women in it: ''Not that they aren't around. But they're not known to drift after an apocalypse, preferring to hang on to whatever nest they may be into.''

This is where *Quake* comes in, supplying the apocalyptic dimension only hinted at in the world-denying outlook of the earlier books. Where *Nog* and *Flats* were inversions of the American road novel, substituting passivity and inertia for purposive movement and change, *Quake* is a California novel drenched in the facile paranoia and apocalypticism that seem endemic there. The book begins in the aftermath of a powerful earthquake. The plastic face of society has been cracked like a toy. Mile-deep chasms yawn temptingly. Dead and wounded mingle in the rubble of large buildings. As rescue operations proceed, it becomes clear that mysterious Minuteman-style groups are struggling to seize power and an outbreak of urban guerrilla warfare is adding to the havoc and carnage. Starting from a strictly realistic description of this situation, the book's narrative gradually begins to blur, and finally descends into an orgy of surreal, arbitrary violence, until the narrator grunts his last and the book ends.

In technique at least, *Quake* was a striking departure for Wurlitzer. Despite a portentous vagueness around the edges, it is his most realistic and conventional novel, his first with genuine narrative thrust. Gone are the bizarre transitions and alienation effects that made his previous books seem four times longer than they were. Gone too, alas, is the imaginative complexity that often accompanied those hardships. The stripping away of social identity, the fear of entrapment, the resumption of undifferentiated being—all of which were part of the formal grain of the earlier books—are here cast in the accessible but banal form of a futuristic fable. But in this case the primitive takes a sinister turn, a catastrophic descent into anarchy, a drift toward apocalypse. Unfortunately this sort of parable has been done again and again. It reads like *Lord of the Flies* as Burroughs might have written it, and, considering that Golding's book was already a pop version of Conrad's *Heart of Darkness*, the version Wurlitzer has written is pure cliché.

Though the book's emphasis isn't political, Wurlitzer has clearly put in time in Southern California, and become alarmed that vigilante groups may be squirreling away arms for the day of reckoning. (Instead, the evidence of recent history seems to suggest that if fascism does come to America it won't be from beefy Minutemen and hard-hats but from the smiling, distinguished faces in board rooms, cabinet rooms, bugged executive suites, and Pentagon offices.) Wurlitzer is afraid that They will take over, not just crackers and rednecks but the peaceful guy next door, the quiet killer in all of us. He fears that in the meeting of victim and executioner he will join the winning side, as his narrator longs to do; he fears that all precivilized reversions are concessions to the killer within us. These are humane discoveries, especially for Wurlitzer, whose imagination is so attracted to primitive states of being.

But by presenting scene after scene of gratuitous and nauseating violence, all blankly recounted by a catatonic narrator, who may or may not be in shock, who claims to be feeling deep changes but in fact shows hardly any response at all, Wurlitzer has already gone over to Them and yielded up the battle. The cool of the drifter and this flat phantasmagoria of lust, murder, and apocalypse make a strange and increasingly unpleasant combination.

Whether Wurlitzer's more fervent admirers have found this brew as unpleasant as I did I have no way of knowing. One enraged young man sent me reams of hate mail when I first published some of these critical comments. He swore generational vengeance, not knowing that I had neither the years nor the inclination to bear the standard of the Fathers in their oedipal warfare against the Sons. He found in Wurlitzer a profound diagnosis of the malaise of affect and feeling in our time, where I found the malaise to be largely Wurlitzer's own. But in seeing it as an illness my correspondent differed from many other young people in the Weatherman phase of the sixties and early seventies, who came to believe that private emotions were a crock, that rooted relationships and traditions were a fraud, that history itself is bullshit. "The Novel of Bullshit is dead," Pynchon announced in his acclamatory blurb for *Nog,* as if the texture of human relations that informs traditional fiction (or his own best fiction) were so much blather. If there were many who believed such things, the drifter mentality of Wurlitzer's books was just the music for them to hang loose by.

I I I

Pynchon's comment illustrates the extent to which writers of experimental fiction were prone to make apocalyptic assumptions about culture and art, assumptions that their critics and opponents tended to share, often hysterically, during the sixties. If we take a longer and calmer view we observe that one form of art scarcely ever abolishes another, though it can alter its place and even sap its spirit. Right now it appears that realism is in eclipse rather than decline; its exhaustion may be temporary rather than terminal. It's not inconceivable that a great Tolstoyan writer could appear tomorrow, though if he were really good his work would look very different from Tolstoy's or George Eliot's. What plagues experimental writers more than realists is the inherent instability of avant-garde techniques, which frequently resist both imitation and development and lead to movements that are notoriously short-lived, like dada and surrealism, op art, or minimal art. (Sometimes these movements evolve only by being domesticated, as surrealism is integrated into a realistic framework, wonderfully, in Vigo's *Zéro de conduite* or in the later movies of Buñuel, including some of his Mexican potboilers.)

I believe this helps explain the problems that have afflicted experimental writers since the end of the sixties: after you've performed a smashing act, what do you do for an encore? We have *Finnegans Wake* to remind us how difficult encores can be, especially when artists, like other would-be revolutionaries, feel endlessly compelled to radicalize their vision and rebuild the world from scratch. If the faith in actuality, the acceptance of the world as it is (or as it once seemed to be), has declined, if practitioners of fiction no longer believe in what Barthelme calls the "enormous diversity of things," the natural abundance of God's creation, they have filled the void with an astonishing variety of their own artifacts. Writers of the seventies are heirs to a liberating chaos of new forms, running from the Borgesian miniatures of Donald Barthelme to gargantuan miscellanies like Nabokov's *Ada*, Gaddis's *JR*, Alan Friedman's *Hermaphrodeity*, and Pynchon's *Gravity's Rainbow*. But freedom can be a burden and a terror as well as an exhilarating opportunity, and in the last part of this chapter I'd like to take another look at some of the experimental short fiction of our period to see how the liberated writer has dealt with his dilemma. I'd like to know what principles underlie the not-so-random successes and failures. I'd like to prove to my unhappy correspondent that generational anthems and apocalyptic slogans are beside the point, that one needn't sign up in one camp or another, that it's possible to be neither swinger nor reactionary but merely what Matthew Arnold liked to call a disinterested critic.

What all these novels and stories I've mentioned have in common is a degree of creative freedom and seriousness about art that was alien to the generation of John O'Hara. American fiction has joined the camp of modernism with a vengeance, and done so at a time when the modernist impulse seemed to be exhausted. But new modernist writing still does not sell; it sells only to the intellectuals and to posterity. The dark side of the healthy abundance and variety of fiction is the collapse of the commercial market, which has driven novelists to little magazines with a minuscule audience and even to self-publishing, an "underground" usually inhabited only by the poets. Publishers stop buying novels or hesitate to promote those they do buy: they retreat to old middlebrow staples like history, biography, and reportage, which provide the narrative element many of the novelists have abandoned, and sometimes even deliver news about a world outside the writer's head. A special issue of *Newsweek* in 1973 on "The Arts in America" gave all its emphasis to the performing arts, almost none to writing. Along with professional sports, the performing arts at least convey a solid reality, a kinetic human presence that today's writers often refuse even to simulate.

How much, then, are writers responsible for their own commercial decline? More seriously, how well has the newest experimental work delivered on the promises of the tumultuous sixties? How do the aims of the younger writers compare to those of the classical modernists, who themselves endured opprobrium and neglect before achieving wide recognition? I won't really answer the last question, except to reiterate that an experimental attitude and a rebellion against nineteenth-century realism were important features of the modernist achievement. But they were accompanied by a heroic effort to master reality, to interpret the world in new ways, through new forms. Though a writer like Kafka may feel anything but heroic, may feel the victim of circumstances at every turn, as an artist he turns his helplessness into mastery by creating a mode of apprehension that we recognize on every page, in every sentence. His work has become a way that *we* see reality, which helps us to grapple with it too. But in the 1960s an impressive and influential body of fictional theory codified the modernist attitude in a way that almost leaves reality out of account. The essays collected in Alain Robbe-Grillet's *For a New Novel*, Richard Gilman's *The Confusion of Realms*, and William H. Gass's *Fiction and the Figures of Life* all stress the aesthetic autonomy of the work of art, its non-referential status as an object in itself—neither mirror nor lamp, neither imitation of life nor emanation of the self—a new reality bodied forth in words.

Robbe-Grillet had the example of the *nouveau roman*, which his essays aimed to validate, but there was little in American fiction in the early sixties to justify so extravagant a theory. The characteristic novels of the period, by writers like Barth, Berger, Pynchon, Heller, and Vonnegut, had indeed broken with the realistic conventions that predominated in the forties and fifties, not by junking them, however, but by subsuming them, as Kafka and Joyce had done, in an immense ironic structure. The worlds they created were virtual or contingent ones, which oddly mixed fact and fantasy and directed much attention to the artist's own ingenuity, but they were worlds nonetheless, full of the same "solidity of specification" that James described as the hallmark of the realistic novelist.

233

Gates of Eden

It remained for the writers of the late sixties to press toward a mode of fiction that would make the novel a body of words *and no more:* its own devices would become its only subject. Using techniques of abstraction, fragmentation, and discontinuity—borrowed from sources as diverse as dada painters, surrealist poets, New Wave filmmakers, Brechtian dramatists, as well as modernist writers of fiction—they wrote stories that deliberately alienate the reader, inhibit his identification with the "characters" or the story, and short-circuit his suspension of disbelief. Barthelme's later stories, whose protagonists have names like Perpetua, "the genius," or "the catechist," announce themselves immediately as fictive constructs, verbal machines with all their gears exposed. Yet all sorts of words and deeds are attributed to the puppet-characters, who imitate life so inexactly that they mock the very principle of imitation. Reduced to a collection of verbal and emotional mannerisms, tics of behavior severed from an elaborated human context, Barthelme's world foppishly parades its superficiality; yet with such themes as "the rise of capitalism" it also toys with an air of portentous generality, even of parable, teasing us with Kafkaesque hints of remote, inaccessible symbolic depths.

All things considered, however, the freshest and most boldly realized experimental fiction of the late sixties, such as the stories I've discussed from Barthelme's *City Life,* does not correspond to the astringent formalism of such critics as Robbe-Grillet, Gilman, Gass, and Susan Sontag. It is not free of that "heavy burden of 'content' " and moral seriousness that Sontag deplores in contemporary literature; it has not abandoned worldly ambition for a purer realm of style. I can explain this by citing some comments made by Philip Rahv in 1949 on the Kafka vogue of the late forties, which resulted in some good examples of fake modernism, misconceived imitations of that most elusive of models:

> To know how to take apart the recognizable world is not enough, is in fact merely a way of letting oneself go and striving for originality at all costs. But originality of this sort is nothing but a professional mannerism of the avant-garde. The genuine innovator is always trying to make us actually

experience his creative contradictions. He therefore employs means that are subtler and more complex: *at the very same time that he takes the world apart he puts it together again.* For to proceed otherwise is to dissipate rather than alter our sense of reality, to weaken and compromise rather than change in any significant fashion our feeling of relatedness to the world. ["Notes on the Decline of Naturalism"]

The limitations of this position are evident enough: under the guise of high standards and loyalty to the "true" avant-garde (read: some *previous* avant-garde) it can become a conservative defense of established forms and of acceptably humanist feelings of "relatedness to the world." Much later, in the sixties, Rahv himself fell victim to this sort of embattled traditionalism, and became an indiscriminate foe of all attempts at innovation in literature. The seeds of this decline are already present in these earlier gibes at "letting oneself go," "originality at all costs," and the "professional mannerisms of the avant-garde."

Yet, however easily misapplied, Rahv's dictum is basically sound. All modernist writing is in some ways experimental and revisionary, thriving on the decadence of previous forms and norms like Swift's tulips rising out of dung. Modernist writing is ebulliently parricidal and cannibalistic. It revels apocalyptically in the end of culture—the death of the novel, the death of rhyme, the exhaustion of narrative, the end of the nineteenth century—yet feeds lustily on its murdered forebears, as Kafka sups ironically on the techniques of realism while undermining their grip on causality and "reality," as Joyce turns *Ulysses* into a parodistic anthology of traditional styles.

But in all the best modernist writing, this negative and parodistic element never predominates, however largely it bulks. Some modernist techniques do aim at pure destruction and chaos, a form of aesthetic terrorism, but where this polemical side is dominant we often find publicists rather than artists, dada rather than symbolism, Dali rather than Picasso. Otherwise, where modernist or experimental art seems unstructured, incoherent, anarchic, even nihilistic, as is often the case, it usually means that we have not yet recognized the new norm, the new principle of coherence or mode of awareness that the artist has invented. Often enough though, we *sense* that it is there, for our instinct is sounder than our aesthetic, which is still grounded in the *idées reçues* of the past. The function of criticism is to interrogate that feeling, to turn it into new categories, a new aesthetic. Bad criticism spins clever theories; good criticism justifies unexpected intuitions.

In the experimental fiction of the late sixties, the largely negative strain shows itself most clearly in Barth's stories in *Lost in the Funhouse*, in Coover's *Pricksongs & Descants*, in Barthelme's novella *Snow White*, in the insubstantial and self-indulgent antiworld ("Antiterra") of Nabokov's *Ada*, and in the catatonic ambiance of Wurlitzer's *Nog* and *Flats*, to list mainly examples I've already discussed. There is much to praise in all these books: corrosive ironies, flights of fantasy, nuance of language that we expect more from poetry than fiction. What they too frequently lack is poignancy, intensity, a recognizably human framework. I don't mean realism, which is only one of many conventions by which art approximates the human. Without being representational, the paintings of Kline and Pollock, with their sweeping swathes or dense multiple layers of paint, boldly suggest the energies of their composition, the turbulent circumstances of their own inception. These works are not really "about" themselves, however, because their reflexiveness takes us through and beyond technique, back to a world of gesture, feeling, and movement, as well as shape and color. But some of the new fiction is really about fiction itself, paralyzed by self-consciousness, caught in an infinite regress of writing about writing. Thus, bereft of a full human subject, embroiled in problems of craft rather than art, it readily devolves into a parochial whine or ascends to a cerebral high, manipulating words and worlds with a meaningless impunity.

At its best, this fiction evades such criticism to achieve a genuine if narrow intensity. Nabokov's *Pale Fire* is partly saved from mere cleverness by its obsessiveness, which well accords with the problem-solving mania it depicts. Some of Barth's stories, like "Lost in the Funhouse," "Title," and "Life-Story," make of the prisonhouse of authorial self-consciousness an almost adequate subject, especially when set off against an impotent nostalgia for the happy credulities of tradition. Here, more extensively, is a passage I began to quote earlier:

> Another story about a writer writing a story! Another regressus in infinitum! Who doesn't prefer art that at least overtly imitates something other than its own processes? That doesn't continually proclaim "Don't forget I'm an artifice!"? . . . Though his critics sympathetic and otherwise described his own work as avant-garde, in his heart of hearts he disliked literature of an experimental, self-despising, or overtly metaphysical character, like Samuel Beckett's, Marian Cutler's, Jorge Borges's. The logical fantasies of Lewis Carroll pleased him less than straightforward tales of adventure, subtly sentimental romances, even densely circumstantial realisms like Tolstoy's. . . .
>
> By Jove he exclaimed to himself. It's particularly disquieting to suspect not only that one is a fictional character but that the fiction one's in—the fiction one is—is quite the sort one least prefers. ["Life-Story"]

This may not be great fiction—what is?—but it has a certain wry precision and point. Its self-referential quality is earned, dramatized, by the playful dialectic of unwillingness. Like the proverbial cynic with a sentimental core, Barth in all his fiction oscillates between a mock traditionalism and a coyly hesitant vanguardism, in a way that at least approximates Rahv's formula that "the genuine innovator is always trying to make us actually experience his creative contradictions."

The weakness of such writing, as Barth himself indicates, is that it has no subject apart from the writer's problem in being a writer. This can be a rich theme, as it is for Henry James in his fables about artists and writers, but only if problems of technique and creative choice come to represent more general features of our common fate. Since the early Romantics of the late eighteenth century, the fate of the artist has repeatedly become an intensified version of the whole human situation. For this to happen convincingly, however, the writer must genuinely risk and expose himself; he cannot simply dawdle about the private, parochial problems of his craft, no matter how apocalyptically he interprets them. But the Barthian apocalypse is a game without risk, a purely intellectual game that scribbles in the margins of the history of art without adding to the basic text. Recent critical theory endows fiction with total imaginative freedom, making it no longer "subservient to the actuality from which it draws its instigations and energies." But what the Barthian writer, caught in his dead-end self-consciousness, most completely lacks is imagination, the deep subjectivity that enables the imagination to take wing. For all their personal reference, his cerebral musings about art foster an escape from subjectivity, an escape from personality; he eschews not only characters but character, including his own; his incursions into the self are as hollow as his excursus into the world.

This escape from personality, perhaps an understandable reaction to the fury of self-assertion that predominated in the sixties, threatens to rob the writer of everything but his "voice," the distinctive accent of his prose (distinctiveness we associate with poetry more than with fiction). At the same time it makes possible the celebrated "cool" tone of much recent experimental fiction, a cleanness of manner that partly redeems the pervasive irony and emotional distance. Experimental fiction clears away the debris of prevailing styles—such as popular realism—which are usually debased versions of styles that were radical in their own day. (Eliot's poetry challenges Swinburne and Robert Bridges, not Blake and Wordsworth; Barthelme undermines Bellow, not Balzac.) After we've read Barthelme and Borges, it's hard to be told that so-and-so got into a car, slammed the door, turned his key in the ignition, pressed his foot on the gas pedal, etc., unless this sequence of gestures advances the meaning (as it does, for example, in Truffaut's neo-Hitchcock film *The Soft Skin*). In most popular (and some serious) fiction, however, such filler merely aspires to verisimilitude: to convince the reader, as Robbe-Grillet remarks, "that the adventures he is hearing about have really happened to real characters." In Balzac setting and description imply and foreshadow the whole work, like an overture that introduces a mesh of musical themes; in contemporary realism they merely strain to convince us we're in a world.

Faced with the debasement of realism into lazy conventions the writer can clear the ground by abstracting from reality, perhaps by condensing the story from thirty to three pages, essentializing it into pure narration; but unlike the painter he cannot recoil wholly from representation into pure abstraction. A painting by Jules Olitski can be "about" its acrylic surface, or about other layers of paint the surface suggests but half-conceals. Still the canvas remains an object of sensuous contemplation. But words are abstract to begin with; they lack sensuous address. The pulpiest novel, dead on the page, can make a good movie; the sounds and images, the moving presence of the actors, can bring the thing to life. As Mary McCarthy puts it: "Language, unlike paint and sound, cannot slough off its primary function of saying something. When it tries, we simply stop listening. This is why large audiences can be attracted by every sort of non-objective art and 'concrete' music but so very few people will consent to turn pages from which no meaning emerges."

Admittedly Miss McCarthy is discussing an extreme example, the French "*new* new novel," which, like so many other "new" developments in French cultural life, is more a triumph of publicity and fashion than a true avant-garde. But some of the younger American writers of the seventies *have* been moving toward this kind of abstraction, insulating themselves from criticism by a coterie mentality and donning tattered modernist robes of neglect and artistic martyrdom. Abetted by the genuine foolishness of publishers, critics, and lazy readers, they have begun to create an underground fiction that even in its weaknesses resembles the so-called underground cinema of the early sixties, and that will remain underground until it overcomes its own conceptual limitations. Few will consent to turn the pages because their work neglects the sequential, durational element that is much more important in fiction than in painting or poetry, and more important in long fiction (or films) than in short.

As John Barth's *Chimera* (1972) made clear, even a novella can seem interminable when it doesn't move on its own, when like a stubborn nag the author must prod it onward from page to page. This kind of arbitrary sequence is connected to a lack of affect, the absence of deep subjectivity, the failure to engage the reader's full being. Philip Stevick, in his fine essay on the new fiction in *TriQuar-*

terly (Winter 1973), acknowledges this when he quotes Kenneth Burke's point that *"Form* in literature is an arousing and fulfillment of desires. A work has form in so far as one part of it leads a reader to anticipate another part, to be gratified by the sequence." Barth, whose recent work almost disarms criticism by forever saying the worst that can be said about it, himself admits as much in one of his self-reflective digressions:

> How does one write a novella? How find the channel, bewildered in these creeks and crannies? Storytelling isn't my cup of wine; isn't somebody's; my plot doesn't rise and fall in meaningful stages but winds upon itself like a whelk-shell or the snakes on Hermes's caduceus: digresses, retreats, hesitates, groans from its utter et cetera, collapses, dies. ["Bellerophoniad"]

Barth deliberately directs the three novellas in *Chimera* at the crisis of self-consciousness that he perceives in experimental writing, which had been the problematic subject of *Lost in the Funhouse* and had subsequently given him his first taste of writer's block. He is caught in a conflict between his affinity for traditional fiction and his acute sense of its exhaustion, a feeling that its historical moment has passed. His solution in *The Sot-Weed Factor* in 1960 was to outflank the social and psychological realism of the nineteenth century by mimicking an earlier mode. His solution in *Chimera* is to leapfrog even further beyond the conventional novel, "back to the original springs of narrative"; he will return to the earliest myths and legends like those of Scheherazade and Greek mythology, whose patterns, repeated instinctively in so many later stories, he will *consciously* develop and modernize (on the premise, false in my view, that "to write realistic fictions which point always to mythic archetypes is in my opinion to take the wrong end of the mythopoeic stick. . . . Better to address the archetypes directly"). As Barth puts it earlier, "He declared with pleasure that thanks to the inspiration of Scheherazade and to the thousand comforts of his loving wife, he believed he had found his way out of that slough of imagination in which he'd felt himself bogged: . . . he had gone forward by going back, to the very roots and springs of story." Thus, he hopes, without suppressing his self-consciousness by flatly mimicking an archaic mode, he can write stories that are aware that they are stories but also "manage to be seriously, even passionately, *about* some things as well."

Barth's recognition of the value of a subject makes him something of a conservative on the fiction scene of the early seventies, but it does little to save his book. Greek mythology and the Arabian Nights are tough leagues to bat in, and Barth's three novellas manage few palpable hits. Caught between the simple integrity of traditional stories and the demystifying problematics of modernist self-consciousness, Barth realizes neither one nor the other. In *The Sot-Weed Factor,* whatever its limitations, Barth almost had it *both* ways by writing a half-loving, half-mocking version of the eighteenth-century picaresque novel. *There* he invented stories, not yet knowing it couldn't be done. But nothing could seem further from "the original springs of narrative" than the chatty, trivializing tone of *Chimera,* punctuated only by mock-literary pomposities, never by the unself-conscious simplicity of the storyteller. Storytelling is rooted in wonder, in the marvelous, in magical charm, enchantment, even possession. Barth's versions utterly lack vividness, let alone the power to charm or possess. The stories themselves are pallid and hard to follow, swamped by digression and commentary. Barth babbles on about domestic problems, his writer's block, quotes verbatim from his sources, even delivers a critical lecture on his work to date. Some of this is funny, ingenious, and even enlightening, but it all belongs to what Walter Benjamin calls "information," the modern journalistic mode that is the fatal enemy of traditional storytelling, however many stories it claims to tell. As Benjamin puts it,

> Every morning brings us news of the globe, and yet we are poor in noteworthy stories. This is because no event any longer comes to us without being shot through with explanation. . . . Actually, it is half the art of storytelling to keep a story free from explanation as one reproduces it. . . . The most extraordinary things, marvelous things, are related with the greatest accuracy, but the psychological connection of the events is not forced on the reader. ["The Storyteller"]

Instead Barth tries to control the reader's response at every turn, substituting cleverness for imagination, gossipy prattle for myth, the manipulations of the will for spontaneous affect (or effect). There's more feeling for Greek myth in the two pages of Freud's little essay on "Medusa's Head," though Freud makes no pretense at story-telling, than in Barth's laborious novelistic version of the same myth. Barth frequently tries to identify his characters' situation with his own—they too are storytellers, or are entering middle age, or are minor celebrities and feel past it, etc.—but the connections are willed and superficial. For all their comic intent the three stories betray the fear of intersubjectivity that Paul Goodman identified as a prime cause of writer's block.

The relative failure of *Chimera* underlines the limitations of nostalgia as a solution to the dilemmas of experimental fiction. Nostalgia really does take the writer backward rather than forward. Traditional stories, however conscious they may make us of the writer's "creative contradictions," in themselves provide no instrument of creative breakthrough unless the writer experiences them in a new way. Barthelme's *Snow White,* though circumscribed by its linguistic and satirical rigor, was a much more successful book, for in its purity of intention it breaks more drastically with its traditional source. Where Barth's style is mock-dainty, or chatty and low, a lesson in the art of sinking in fiction, Barthelme's language is a model of planned incongruity. Like some of the New York poets, whose playfully surreal styles have similar roots, Barthelme has a background in the visual arts; he edited art journals, did the design for *Fiction* magazine, and illustrated many of his own stories, including a children's book. All his books are attractive objects, informed by an easy elegance and urbanity, and his fictional method is similar to his visual one. Barthelme the designer is principally a collector, who does bizarre collages of nineteenth-century engravings, the effect of which is neither wholly satiric, antiquarian, nor camp, but poised in a vacant eerie zone between nostalgia and irony, mad and mod. Barthelme the writer is also a connoisseur of other people's styles, not so much literary as sub-literary ones—the punishment corner of language, where curious things happen—from Victorian kitsch to modern pop, from professional jargon and journalistic formula to the capacious regions of contemporary cliché. His puckish feeling for other people's oddities of style is what makes *Guilty Pleasures*, his 1974 collection of fables and parodies, such an engaging book. The trash of inert language is his meat and drink. *Snow White* is a book about language, a collage of styles bleached and truncated into one pure and rigorous style of its own. Its fairy-tale subject is a hollow sham, the eye of a word-storm, the common theme of an anthology of ways of not saying anything. Its purity of purpose is cold and bracing: a good book for writers to read, like a verbal purge; or like ordinary-language philosophy, always sharpening the tools. But the book suits the theory of the new fiction a little too well: its surface is rarely ruffled, let alone subverted, by any actuality.

Snow White is an extreme case. Dominated by an austere, bookish wit and a negative appetite for verbal trash, it is a work of severe ironic distance. The perfection of Barthelme's method, now so widely and ineptly imitated, comes in half a dozen stories of *Unspeakable Practices, Unnatural Acts* and nearly everything in its successor, *City Life,* still the most brilliant collection of experimental fiction these last years have produced. In stories like "Brain Damage," "At the Tolstoy Museum," and "Robert Kennedy Saved from Drowning," as I tried to show earlier, the cool mode heats up electrically, and experimental writing proceeds from critique to creation. Where *Snow White* is a clearing of the ground, these stories construct a new fictional reality. They show what even *Snow White* made clear; that Barthelme is no mere collector, but a writer who juxtaposes strange forms and fragments in a way that creates new form and releases new meanings. Where *Snow White* is mainly an ironic book, *City Life* is also an impassioned one. *Snow White* is more sophisticated and condescending but it is experientially vacuous; *City Life* gives free play to that other side of Barthelme's temperament, the melancholy nostalgia for traditional art and old-fashioned feelings, unlike Barth's a nostalgia that animates rather than inhibits him. The longing is hopeless of course—he can't try to be Tolstoy. But he can plumb his ambivalence and make that contribute to the enigma, adding thick shadows to his subject. The Barthian writer escapes from personality; though he babbles about himself incessantly he discovers very little and achieves no deep subjectivity; his self-consciousness tells him that no art, no imagination, is still possible, and the prophecy is self-fulfilling. The Barthelmian writer is scarcely ever present; he loses himself in the oddest, most unpromising subjects—Kierkegaard, Robert Kennedy, angels, the Phantom of the Opera—but the space between passion and irony is filled with new perceptions and connections, self-discoveries, as in all the best fiction. The art is not confessional but it is hauntingly personal, full of mood and mystery, and the author is arrestingly present. Where writers like Wurlitzer, proclaiming the death of feeling, merely betray their own emotional poverty, Barthelme finds new imaginative life in the heart of the contemporary wasteland, in the land of "brain damage," where art shacks up with kitsch and tradition lies down with the New. This art of incongruity brings Barthelme's stories closer to the work of the comic-apocalyptic writers of the early sixties, such as Pynchon, Heller, and Vonnegut—who meet reality halfway, and strike a Faustian bargain— than to the verbal austerities of, say, Gass's fiction, or of his own younger admirers.

Unfortunately Barthelme was unable fully to maintain his creative élan in the early seventies, and his difficulties are symptomatic of the problems of experimental writing during this period. Fiction is one of the few areas of our cultural life where the breakthroughs of the sixties have been sustained, if not carried forward. By the fall of 1973 *Newsweek* could inform its readers that Barthelme had become the greatest influence on our newer writers, but by then it seemed clear that neither the established nor the younger talents had delivered the body of innovative work the late sixties had seemed to promise. Other writers imitated Barthelme's manner rather than his inventive rigor, while he himself fell frequently into shallowness, decadence, and self-imitation. On both sides this resulted not in the kinds of stunning collage and fable that made *City Life* fresh and important but in an epidemic of easy-to-write pastiche or put-on which would have been at home in a college humor magazine of the 1950s.

It was to the credit of Barthelme's next (but weakest) collection of stories, *Sadness* (1972), that he became very conscious of the perils of repetition and self-parody. His main sadness is the fear that he's already said what he has to say:

> When one has spoken a lot one has already used up all of the ideas one has. You must change the people you are speaking to so that you appear, to yourself, to be still alive. ["The Party"]

> It is difficult to keep the public interested.
>   The public demands new wonders piled on new wonders.
>   Often we don't know where our next marvel is coming from.
>   The supply of strange ideas is not endless. . . .
> The new volcano we have just placed under contract seems very promising.
> . . . ["The Flight of the Pigeons from the Palace"]

The realistic writer, who may take his form for granted, in principle need only find another corner of reality to portray, another "subject" for a novel. If he has the energy he can write a *Comédie Humaine;* this may be why writers like Updike and Joyce Carol Oates are so prolific. But the writer who interrogates and subverts his form at every turn has no such luck. He can run out of new wonders very easily, or stick to a manner that quickly degenerates into mannerisms.

Though it contains a few good stories, *Sadness* is a sad case in point, for it exposes the underside of all the writer's virtues. It shows how the collage method fails when the fragments remain disjunctive, unillumined. It shows how the fascination with cultural trash can devolve into a taste for trivia, lovingly collected but barely transformed. It exposes the merely campy side of Barthelme's interest in melodrama, kitsch, and old-fashioned iconography, or the snobbish side, in which the artist flaunts his cultural status while slumming and loving it. The book even betrays the limitations of Barthelme's most basic virtue, his purity of language and narrative technique, which cleans up too much—psychology, description, interaction—leaving only plastic figures with curious names, leaving elegant surfaces that mesh too well with *The New Yorker*'s waning cult of style.

Gates of Eden

Barthelme is at his worst where the realistic writer is best: in describing the relations between men and women. Here he retreats entirely into the satiric and ironic mode of *Snow White* but without that book's freshness and wit. (I suspect this accounts for some of the difficulties he had in writing a second novel.) *Sadness* is much too full of the trivial and the inconsequential, the merely decorative or the merely enigmatic. I have no idea why Barthelme regressed in *Sadness* from the passionate fabulistic manner of his two previous books, except for the reasons he himself suggests, but the lesson for experimental fiction is clear enough. The "cool" mode has its limitations, especially in a period of disengagement and disintegration like our own. When "Robert Kennedy Saved from Drowning" (arguably Barthelme's best story) appeared in book form in the late sixties, an otherwise admiring William Gass dismissed it, no doubt in alarm over its topicality. But the story is both fervently engaged and formally daring. Barthelme needs a great subject, an immediate subject, to draw him at least halfway out of his irony and aesthetic detachment. The feverish immediacy of life in the late sixties, the energy and pressure and swirl, which affected all of us, worked their way into his fiction with a fascinating indirection, just as it ruined some writers who tried to devour it too directly. Without that stimulus, without the pull of social ferment and spiritual possibility, Barthelme's work in *Sadness* looks the same but feels listless and remote, sketched rather than imagined.*

Given the depressed character of the age, the young writer is at a dangerous crossroads. He can pursue his quest for new forms, new spectacles, new shapes for our consciousness, but he must try to do so without abandoning experiential vividness, emotion, actuality. (I assume, perhaps wrongly, that he has a choice.) Whether or not he makes peace with realism he must somehow cope with reality—if

* *The Dead Father* (1975), his second novel, is better but not much better. It abandons the satiric language of *Snow White* for the gusto of Rabelaisian catalogues and word-heaps. Only one segment shows Barthelme at his best: an utterly brilliant but entirely tangential text-within-a-text called "A Manual for Sons," which once appeared separately in *The New Yorker*.

possible in a fresh way—as the early sixties writers did, as the Latin American novelists do. If the sixties were hysterical (in more ways than one), the seventies risk becoming sterile and catatonic, and the writer, bent on refining his instruments, risks becoming part of that reaction. The times have gone from bad to worse, but the artist who is not part of the solution may become part of the problem.

9

Epilogue:
Remembering the
Sixties, Surviving
the Seventies

ONE of the healthier things we learned in the sixties, and are unlikely to forget, was to be more skeptical of the pose of objectivity. When we hear words of wisdom, we want to know who is talking. When the voice of reason speaks, we're inclined to ask what unconscious needs are at work. When we look at the social or economic structure, we want to know whose interests are being served. This skepticism about appearances hardly originated in the sixties; like so much else that happened then, it had its roots in some of the main tendencies of modern art and thought. It was Marx and Freud, among others, who showed us the duplicity of many of our civilized disguises and taught us to look to the mainsprings of power, desire, and personality, just as it was Rousseau and Wordsworth who first showed how much the root of truth lay in the self rather than in any abstract set of values.

It was the artists, with their inherently intense subjectivity, who were quickest to learn that if they expected our credence they had to declare themselves. In the conventions of artistic form, as in religion and philosophy, the old modes of belief and illusion had broken down. The visible brushstroke of the impressionists was a constant reminder that a real man, with actual brush and paint, had worked at an easel to create this object, just as the modernist novel—or the post-Brechtian drama—never lets us fall into the lazy assumption that all this "really happened" to real people. In time we've come to learn the limitations of this galloping self-consciousness: the illusions it still sustains, the thinness and constriction it can impose, the vital (if primitive) satisfactions it can choke off. Periodically, then, each of the arts returns to some of the primary techniques that the avant-garde has called into question—whether it is narrative in fiction, representation in painting, or melody and tonality in music. Yet each time we discover that a naive state of mind can only be approached or imitated, never wholly restored; the fundamental fact of the modern consciousness, what Matthew Arnold called "the dialogue of the mind with itself," cannot really be repealed.

The experimental élan of the arts in the sixties thus had a long prehistory; what was notable about the period was the great extension of self-consciousness to areas other than the arts, to professions and institutions that had greater pretensions to objectivity. Social science, journalism, the law, and even literary criticism conventionally put a premium on impersonality—or on a "value-free" neutrality said to exist in the physical sciences—that would have been unthinkable in the arts. Journalists learned that it was not only safe to participate in the events they described but that their presence and private feelings belonged in the final account. Critics like Daniel Hoffman (in his book on Poe) began to include the affective and subjective elements they had been taught to censor out. A historian like Martin Duberman, also trained in the objective mode, turned his book on Black Mountain College into an illuminating personal dialogue with his well-researched material.

This transformation altered not only the methodology of the observer but the dimensions of the subject. If the critic or historian could bring his own idiosyncratic humanity into the picture, he also could deal more freely with the complex humanity of his material.

249

Gates of Eden

What in criticism was called the Biographical Fallacy collapsed along with the Affective one, and we learned to examine not only texts and institutions but the complex interaction of man and his works. At the same time in social criticism, contemporary institutions came under increasing scrutiny on the old radical principle of "Who? Whom?" (In other words: Who gets the bacon? Who gets screwed?). Social scientists learned how much their doctrine of neutrality served the status quo and the powers that be. Every segment of society, especially where younger professionals had access if not power, spawned its own reformist movement, which today is still far from exhausting its effect on our institutions. Even in a state of economic retrenchment, when many of the innovations and reforms of the sixties get shoved to the back burner, our skeptical, critical habits of mind have proved to be among the sixties' most durable legacies. As our emphasis has shifted from reform to survival we've still managed to preserve the critical framework that enables us to think about alternatives, even when we're told we can no longer afford them.

In the critical and existential climate left to us by the sixties it was inevitable that when the cultural history of the period came to be written, it couldn't be done in a wholly impersonal way. The sixties forced people to declare themselves, and the rifts and polarizations that ensued have only now begun to be bridged. The sixties encouraged us not simply to take sides but to find out who we really were or had the capacity to become. There was a surge of autobiography during the decade, and it's been swelled since by those activist types who were too busy to write then, but found much to write about. My own direct experience of the flow of history in the sixties was intense but peripheral to the great events; having no desire to add to the din, I've tried to keep the impulse to autobiography under control in this book, without falling into a spurious and colorless impersonality. (In any case, the sixties alerted us as much to the distortions of subjectivity as to the fraud and bias of standing above the fray.) It's foolish to make the self the measure of all events, or to aggrandize one's role or importance. But the very act of sitting down to

Remembering the Sixties, Surviving the Seventies

write contains its inevitable portion of egotism. It has taken some pains for writers to learn not to fear the first-person singular, for in the fifties it was forbidden to appear in public without a mask; there were rigidly ascribed roles that made certain personal sentiments look like the height of bad taste. But other people's experience of postwar America will undoubtedly differ in significant ways from mine; I'd like to say more about the tenor of cultural change as I've perceived it, for this study will remain incomplete unless I indicate where it comes from, and how it's rooted in my own life and circumstances.

For me the character of life in the fifties was conditioned above all by an orthodox Jewish background and the chance which brought me to a university that had strong links to the intellectual life of New York. Too much has been written, both in memoir and fiction, about the acculturation of the children of Jewish immigrants for me to repeat any of it here. I came to Columbia in 1957 with glib intellectual gifts, a cheery and studious temperament, a good deal of emotional immaturity, and a quiet, ferocious competitiveness. My first two years were blotted out by culture shock, brought on by massive exposure to Western literature and thought, as well as the whole world of art and performance of New York City, which I had barely penetrated in my cloistered school years. It was an experience of awakening and conversion. The culture of the classics, the play of ideas, and the shock of contemporary art sent tremors through the framework of my old world. Like generations of Jews before me, I had always been oriented toward books and ideas; but orthodox Judaism had built a fence of Law around the Book and had put strict limits on the play of concepts, the adventures of the dialectic. Now I was hungry to read everything, see everything, know everything. The secular culture became like a new religion, with its sacred texts and its oral traditions—though I still kept to much of the old—just as the university became as much a home as the home I had left.

Gradually it dawned on me that my courses were good for something other than grades, and by the middle of my sophomore year I

251

found my friendships shifting from those who shared my background to those who shared my budding intellectual interests. By slow stages we became quite a purposeful and self-confident little group; we followed politics and poetry; we wrote for student journals and began to read *Partisan Review* and *Commentary*. It didn't take long for us to become nostalgic for the thirties, when we hadn't even been born. We started seeing more of our teachers outside of class, hotly arguing with them about the great ideas. Just by being taken seriously, we were quietly being inducted into the intellectual life, whose character was to change quite drastically in the ensuing years.

The New York intellectuals did not yet have much influence in universities in the late fifties, when the New Criticism and Wasp traditions of gentility still reigned; the palmy days of academic acceptance and commercial success did not come until the sixties. Columbia was different, however. Its alumni dominated the publishing world. Its faculty included many of the city's most powerful and elegant minds. The periodicals they wrote for had already played a unique minority role in the nation's cultural life. Passionate about politics and ideas at a time when neither was ascendant in most academic disciplines, they were closer in temperament to zestfully committed European intellectuals than to more dryly professional American academics.

It was surely no accident that the grandly spacious Columbia curriculum was neatly consonant with the aims and ambitious interests of these men. It had been revised in the twenties and thirties to diminish the role of separate departments and to create an interdisciplinary program of general education for all freshmen and sophomores. Instead of an Eng. Lit. survey using anthology snippets, freshmen were plunged directly into the masterworks of literature and philosophy from Homer to Dostoevsky. In place of the introductory course in history or economics there was an intensive study of the evolution of Western civilization that overrode the divisions of the social science disciplines. It was a heady atmosphere of big ideas, great books, and long perspectives. Inevitably, it had its superficial side; in quest of the big picture it touched too many points too rapidly, and the excitement was vulnerable to routinization. But at its best it produced students and teachers who, like European intellectuals, ate, slept, and breathed for ideas. It was this passion which prevented the great books from becoming a remote pantheon of classics. The supposed conflict between tradition and the new was muted or obliterated. Long before the cry of relevance went up in the sixties, the great books were taught, at least at Columbia, in a way that sought to connect them with contemporary life and personal feeling.

When the student uprising ten years later seemed to signal that this connection had lapsed, many senior professors felt deeply betrayed, for the rebels' values and slogans had a distressing resemblance to their own. It was they who had taught that the great books were not only relevant but subversive, that the great writer was, as Solzhenitsyn has put it, not only a center of conscience but a separate government in his country. The critical work of Lionel Trilling, which was central to the ethos of both the Columbia curriculum and the New York intellectuals, assumes this is true of the modern period almost as an axiom: "Any historian of the literature of the modern age will take virtually for granted the adversary intention, the actually subversive intention, that characterizes modern writing—he will perceive its clear purpose of detaching the reader from the habits of thought and feeling that the larger culture imposes, of giving him a ground and a vantage point from which to judge and condemn, and perhaps revise, the culture that produced him." The thread of ambivalence that ran through all of Trilling's work, that gave it its dialectical character, came from his never quite making up his mind about this adversary or subversive intention, from suspending his judgment over it and oscillating with it. But when the students of the sixties rebelled against the adversary culture itself, when they treated it as another conservatism, another establishment against which they could exercise their own adversary impulses, all in the impeccable name of relevance, radicalism, and existential truth, many on the faculty felt that a spiritual abyss had opened up at their feet, ready to swallow them.

At the heart of the rift between the established intellectuals and their rebellious students were differences in their conceptions of culture. What Trilling called the ''adversary culture'' of artists and intellectuals had come by the 1950s to be identified exclusively with high culture. A Columbia education taught a young man to dwell in thought only with the very great, but during the fifties we tended to forget the toil and sweat and compromise on which greatness was often built. As modernism became a religion of the elite, many of the cruder, more popular elements that had sustained modern writers from Dickens to T. S. Eliot had been filtered out. The nasty and difficult personal circumstances—and sometimes even nastier political opinions—of some of these writers were lost to view. The modern writers had indeed become a pantheon, and the culture they sustained, the new writing and criticism they engendered, had become less an engaged and political culture than a purely literary one.

Still, whatever the limitations of being at Columbia and in New York in the late fifties, it was better than almost any place we could have been. Our intense involvement with the modern writers kept us from the exegetical narrowness and remoteness of the New Criticism, or the fatuities of conventional scholarship, which then held sway in most other universities. If the culture of the Great Books had been depoliticized it never ceased to approach literature as a ''criticism of life,'' and thus remained a potent repository of critical and even utopian ideas. If the New York intellectuals had also become increasingly depoliticized after their struggles with Stalinism in the thirties and forties, they remained saturated with history and criticism; schooled on alienation, they never fully took to celebrating the American way of life of the 1950s. Yet their culture had finally become more literary, more belletristic even, than they were ready to admit.

For the impatient students of ten years later, however—whose ''counterculture'' actually inherited many of the ideas of the ''adversary culture'' that had spawned some of their older gurus and theoreticians, such as Paul Goodman and Herbert Marcuse—culture was to be seen above all in its practical and political possibilities. If literature had its utopian and subversive import, if literature was full of incitement to rebellion and self-creation, if it taught us to judge man's life by the standard of quality rather than quantity, by the standard of imagination and full humanity rather than material success, then such visions could not be left to literature alone: they could be fulfilled in actuality. It was paradise now or never.

By the early seventies, of course, time had once again revealed to us the illusions and even dangers of ''paradise now,'' and had disclosed virtues we had slighted in the more traditional literary culture of the fifties. What probably has marked me more than anything was that I came to consciousness between the generations; my formative experiences bridged both the fifties and the sixties, and I never felt wholly comfortable in either world, though both were passionately important to me in their turn. As a personal paradigm, which may have some larger cultural import, I'd like to look more closely at the periods symbolized by the years 1958 and 1968. During the first period I was an undergraduate at Columbia; during the second I was a junior faculty member there, after some years of graduate work in English at Yale and Cambridge.

I came back to teach at Columbia in 1966, after five years' absence, and my first impression was how little had changed. The same men, the same values, dominated the faculty and the administration; the same books that had first plunged me into the life of the mind were the ones I would be teaching to a new wave of freshmen, who were scarcely greener and looked hardly younger than their fresh young instructors. These students had all the bright, eager, unruly articulateness that I remembered from my first classroom days, something I had missed in the undergraduates I had encountered as a graduate assistant at Yale. Soon I discovered the kind of rich, frantic education that goes into the first years of teaching. In the back-breaking humanities course I learned the exhilaration of racing to keep a few steps ahead of one's students. Books I had once studied casually, offhandedly, I now read with a furious intensity: in a few hours I would have to stand and deliver. The Western classics were imprinted on my brain as with a branding iron; I suspected I would never again feel so alive, or so harried.

Gates of Eden

But if the ethos of the university and its cherished texts were unchanged, the world around it had changed considerably. The election of Kennedy and the rhetoric of his inauguration had given my senior year in college a hopeful, activist glow. A spirit of reform would soon undo the lazy, phlegmatic mood of the fifties, or at least so we hoped. But by 1966 it was clear that the activist spirit had fallen into the hands of malevolent demons, determined to establish their masculinity at others' expense. The bombing of North Vietnam, begun by a ruse, had continued daily for over a year and a half, while the ground war was being escalated by stealth and guile. A fear and hatred of military service already hung over the students; they felt locked in and fell prey to gloomy feelings of disaffection and alienation—not directed especially at the university—yet they also began to enjoy a boisterous freedom from social constraint. Between this malaise of feeling and a casual hedonism, between spiritual hunger and a radical politics, the adversary ethos of modernism was becoming real, in the flesh, in a generation that found little in society to trust or believe.

The effects of this mood showed up very little in the classroom, especially where the instructor shared its premises. The curriculum of Columbia College was geared as little toward professionalism and as much toward the liberal arts as can be imagined; the books we read together, from the Greeks through Shakespeare and the nineteenth century, were not recent or trendy but they were supremely relevant, and had their own adversary implications. They had an uncanny way of giving historical dimension to our own immediate joys and griefs. There was something phantasmagorical about studying Thucydides during the Vietnam war. His account of the moral and military decline of Athens and especially the doomed Sicilian expedition had just the exemplary meaning he intended; the parallel to America's overseas adventure was overwhelming and inescapable. Only the last chapter remained to be written.

If a community of feeling between students and young instructors left the student body looking less changed than it was, in one respect it was visibly different. Columbia had begun active recruiting among

256

minority groups, and the first large number arrived in 1966. In the Columbia of the fifties—only two blocks from Harlem—a black face was almost as rare as a woman with tenure. (I never had a course with a woman in four years of college.) In 1963 Martin Luther King had told a historic rally in Washington that he had a dream. Three years later, thanks to the pressures of the civil rights movement, some of the children of the dream were sitting in my classes. In April 1968 they would emerge into the national spotlight, playing a fateful and distinctive role in the campus uprising.

By the late sixties, however, black separatism and nationalism were altering the character of the civil rights movement. Most whites no longer felt welcome, and in 1968 black students actually asked white radicals to leave Hamilton Hall not long after its seizure: it became a strictly segregated revolution. Thus, during the most hectic years of the protest movement, from 1966 to 1969, it was antiwar feeling and, finally, university reform, not racial injustice, that most galvanized white middle-class students. While the university changed very little, the tenor of life around it, within it, altered and quickened. A canker of rage and frustration was eating away at America; the university was only a flash-point. For someone like me, not given to physical bravura, the succession of marches and demonstrations, each necessary in its own way, was like learning a new language. There were moments of ironic conjunction, when we had to speak both languages almost at once. I recall a day in April 1967 when I finished my thesis in the morning, went downtown to march against the war in the afternoon, and raced up to New Haven to deposit the manuscript in the evening. Another ironic scene occurred at an early morning anti-draft demonstration on Whitehall Street in New York a year later. A group of craggy, burly longshoremen on their way to work began heckling some of the protesters with comments like "Get washed, hippies!" and "Take a bath!" A typical moment, except that in this case the immediate objects of their scorn were some impeccably groomed suburban matrons. The social abyss between protesters and hard-hats gave their relationship a purely abstract, mythmaking character. It was one of the ironies of the sixties that protest was so much a middle-class phenomenon, while the children of the working class, who were less likely to have the protection of college deferments, were actually dying in the war.

This may help explain why so many instances of class resentment occurred between young protesters and the police. To the students the police, the agents of repressive authority, became dehumanized into "pigs," while the police in many celebrated instances took their revenge in the flesh with their billy clubs. This happened most dramatically during the Democratic convention in Chicago in 1968, but the same thing had occurred on a smaller scale a few months earlier when police were finally called in to remove the Columbia students from the buildings they occupied. While handling the black students in Hamilton Hall with precision and restraint, elsewhere they let loose with a wanton brutality and a good deal of unnecessary damage to the university itself. The overall effect, not unwelcome to the SDS, was to cripple the moral legitimacy of the administration and to "radicalize" the large moderate mass of students. Why did the cops behave this way? Though personal frustration and resentment undoubtedly played their part, there was clearly an explosion of class anger at the whole elite institution and at frivolous middle-class kids who were squandering an educational opportunity that they and their children would never have. While some of the officers stood in visible awe before the august rotunda of Low Library, a few yards away a flippant young radical poet sat with a cigar in his mouth and his feet on the president's desk. (Like everyone else, cops and kids included, he'd seen too many movies.)

What the policemen failed to understand was the different forms education can take. (Obviously their view of the learning process inclined them toward corporal punishment.) During the entire week when many on the faculty were working to conciliate the situation and keep the police from being called, what was going on was nonstop education. The students were completely existential revolutionaries, learning the whole gamut of political strategies and possibilities as they went along. The faculty were putting their abstract liberalism to the most immediate test, trying to distinguish between protest, disobedience, obstruction, disruption, intimidation, and a dozen other shades of activist strategy. We thought about the difference between force and consent. We thought about academic freedom. We thought about the relation of scientists and intellectuals to the war machine. We thought about the relations between the university and the outside world, including its own local community. We thought about the service functions of the university as against its commitment to the disinterested pursuit of knowledge. We thought about who owned the university, and whether it was truly equipped to play an oppositional role in society.

For me in particular there was one rude personal shock. The university had always centered for me on the literary culture, the community of ideas, the culture of the great books, which had helped form me and which I had come to love. Actually, however, unlike the other Ivy League schools, we were a rather small college in a large, disparate, and impersonal university, which had always been administered, as Jacques Barzun once said (before he himself became an administrator), like a bank. Now all the other Columbias came crawling out of the woodwork, including a handful of flaming Luddite students and stiff-necked administrators who had no commitment at all to our idea of a university, who were quite ready to risk destroying it to forward their own aims. In this situation the faculty were thrown back on their conscience and whatever quantum of vision illuminated it. At the furthest extremes a few faculty members were eager to smash heads, and said so repeatedly, while a few others regretted that they couldn't join the students occupying the buildings. Among the larger majority, some faculty members discovered that their liberalism meant mainly order and peace, whatever the cost; for others it meant protest and reform, even at the risk of abridging some personal rights, such as the rights of non-protesting students to attend classes. Astoundingly, the university had no representative governing body in which the crisis could be discussed. Its trustees and its president were living in another century. Each faction on campus wore its own colored armband and published its own set of theses and broadsides. I belonged to a self-constituted group of concerned faculty who stayed in session day and night to discuss the issues, to conciliate the factions, to advance the cause of reform and preserve an atmosphere of consensus and rational debate. Unfortunately the students and administrators only pretended to negotiate through us; each sought total capitulation, and since that was hardly likely, both were hell-bent on bringing in the police, the one "solution" we were working to avoid. My hopes for a peaceful solution, which in retrospect proved so futile, finally showed me that I *was* a liberal rather than a radical, but it also made me more antipathetic to the law-and-order liberalism that was just beginning to crystallize and which, by a backlash effect, would mushroom in strength over the ensuing years.

It was precisely my liberalism and my pacific, law-abiding temperament that made the last years of the sixties so full of conflict for me. The antiwar movement and the push for domestic equality and justice seemed absolutely right and honorable to me, but when the movement went from dissent to resistance I followed it more in spirit than in practice. I never burned my draft card, never withheld my taxes, and was never arrested, though there were a few times when I could have been. I'll never forget how my heart pounded at the Pentagon in the fall of 1967, when my wife and I crossed a gully and trampled a fence that separated the legally designated protest area (a barren, meaningless parking lot) from the lawn that lay at the steps of the Pentagon. It was but a modest example of the way conscience and frustration forced people to overstep the "law" in the sixties, but for me it was a Rubicon, it meant a great deal.*

The parking field epitomized the pointless, frustrating, isolated lot

* Growing up, I had always been a good boy. It was hard to know what "good" meant anymore. Was killing people good? Was smoking dope good? Was group sex good? Was it good if it felt good, as Hemingway said, or only if it were conducive to the Good? The sixties were more given to the collective loss of inhibition, the assertion of group ethos and solidarity, than to collective law-breaking. Not since Prohibition had there developed such a gap between the stated norms of society and the actual behavior. In one way or another a large number of Americans learned to live outside the pale, as it were, in a separate state, an alternative culture. Later, some of the wide-eyed, clean-cut malefactors of Watergate used this to validate their own special norms and "dissident" behavior.

the government had relegated to the dissenters. Our feelings oscillated wildly at each of the marches and demonstrations. At times we felt that because of our numbers and the justice of our cause the nation couldn't fail to take notice: policy would change, the voice of the people would have spoken. At other times, especially after years of similar manifestations, we recognized the practical futility of what we were doing. Yet somehow this feeling redoubled the need to do it. The prevailing mood on these occasions demanded a gesture of conscience; it arose from a compulsion to bear personal witness. As with so much associated with the New Left, stringent moral categories predominated over realistic political ones. Vietnam made us sick, made us feel like exiles, robbed us of an image of this nation that we desperately needed. By marching we tried to purge ourselves of the least trace of inner complicity with the war; we stepped outside the national consensus and reached out for solidarity with others who shared an alternative idea of America. This is why the marches were invariably better than the rallies that followed: at the rallies the rhetoric and politics took over again.

This feeling of solidarity and community gave many of these protest events a festive air; at times they were hard to distinguish from the colorful human be-ins and other countercultural celebrations, which also aimed at preserving a utopian communal ideal in a period of strife and polarization. The atmosphere resembled the festivities of an ethnic group coming together to reaffirm its common identity: a shared culture, shared values, shared music and language, and a common feeling of special virtue and distinctness, which the culture at large helped to solidify. At times the benign, generous texture of life, the heady human atmosphere, was a wonder to behold, even under trying circumstances. I remember bringing my two-year-old son to the Columbia campus one day during the occupation of the buildings. It was the first warm day of spring, everyone was in a dreamlike mood, and as we sat on the grass the campus looked more tranquil and serene than ever. Two days later, mounted police would be chasing students and bystanders across the lawn, backing them up against the stone walls of the library. But for an instant the illusory ideal of an open university in an open society, without hierarchy, with everyone doing his thing, seemed like a reality. It felt like Paris under the Commune, and proved equally fragile. The sixties were a lesson in the inspiriting power and irrationality of utopian visions. I suspect that they'll continue to exercise a secret fascination over the minds of a whole generation that experienced them most dramatically.

What was most amazing was that my own fifties education had not unfitted me for utopian visions of any sort. It was reading Trilling's *The Liberal Imagination* at the end of my sophomore year of college that most crystallized my desire to become a critic and writer, and in many ways I could not have had a better model. Trilling not only wrote well but wrote as a man speaking to men, not an academic specialist plying his trade. (The opaque, private quality of much recent French and American criticism must have been deeply offensive to him.) In his writing, literature exfoliated into issues of politics and culture, psychoanalysis and personal destiny. Coming directly out of a religious tradition, I couldn't fail to respond powerfully to a treatment of texts that brought them to bear so directly on experience, on morality, on behavior. But politically *The Liberal Imagination* was characteristic of the postwar period (and characteristic of the New York intellectuals) in its attack on ideology, whether the object of its attack was liberalism or, by implication, socialism. Liberalism, he says in his preface, as it aims for a rational organization of life, drifts toward an impoverished human ideal, drifts toward a denial of the emotions and the imagination, a restraint upon human "variousness and possibility." It was exactly the same criticism that the Victorian culture critics had leveled against Benthamite utilitarianism and later against popular democracy. They accused Bentham of a mechanical, quantitative notion of personality, against which they set up the qualitative standards and humane visions that were enshrined above all in the arts. Their prescient criticisms could be applied just as well to modern Stalinism and vulgar Marxism, as many conservatives since have done. Yet the Victorians did not confine themselves to criticizing the Benthamite "left"; they rightly discerned the same mechanical norms and values in the prevailing industrial society of the bourgeoisie, which had adopted laissez-faire liberalism as its official rationale. Thus men like Carlyle, Dickens, and Ruskin, by instinct conservative, became both critics of society and critics of the dominant alternatives, critics of the entrenched liberalism as well as the Benthamite pragmatic radicalism.

It was this ambiguous ground, neither left nor right—though in some ways to the left of the left—that Trilling tried to occupy in *The Liberal Imagination*. Along with Leavis in England, he lay claim to a tradition of cultural criticism that was as applicable to the present as it had been a hundred years earlier. Like his mentor Arnold, but without the *éclat* and impact that Arnold could have in a smaller, more cohesive culture, he aimed to become the gadfly of liberalism from within, "to recall liberalism to its first essential imagination of variousness and possibility." Unlike Arnold, who had only literature as his ally—literature and theology, really—Trilling had not only literature but the complex imagination of modernism and the paradoxical discoveries of psychoanalysis. His goal was to convince the political mind, the ideological mind, to enlarge its range of human awareness. But equally he would try to restore to the literary mind some of the social and historical awareness *it* was rapidly losing.

It was an inherently ambiguous project. It involved not only a shifting dialectic between politics and literature but a reorientation of the relations between liberalism, radicalism, and conservatism. As with the Victorians, Trilling's critique of liberalism worked equally well from the left or the right, for it was an expression of Tory radicalism or what Mailer liked to call "left conservatism." By attacking vulgar leftism in the name of a more ample, more qualitative human vision, it was consistent with both conservatism and a truly humanist radicalism, such as the revisionist Marxism of the early Lukács and the Frankfurt school. With this ambiguous legacy it was no surprise that so many of Trilling's followers, whom he rarely encouraged, took sharply different routes in their own careers. Some became rarefied fifties aesthetes, remote from all interest in politics, some ended up in the New Left, while others turned up in the pages

Gates of Eden

of the *National Review*; all remained true to the implications of his work, in their fashion. At the same time his own writing became ever more Hamlet-like, more sad and ironic, and more detached.

It would be presumptuous of me to speak for others, but I can now see more clearly why Trilling's earlier work had so great an impact on me, which paradoxically led me to diverge from the course he himself was taking. Even as a child I had always been fascinated by politics, including the crass electoral kind, just as my father was. I remember sitting up late one night in 1948 listening to the electoral returns on the radio while my father, a union man, explained, probably for the hundredth time, why he supported Truman over Henry Wallace. (Twenty years later I would find myself in a similar fix with friends, groping to justify a last-minute vote for Hubert Humphrey.) *The Liberal Imagination* seemed to suggest a new way of bringing literature and politics into conjunction. Overtly, it was a defense of the imagination against the encroachments of political thinking, whether Marxist, populist, or liberal. But although it discredited the mobilization of culture to serve an ideological cause, it fostered a more complex ideological consciousness, a more subtle politics, a more oblique *engagement*, modeled upon literature and the imagination. When such a new consciousness began to emerge in the late fifties, and came to fruition in the sixties, Trilling's work had helped prepare me to receive it. For reasons of his own, however, he reacted with ambivalence, which gradually turned to deep hostility, as if he himself felt somehow implicated.

Trilling never joined the ranks of backlash intellectuals who devoted themselves to polemics in the sixties, whose work became so tendentious that it vitiated the qualities of rational disinterestedness they claimed to defend. Instead his later work is marked by a high degree of withdrawal—an increasing remoteness from politics and from contemporary literature, a vein of quietism which comes into *The Opposing Self* (1955), an echo-chamber of ironies that puzzled readers and reviewers of *Beyond Culture* (1965). In an essay on Freud in the mid-fifties, when the pressures of social conformity were at their greatest, Trilling wrote that the "intense conviction of the existence of the self apart from culture is, as culture well knows, its noblest and most generous achievement. At the present moment it must be thought of as a liberating idea. . . .'' *At the present moment.* By the time of *Sincerity and Authenticity* (1972) Trilling must have surprised even himself by writing a book *against* authenticity, which he defines precisely as the quest for self-definition apart from the norms of the culture. Instead he defends the older, more quaint ideal of ''sincerity,'' which he describes oddly as the acceptance of the conditioned life, an acknowledgement that we are not entirely free, and a willingness to seek self-definition within the terms laid down by society. What Emerson called the ''national sincerity'' of the English, he says, can be ascribed ''to the archaic intractability of the English social organization: the English sincerity depends upon the English class structure.''

Trilling isn't unaware of the paradoxical character of such a statement, or the extent to which it might be taken as a piece of self-betrayal. For centuries foreign observers have described hypocrisy as *le vice anglais;* for Trilling to convince us to substitute sincerity was scarcely to be expected, even on the authority of Emerson. The passage must be understood as the culmination of Trilling's quarrel with the modern, especially the American, temperament, which had been developing inexorably for two decades. In 1950 in *The Liberal Imagination* Trilling had defended the autonomy of the literary imagination as an antidote to the crude politicization of culture, which he associated with the Stalinists. But in the years that followed, as the pressures of politicization abated and disappeared, he came to be disturbed by a division within the imagination itself—between the minute sense of the conditioned life that he saw in the nineteenth-century social novel and the apocalyptic fierceness and negativity that he saw in the modern writers. For some years Trilling gave a course on these writers in Columbia College, and his affinity for them was very great. As a critic he had helped rout the genteel tradition in American letters and pave the way for the acceptance of modernism. When he came to lecture on Frost he described his belated discovery that he too was a modern writer; only then had he come to admire him.

Trilling was also one of the first to perceive the affinity between modernism and the apocalyptic strain in modern social life. "The predilection for the powerful, the fierce, the assertive, the personally militant, is very strong in our culture," he wrote as early as 1950. Much later in an interview, in one of his few direct comments on the upsurge of radicalism in the sixties, he suggested that the protesting students were practicing "modernism in the streets." * But had there ever been a modernism that was content to remain in the closet or in the library? It was precisely here that the intellectuals of the fifties defaulted, by fashioning an academic modernism that was a threat to no one. Trilling, on the other hand, always took modernism seriously, and insisted (I think excessively) that it was grounded in alienation and opposition. But as he grew older and more conservative, his sensibility, like that of Leavis and Lukács, became increasingly rooted in the great novels of bourgeois realism and the solid character-building values of bourgeois society. What he says of Marcuse near the end of *Sincerity and Authenticity* undoubtedly applies to himself as well: Marcuse "prefers the character-structure shaped by a non-permissive society. . . . He *likes* people to have 'character', cost what it may in frustration." But there's a distinction here that Trilling doesn't adequately draw. For Marcuse the paternalistic structure of bourgeois society gives the young person something firm to rebel against, something outside the self that can temper its mettle. But Trilling came increasingly to admire and defend bourgeois values themselves.

To most young people of my generation the "non-permissive society" of the fifties seemed anything but character-building, though it had built us. There seemed to be little virtue and much neurosis and suffering to be gained from growing up in a world that was sanctimonious, repressive, prudish, hypocritical, and intolerant. When the radical prophets of a new consciousness appeared toward the end of the fifties—some of them, like Norman O. Brown, under Trilling's

---

* Compare Saul Bellow on the sixties: "The dreams of nineteenth-century poets polluted the psychic atmosphere of the great boroughs and suburbs of New York." (*Mr. Sammler's Planet*)

patronage—it seemed like a breath of air from another world, as free from the clichés of Old Left radicalism as from the bromides of social conformity. It was an actualization not only of the subversive possibilities of the literary imagination, which had been such a staple of my education, but of its vision of human "variousness and possibility." As the sixties proceeded, the radicalism of the students developed all the spontaneity and affect that had been missing from the mechanical, systematic ideology of the Old Left, which mirrored the established order in prizing organization and discipline, and in its contempt for empirical truth and personal vision. The New Left, on the contrary, cherished individuality and had a surplus of vision, as if it were aware of its literary roots. As the occupants of the Sorbonne put it in 1968, *L'imagination au pouvoir:* "The bourgeois revolution was judicial; the proletarian revolution was economic. Ours will be social and cultural so that man can become himself" (part of the "Appeal from the Sorbonne" of June 13-14, 1968).

It was not modernism that was responsible for the alienation of the young in the sixties, but modernism contributed to the cultural form and the utopian content which that dissidence took on. To criticize "modernism in the streets" was to slight the reality of war, racism, inequality, and social anomie that had brought the youthful left to birth, that made alienation and opposition the only honorable course, not something perverse and arbitrary. Eventually it did splinter off into something perverse and arbitrary, but only after the frustration of its generous hopes and humanist tactics of nonviolent persuasion. I saw this happen within a period of a few months among my own students at Columbia in 1968. I spoke earlier of the "existential," spontaneous character of the young protesters, and of the New Left in general. It was as if the movement had been designed unconsciously to respond to the criticisms leveled at Stalinism. If the Old Left was Benthamite and materialist, the New Left was almost obsessed with "the quality of life." If the Old Left distrusted emotion and individuality and demanded organizational (even conspiratorial) discipline, the New Left was almost anarchic in its relish for individual display, in its scrupulousness about ends and means, in its moral fervor and utopianism. It aimed not to appropriate the means of production but to change the character of human relations. In that sense its origins *were* literary, and it lacked the hard-headed political outlook that informed the old-line militants. There's no question that the combination of political and cultural radicalism that made the sixties unique was soft on the political side. It saw the whole political arena as compromised, tainted, and only gross abuses like the war could stoke its moral passion and galvanize its political energy.

This became clear at Columbia in the difficulty the students had in defining their goals and demands. One need not agree with Trilling, who said in an interview that "the explicit issues were largely factitious," to recognize that the surge of protest was out of proportion to the particular complaints. (These involved the encroachment of a new gym onto Harlem park land and the involvement of the university in an institute for defense research.) The immediate issues were merely symbolic of larger questions of racism, community relations, and the war in Vietnam, just as the university itself was made to symbolize the whole of society. In attacking the university the students were acting on the impeccable principle that radicalism begins at home, not in some distant rice paddies, but in doing so they risked destroying one of the few institutions in society that was sympathetic to their needs, that was relatively insulated from the social consensus and capable of playing an adversary role (or at least protecting those who did). Beneath the political demands the students were playing out a psychodrama of self-validation, which involved above all the demystification of authority. The radical poet with his feet on the president's desk was making a calculated, insouciant affront to the sense of hierarchy and decorum that shields society and its institutions from searching criticism and structural change. We can recognize the same kind of theater, the same significant mockery, in all the manifestations of "dirty" words, exhibitionistic sex, and personal unconventionality of the young rebels of the sixties. It was an assertion of self, yes, but in a way that proved once again that the personal *is* political, for it also aimed at democratizing our institutions and making them more participatory. For a brief moment the university was turned into a microcosm, a laboratory, for direct democracy in society as a whole.

Eventually, after the initial shock, most of our institutions learned how to defuse this democratic thrust, by changing just enough, and transferring power to slick and flexible new elites that schooled themselves in specially developed techniques of counter-insurgency. Our institutions learned to contain protest in the same existential way the protesters had learned to make trouble. But the students themselves were also responsible for the waning of the democratic spirit, for they gradually developed their own leadership elites that were contemptuous of the torpor and impurity of the mass of ordinary men. I mentioned earlier how the use of the police and their resort to excessive force had "radicalized" a large part of the student body and faculty. But there was something about this inchoate moral indignation that didn't satisfy the increasingly militant leaders of the SDS. For six weeks the campus became a colorful bazaar of experimental courses and political rap-sessions. Looking back to that period, I can't help but think of every exhilarated description of revolutionary situations in the brief utopian interval between birth and betrayal, as Wordsworth in *The Prelude* described post-revolutionary Europe "thrilled with joy,/ France standing on the top of golden hours,/ And human nature seeming born again." * When the summer vacation came it merely seemed like a recess; instead it would prove fatal to this whole atmosphere. Early in June came the assassination of Robert Kennedy, which effectively shattered hopes for change within the system, and then in August the confrontation with the police in the streets of Chicago. I was working that summer on a task force charged by the faculty with "restructuring" the university, and I was glumly aware how few of our proposals could ever be adopted. But the SDS leaders were busy turning themselves into a cell of committed revolutionaries, a Leninist vanguard that was becoming disdainful of the mass of students it felt called upon to educate and lead. They were looking for a systematic, Marxist analysis.

* As he puts it later, even more extravagantly: "Bliss was it in that dawn to be alive,/ But to be young was very Heaven."

Gates of Eden

They were looking to trade in spontaneity and openness for revolutionary purity. Each time I met one of them, including students I had known for two years, I caught more of the opaque rhetoric and puritanical zeal of the Old Left, but without its genuine feeling for the strenuous, difficult lives of workers and social outcasts. Words like *fascism, imperialism,* and *neo-colonialism* began to cloud the air and make thinking and communication next to impossible. There wasn't yet a Weatherman faction, but by August 1968 I could see its self-destructive outlines with dismaying clarity. By the time of the "days of rage" a year later in Chicago, which forced many SDS leaders to go underground, Nixon was president and student radicalism was just another way of venting frustration and anger. Student dropouts solicited "bail money" from their old instructors . . . to help stock a bomb factory on West 11th Street. Like the hapless anarchists in Conrad's *Secret Agent,* they managed to blow up only their own. The student movement had come at last to fulfill the destructive irrational image that many older people had long since projected on it. In its impulse toward ever-increasing radicalism, always upping the ante to keep up revolutionary purity, it lost most of its followers and played directly into the hands of its enemies; violence and outright criminality, *that* they knew how to deal with, that made no disturbing moral claim upon them.

There's certainly no reason to take satisfaction in what happened, especially now that the poisonous mood in which the sixties ended has given way to the torpid, constricted climate of the seventies. Though 1968 was one of the nodal years in American history, it's hard to think of a single good thing that happened then. The Tet offensive broke the back of our escalation in Vietnam and led to Johnson's withdrawal, but the assassinations of King and Kennedy dashed hopes for nonviolent change, as did the repression in Chicago, the nomination of Humphrey, and the election of Nixon. Within the space of a year the protest movement crested and shattered, and a pernicious right-wing government without principle but with an insidious appetite for power was installed. In retrospect, what followed has all the hallmarks of inevitability. The three chief developments in American public life in the early seventies were not the result of a new phase but merely the garbage of an older one, the unfinished business of the sixties.

In a way the Watergate affair was an oblique postmortem triumph for the New Left, even more than the withdrawal of Johnson. The presence of dissenters fed the paranoid fantasies of the new men in Washington; it fueled and, in their minds, justified their pursuit of power by any means. And Nixon's complete defeat of the Left led to a feeling of omnipotence, as if to say: "Congress and the press are on the run, the left is weak and demoralized, and we own the organs of justice. They can never touch us." This was in essence the reasoning that led to otherwise incomprehensible and foolhardy acts of overreaching. Unshaken from without, the governing clique collapsed on its own from overconfidence and inanition. I needn't apply such subtle reasoning to the collapse of our client state in Vietnam to show that it too belonged among the unfinished business of the sixties. In Vietnam we lost not only a war and a subcontinent; we also lost our pervasive confidence that American arms and American aims were linked somehow to justice and morality, not merely to the quest for power. America was defeated militarily but the "idea" of America, the cherished myth of America, received an even more shattering blow. The third collapse of the seventies, the collapse of the economy, can also be traced back to the sixties, particularly to Johnson's duplicitous prosecution of the war. According to some economists, it was Johnson's failure to press for a tax increase early in 1967—his refusal to admit that we actually were fighting a full-scale war—that led to the first waves of inflation and finally, with the help of the oil cartel, to the disastrous combination of inflation, recession, and unemployment that hit the country so hard by the fall of 1973.

The temporary breakdown of the economy by 1974–75, our severest recession since World War II, made a more drastic alteration in the ambiance inherited from the sixties than anything else I have mentioned. At first it seemed as if the seventies would treat us to a rerun of the 1950s, but the fifties were a period of growing affluence:

it took money to foot the bill for all that complacency. The sixties were more affluent still; a relaxed, abundant economic climate gives more prominence to leisure, more latitude to culture and consciousness. It takes a firm structure to support a large superstructure; culture and sensibility belong to the superstructure, and their importance has diminished in the climate of mere survival that has developed in the seventies. If the watchwords of the sixties were self-expression and self-development, now many were content with simply getting by. (Students, for example, shifted from the liberal arts to bread-and-butter courses and desperate grade-grubbing.) The reasons involve more than our fiscal resources: depression is a psychological fact, not simply an economic one. We've been through nothing comparable to the great Depression, and the economic situation affected Americans very unevenly. But a sense of pinched possibilities, failed utopian visions, and exhausted psychological resources had a constricting effect on the arts, which in this case accurately mirrors the constrictions of consciousness in our ordinary lives. Getting and spending continue, and many have recoiled from Promethean hopes to discover the pleasures of domesticity, family, and the private life, or the satisfactions of professionalism and disciplined work. Many who delayed child-bearing in the sixties have begun raising a family; some are discovering with surprise how much it can tell them about their own identities. The success of the women's movement in surviving the debacle of sixties radicalism undoubtedly depends on its intimate rapport with problems of personal identity, which other kinds of activism tended to blur. The persistence of occultism and the vogue of meditation techniques are another version of the same inward shift in American culture.

Cultural change always includes a great deal of persistence and continuity along with dramatic shifts in emphasis. There is a sense in which certain doors, having once been opened, can never quite be shut again. Less than an epoch but more than an episode, the sixties are likely to remain a permanent point of reference for the way we think and behave, just as the thirties were. The sexual freedoms that were granted or seized in the sixties have not been repealed, though some more flamboyant kinds of sexual experimentation may have diminished; the promised nirvana never materialized, and sex without feeling was found to have its drawbacks. We've learned anew that after the death of God everything is possible, everything is permitted, but, alas, not everything is necessary. Personal relationships have remained more tentative and experimental, perhaps less anxiety-ridden, while the divorce rate shows that our private lives have fewer solid moorings than ever. The public appetite for sexual display has certainly not abated, and it's hard to imagine returning to the moralism and hypocrisy that preceded the sixties.

Neither have we witnessed a complete about-face in the political sphere. The politics of radical activism made available to us not only critical habits of mind but strategies of direct action that continue to be used on particular issues and in local encounters. Even the fiscal crisis in New York, although it stymied and disheartened liberals with a sense of diminished resources and shrinking options, did not cow the populace into the complete passivity that was characteristic of the fifties. The resurgence of group identity among ethnic groups, which took its early cues from black militance, has continued. The fifties' belief in the old American ideal of the melting pot, with its implications of conformity, homogenization, and hundred-percent Americanism, seems irrevocably shattered. It sacrificed too much, demanded that too much be repressed; like so much else in the fifties it conflicted with the exigencies of personal identity, which the fifties claimed to value so highly.

Yet the inward turning of recent years lacks the radical subjectivity that marked the search for authentic selfhood in the sixties. The meditating self is really an abeyance of self: it seeks less its own individuality than a generalized tranquility that reminds us of those promises of "peace of mind" that we heard in the fifties. Nor do any of the other quickie therapies that have displaced Freudianism show much tolerance for the strenuous labors of individuation. It can scarcely be said that the seventies have yet shown a cultural accent of their own, but there are a few straws in the wind that seem to confirm this decline of interest in the individual self. The most dramatic and widely debated new idea in literary criticism, Harold Bloom's theory of "the anxiety of influence," emphasizes the intersubjectivity of poets as poets rather than the individuality of the poet as a person, a living subject. The contemporary poets that Bloom favors—John Ashbery and A. R. Ammons, for example, or the later John Hollander—write in a cooler, less subjective mode than the poets of the sixties, in a mode that tends toward meditative abstraction. An elusive and daunting intellectuality, whose exemplar is Wallace Stevens, has begun to displace the bardic directness of Whitman and his brood. The belated arrival of structuralism and post-structuralist French thought in our academic life contributes to new methods that eliminate the living subject entirely, as Bloom does not.

A similar emphasis on structure and system over personality can be found in Robert M. Pirsig's widely read autobiographical work, *Zen and the Art of Motorcycle Maintenance*, which appeared in 1974. If any single book reveals a distinct post-sixties outlook it is this one. At first Pirsig entices us with narrative and personal mystery, but as the book goes on he eschews the novelistic strategies that first drew our interest. He wants to catapult us beyond the sphere of personality, beyond his own experiences, into a platonic realm of Truth itself. Thus he distinguishes between "romantic" knowledge, which in his view is of the surface, subjective and emotional, and "classical" knowledge, which inheres in the system of life itself. The romantic type in Pirsig's book values the motorcycle for its energy and thrust but has no interest in it as a machine, whereas the classical mind is engaged by the machine as a system in itself, an underlying form, rather than simply a vehicle for experience. Clearly the romantic mind, which Pirsig caricatures by relegating it to aesthetics and surfaces, is the mind of the sixties, with its fascination with movement, flow, and energy, its experiential appetite, its contempt for the machine. Part of the dissident spirit of the sixties was surely Luddite. It saw machines everywhere, and was determined to break them or shut them down: the war was a machine, society was a machine, even the university was a machine producing cogs for society. Chaplin's vision of the assembly line was the students' image of the world into which they had been born. If the Old Left would have been content to take over the machine, the young in the sixties were determined either to stop it from functioning or drop out of the whole system. Pirsig's classical attitude is just as clearly a post-sixties perspective: systems-analysis rather than dropping out of the system. How widespread it may become is anyone's guess. It's already been applied in the fiscal crisis, where those decreeing the cutbacks, including many longtime liberals, have swallowed their qualms and learned to treat people as economic ciphers. In New York the bankers have tried to repeal not only the sixties but liberalism in general.

I hope I haven't left the impression that all the signs of the present decade have been negative. Every cultural phase, whatever its limitations, has its distinct accent, its own contribution. The shift away from subjectivity and romantic "excess," for example, has given new life and patronage to dance companies that had struggled for many years to gain attention. Dance in the sixties was amateur, free-form, and expressive, something everyone did for himself. It suggested that each of us could find the contours of his own energy, however gauche or unaesthetic the result might be. (The jerky stage mannerisms of rock musicians, for example, were always palpably sexual rather than aesthetic.) Like everything else in the sixties, the music was a siren song telling us to let go, to be ourselves, not to follow any formal steps. In the seventies, however, we have come more to appreciate the grace and intelligence of disciplined movement, whether in Balanchine's dancers or in professional athletes. This kind of movement requires more than liberating one's energy and overcoming physical inhibition; on the contrary, it demands years of laborious training and control. Its expressiveness is great but different, for it treats the whole body as an expressive instrument, not as a self-justifying, self-delighting entity in itself.

This may be the crux of our most recent cultural phase. It's not simply that our mood shifts like a pendulum between the classical and romantic attitude. Such shifts are both inevitable and, in some degree, useful. The culture of the sixties had a liberating effect on many of our lives—it certainly did for me—but while we need to remain free, we don't need to be perpetually liberated. The university freed me from a strict and confining religious tradition, just as the sixties freed me not only from physical inhibitions but from some of the more constricting channels of academic work. But once we are liberated we must learn from scratch to do something with our freedom, to make the best use of whatever gifts we have. Sometimes that involves the submission to discipline, perhaps even a revolution of diminished expectations. For whatever it's worth, this book is one way I've tried to use my own freedom and some portion of my talents. Without the sixties I probably couldn't have written it in quite this way, for the combination of literary criticism, cultural history, politics, and personal reminiscence would have seemed less imaginable, more illegitimate. Perhaps my time could have been spent writing a solid book on Wordsworth or Carlyle, or preparing for classes, or lying in the sun. Even so, if it's not the book I might have dreamed of writing, it's at least the one I've actually written.

Inscribing *Finis,* I find this epilogue has become by degrees less personal, more cultural, than the one I expected to write. I suspect that this reticence or reserve, this submission of the self to the idea—along with my continued allegiance to criticism and its traditions—reveals the part of me that remains a child of the fifties, just as another side of me continues to nurture the thwarted millennial aspirations of the sixties. Yes, the sixties survive as more than a memory, more than a reference point or a cautionary tale. They survive in us, survive in those who experienced them most intensely. The sixties generation was not my generation, but it continues to fascinate me nonetheless. I expect we'll hear from it yet, for noisy and visible as it was, it hasn't fully had its say. The members of a generation which made its mark collectively at an abnormally young age have yet to make their mark separately and personally. Some blew their minds or their lives and a few others are dispersed into pockets of radical rage or remnants of communal life, but most have disappeared into families, guilds, and professions in every area of society; the exiles of the sixties, who are also exiled from their own colorful youth, should continue to bring a distinct ethos to bear in their individual work. Utopian hopes may be disappointed but can rarely be forgotten. The gates of Eden, which beckoned to a whole generation in many guises, still glimmer in the distance like Kafka's castle, unapproachable but unavoidable. What Matthew Arnold, who felt he lived in a fallow age, a *dürftige Zeit,* said of the next great age of literature we may say about the transformation of culture: "There is the promised land, towards which criticism can only beckon. . . . But to have desired to enter it, to have saluted it from afar, is already, perhaps, the best distinction among contemporaries. . . ."

SOURCES AND SUGGESTIONS
FOR FURTHER READING

General

Most general works on the sixties, especially those written toward the end of the decade when the culture was still actively in process, lack critical and historical perspective; by and large they're disfigured by polemic, exaggeration, and apocalyptic rhetoric. This is equally true for boosters of the new culture, such as Theodore Roszak in *The Making of a Counter Culture* (Garden City, N.Y.: Doubleday Anchor, 1969) and Charles Reich in *The Greening of America* (New York: Random House, 1970), and for implacable opponents like Robert Brustein in *Revolution as Theatre* (New York: Liveright, 1971). In some journals, such as *Commentary* and *The Public Interest*, the polemical tone continues; otherwise a gradual depolarization has occurred, and many seem ready for a more balanced, disinterested assessment of the griefs and achievements of the period. To date the two best books about the sixties were produced by two writers who figured prominently in the period's cultural life: Norman Mailer's *The Armies of the Night* (New York: New American Library, 1968) and Paul Goodman's *New Reformation* (New York: Random House, 1970). Both are notably ambivalent and complex in their view of the age.

Some valuable things have been written from special viewpoints on subjects treated in this book. The best book on cultural change in the sixties is Richard Poirier's *The Performing Self* (New York: Oxford University Press, 1971). From a sociological angle there is Philip E. Slater's *The Pursuit of Loneliness* (Boston: Beacon, 1970). A handy brief volume by a historian on the whole postwar period is William E. Leuchtenburg's *A Troubled Feast* (Boston: Little, Brown, 1973).

There are a number of comprehensive works on postwar American fiction, including Tony Tanner's *City of Words* (New York: Harper & Row, 1971), Alfred Kazin's *Bright Book of Life* (Boston: Little, Brown, 1973), Raymond Olderman's *Beyond the Waste Land* (New Haven, Conn.: Yale University

Sources and Suggestions for Further Reading

Press, 1972), and Jonathan Baumbach's *The Landscape of Nightmare* (New York: N.Y.U. Press, 1965). Two compendious critical anthologies in paperback are Marcus Klein's *The American Novel Since World War II* (New York: Fawcett, 1969) and Richard Kostelanetz's *On Contemporary Literature* (New York: Avon, 1964, 1968). Richard Howard discusses 41 younger American poets in *Alone With America* (New York: Atheneum, 1969).

In what follows I'll give references and suggestions chapter by chapter. Usually the secondary works are those I found most helpful to my own thinking, but in a few cases, for the convenience of the reader, I've added relevant books that escaped my attention or were published too late for me to use.

Chapter 1

Allen Ginsberg's major poetry collections are *Howl and Other Poems* (1956), *Kaddish and Other Poems* (1961), *Reality Sandwiches* (1963), *Planet News* (1968), and *The Fall of America* (1972), all published in San Francisco by City Lights Books. His early poems were collected in *Empty Mirror* (New York: Corinth, 1961). Some of his best work of the seventies is in songs, now collected in *First Blues* (New York: Full Court Press, 1975). Jane Kramer's two-part *New Yorker* profile of Ginsberg later emerged as *Allen Ginsberg in America* (New York: Random House, 1969). Two interviews I found useful were by Tom Clark in *Writers at Work*, 3d ser. (New York: Viking, 1967) and Paul Carroll in *Playboy* (April 1969). Paul Zweig's review of *Planet News* appeared in *The Nation* (March 10, 1969). John Tytell's impressive study of Burroughs, Kerouac, and Ginsberg, *Naked Angels* (New York: McGraw-Hill, 1976), appeared too late to be of use to me. An earlier, more journalistic account was Bruce Cook's *The Beat Generation* (New York: Scribner's, 1971). Ann Charters has written *Kerouac: A Biography* (San Francisco: Straight Arrow, 1973).

Three of the sharpest early attacks on the Beats all appeared in *Partisan Review*, which also published a few of their poems. The three were John Hollander's review of *Howl* (Spring 1957), Norman Podhoretz's "The Know-Nothing Bohemians" (Spring 1958), and Diana Trilling's "The Other Night at Columbia" (Spring 1959). Podhoretz's essay was reprinted in *Doings and Undoings* (New York: Farrar, Straus, 1964); Mrs. Trilling's piece reappeared in *Claremont Essays* (New York: Harcourt Brace, 1964).

Among the polemics on "the new sensibility," Susan Sontag's "One Culture and the New Sensibility" served as a conclusion to *Against Interpretation* (New York: Farrar, Straus, 1966), while Irving Howe's "The New York Intellectuals," which first appeared in *Commentary* (October 1968), was reprinted in *Decline of the New* (New York: Horizon, 1970). Harold Rosenberg's brilliant early essays, from one of which I take my epigraph for this chapter, were collected in *The Tradition of the New* (New York: Horizon, 1959).

The signal documents in the battle of the poetry anthologies were *New Poets of England and America*, ed. Donald Hall, Robert Pack, and Louis Simpson (New York: Meridian, 1957), a second selection edited by Hall and Pack (1962), and, on the other side, Donald Allen's *The New American Poetry* (New York: Grove Press, 1960). More recent, more comprehensive anthologies, which contain some of the poetry of the sixties as well, include Hayden Carruth's *The Voice That Is Great Within Us* (New York: Bantam, 1970) and John Hollander's *Poems of Our Moment* (New York: Pegasus, 1968). Ron Padgett and David Shapiro edited *An Anthology of New York Poets* (New York: Vintage, 1970).

Readers who have yet to make the acquaintance of other poets I mention in this chapter might be directed to Robert Bly's *The Light Around the Body* (New York: Harper & Row, 1967), James Wright's *The Branch Will Not Break* and *Shall We Gather at the River* (Middletown, Conn.: Wesleyan, 1963, 1968), David Ignatow's *Rescue the Dead* or the more comprehensive *Poems 1934–1969* (Middletown, Conn.: Wesleyan, 1968, 1970), Galway Kinnell's *Body Rags* and *The Book of Nightmares* (Boston: Houghton Mifflin, 1968, 1971), and Kenneth Koch's *Thank You and Other Poems* and *The Pleasures of Peace and Other Poems* (New York: Grove Press, 1962, 1969). John Hollander's virtuoso first book was *A Crackling of Thorns* (New Haven, Conn.: Yale University Press, 1958). His autobiographical sequence, including "Helicon," can be found in *Visions from the Ramble* (New York: Atheneum, 1965). Ralph J. Mills, Jr., discusses Roethke, Ignatow, and Kinnell, along with Donald Hall, Philip Levine, and others, in *Cry of the Human* (Urbana: University of Illinois Press, 1975).

Chapter 2

John Mander's article "In Defence of the 50's" appeared in *Commentary* (September 1969). See also *Commentary*'s symposium, "Liberal Anti-Communism Revisited" (September 1967). On the subvention of fifties intellectuals by the CIA see Christopher Lasch, "The Cultural Cold War: A Short History of the Congress for Cultural Freedom," in *The Agony of the American Left* (New York: Vintage, 1969). For the position of some fifties intellectuals on McCarthyism see *The Radical Right*, ed. Daniel Bell (Garden City, N.Y.: Doubleday Anchor, 1963) and Michael Paul Rogin's critique in

Sources and Suggestions for Further Reading

The Intellectuals and McCarthy (Cambridge, Mass.: M.I.T. Press, 1967). Richard Rovere's eloquent *Senator Joe McCarthy* (New York: Harcourt Brace, 1959) has been widely read. A more recent journalistic treatment is Fred J. Cook's *The Nightmare Decade* (New York: Random House, 1971). Allen J. Matusow has done a handy anthology of materials in *Joseph R. McCarthy* (Englewood Cliffs, N.J.: Prentice-Hall, 1970). Most of the cold war revisionist historians have concentrated on the forties, but Richard M. Freeland has made an important link between the forties and the fifties in *The Truman Doctrine and the Origins of McCarthyism* (New York: Knopf, 1972).

On the blacklist period, especially in the entertainment industry, see Walter Goodman's history of H.U.A.C., *The Committee* (Baltimore: Penguin, 1969), Stefan Kanfer's glib *A Journal of the Plague Years* (New York: Atheneum, 1973), Eric Bentley's huge selection of H.U.A.C. transcripts, *Thirty Years of Treason* (New York: Viking, 1971), and Lillian Hellman's moving memoir *Scoundrel Time* (Boston: Little, Brown, 1976).

The most effective treatments of the Rosenberg case I have read are Walter and Miriam Schneir's *Invitation to an Inquest* (Baltimore: Penguin, 1973) and E. L. Doctorow's novel *The Book of Daniel* (New York: Random House, 1971). The prison letters of the Rosenbergs have been included by their children Robert and Michael Meeropol in *We Are Your Sons* (Boston: Houghton Mifflin, 1975).

Robert Warshow's essay "The 'Idealism' of Julius and Ethel Rosenberg" is reprinted in *The Immediate Experience* (Garden City, N.Y.: Doubleday, 1962). Leslie Fiedler's "Afterthoughts on the Rosenbergs" is in *An End to Innocence* (Boston: Beacon, 1955). On American Communism I profited from Irving Howe and Lewis Coser, *The American Communist Party: A Critical History* (Boston: Beacon, 1957; New York: Praeger, 1962).

On the intellectuals of the thirties see William Phillips' excellent essay "What Happened in the 30's" in *The Sense of the Present* (New York: Chilmark, 1967), Lionel Trilling's novel *The Middle of the Journey* (New York: Avon, 1976), an edition which includes a new preface defending Whittaker Chambers as a "man of honor," Robert Warshow's feverishly anti-Communist "The Legacy of the '30's" in *The Immediate Experience*, which contains his criticism of Trilling's novel, Alfred Kazin's luminous memoir *Starting Out in the Thirties* (Boston: Little, Brown, 1965), Daniel Aaron's *Writers on the Left* (New York: Harcourt Brace, 1961), James B. Gilbert's chronicle of the early years of *Partisan Review* in *Writers and Partisans* (New York: Wiley, 1968), and Richard H. Pells' abstract but wide-ranging *Radical Visions and American Dreams* (New York: Harper & Row, 1973), which contains a thorough bibliography.

Sources and Suggestions for Further Reading

Of the many books on American Jewish writing I would single out Allen Guttmann's *The Jewish Writer in America* (New York: Oxford University Press, 1971), which is no more than an initial synthesis, and Ruth R. Wisse's fine study *The Schlemiel as Modern Hero* (Chicago: University of Chicago Press, 1971). More immediate and more brilliant, however, were the scattered reviews and essays of the leading New York intellectuals, nearly all of whom discussed the Jewish writers at one time or another, especially Irving Howe, Alfred Kazin, and Leslie Fiedler. Many of their pieces are uncollected, but Kazin's review of *The Magic Barrel,* from which I quote, has been reprinted in *Contemporaries* (Boston: Little, Brown, 1962). William Phillips' comments on Bellow can be found in "Notes on the New Style," which is reprinted in *The Sense of the Present* and in Marcus Klein's anthology, *The American Novel Since World War II* (New York: Fawcett, 1969). Steven Marcus deals with Malamud's first four books in "The Novel Again," *Partisan Review* (Spring 1962). Norman Podhoretz discusses the early books of Bellow and Mailer in *Doings and Undoings* (New York: Farrar, Straus, 1964). A recent, fresh treatment of Bellow is Mark Shechner's "Down in the Mouth with Saul Bellow," *American Review* 23 (New York: Bantam, 1975). I have discussed Bellow's polemics against modernism and the intellectuals in "For Art's Sake," *Partisan Review* (Fall 1966), and I've treated Malamud's later work in a review of *The Tenants* for the *New York Times Book Review* (October 3, 1971).

Isaac Rosenfeld's essays were collected posthumously in *An Age of Enormity* (Cleveland: World, 1962) and his stories in *Alpha and Omega* (New York: Viking, 1966). Delmore Schwartz's longer essays were collected by Donald A. Dike and David H. Zucker in *Selected Essays of Delmore Schwartz* (Chicago: University of Chicago Press, 1970). His two volumes of stories are *The World Is a Wedding* (Norfolk, Conn.: New Directions, 1948) and *Successful Love and Other Stories* (New York: Corinth, 1961). His selected poems were published as *Summer Knowledge* (Garden City, N.Y.: Doubleday, 1959; New York: New Directions, 1967). William Barrett's tender memoir "Delmore" appeared in *Commentary* (September 1974). Philip Rahv's review of *Selected Essays* came out in the *New York Review of Books* (May 20, 1971). Alfred Kazin's discriminating obituary essay was published in *Book Week* (October 9, 1966). Irving Howe comments briefly but incisively on Schwartz and other Jewish American novelists near the end of *World of Our Fathers* (New York: Harcourt Brace, 1976).

Sources and Suggestions for Further Reading

Chapter 3

Mailer's "The White Negro" (1957) was reprinted in *Advertisements for Myself* (New York: Putnam's, 1959) and his comments on Paul Goodman can be found in *The Armies of the Night* (New York: New American Library, 1968).

The essays of C. Wright Mills, including "Culture and Politics" and "The New Left," were collected by Irving Louis Horowitz in *Power, Politics and People* (New York: Oxford University Press, 1963). His other books include *White Collar* (1951) and *The Power Elite* (1956), also published by Oxford.

Norman Podhoretz's article on "The Young Generation" was reprinted in *Doings and Undoings* (New York: Farrar, Straus, 1964). Doubleday published Richard Chase's book *The Democratic Vista* (1958). His essay on "The Fate of the Avant-Garde" was included by Irving Howe in his excellent anthology *Literary Modernism* (New York: Fawcett, 1967). Besides *The Tradition of the New* (New York: Horizon, 1959), another selection from Harold Rosenberg's early essays is *Discovering the Present* (Chicago: University of Chicago Press, 1973). Leslie Fiedler's *Love and Death in the American Novel* (1960) is available in a revised edition (New York: Stein and Day, 1966). Quentin Anderson's long review appeared in the literary supplement of the *Columbia Daily Spectator* (April 27, 1960). Fiedler's essay "The New Mutants" was published in *Partisan Review* (Fall 1965).

There are two intelligent books on Freudian radicalism, Paul A. Robinson's *The Freudian Left* (New York: Harper & Row, 1969), on Reich, Roheim, and Marcuse, and Richard A. King's *The Party of Eros* (New York: Dell, 1973), on Reich, Goodman, Marcuse, and Brown. Marcuse's books include *Reason and Revolution* (1941), *Eros and Civilization* (1955), *Soviet Marxism* (1958), *One-Dimensional Man* (1964), *An Essay on Liberation* (1969), and *Counterrevolution and Revolt* (1972). Among the many things written about his work, see Alasdair MacIntyre's highly critical volume in the Modern Masters series, *Herbert Marcuse* (New York: Viking, 1970) and Marshall Berman's long, penetrating review of *One-Dimensional Man* in *Partisan Review* (Fall 1964). A full bibliography of Marcuse's writings can be found in a Festschrift, *The Critical Spirit,* ed. Kurt H. Wolff and Barrington Moore, Jr. (Boston: Beacon, 1967). Marcuse's context and ideas are greatly illuminated by a knowledge of the work of other members of the Frankfurt school. Martin Jay has written a history of the group through 1950, *The Dialectical Imagination* (Boston: Little, Brown, 1973). The Seabury Press has recently published English translations of some writings, including

Sources and Suggestions for Further Reading

Max Horkheimer's *Critical Theory* and Horkheimer's and T. W. Adorno's *Dialectic of Enlightenment* (both 1972). Adorno's essay "The Culture Industry Reconsidered" has appeared in English in *New German Critique* 6 (Fall 1975), with an introductory essay by Andreas Huyssen. Samuel and Shierry Weber translated Adorno's *Prisms* (London: Neville Spearman, 1967).

Besides *Growing Up Absurd* (1960), Paul Goodman's books of social criticism include *Utopian Essays and Practical Proposals* (1962), *The Community of Scholars* (1962), *Compulsory Mis-education* (1964), *People or Personnel* (1965), *Like a Conquered Province* (1967), and *New Reformation* (1970). He died in 1972. Henry Pachter discussed his work in *Salmagundi* 24 (Fall 1973), and George Dennison wrote a fine memoir which appeared as an introduction to Goodman's *Collected Poems,* ed. Taylor Stoehr (New York: Random House, 1973).

Norman O. Brown's books after *Life Against Death* (1959) were *Love's Body* (1966) and *Closing Time* (1973). His important address, "Apocalypse: The Place of Mystery in the Life of the Mind," was published in *Harper's* (May 1961) with a cautionary introduction by Benjamin Nelson. His comments on Philip Rieff were transcribed in *Salmagundi* 24 (Fall 1973). Two significant critiques were by Frederick Crews, "Love in the Western World," *Partisan Review* (Spring 1967), reprinted in *Out of My System* (New York: Oxford, 1975), and Herbert Marcuse's "Love Mystified," *Commentary* (February 1967), with Brown's reply (March 1967), reprinted in Marcuse's *Negations* (Boston: Beacon, 1968).

Chapter 4

In *The Situation of the Novel* (London: Macmillan, 1970), mainly about the English novel, Bernard Bergonzi devoted a chapter to the American "comic-apocalyptic" writers. Bruce Jay Friedman edited an anthology called *Black Humor* (New York: Bantam, 1965) which included both contemporaries and recent ancestors. Though unique and *sui generis,* Lenny Bruce is a pivotal figure in Jewish black humor. Transcriptions of his routines were collected by John Cohen in *The Essential Lenny Bruce* (New York: Ballantine, 1967). His act, his life, and his ambiance have been recreated by Albert Goldman in *Ladies and Gentlemen Lenny Bruce!!* (New York: Ballantine, 1974). Lore Dickstein has discussed Thomas Berger's work in a review of *Regiment of Women* in *Ms.* (August 1973). Richard Condon is another writer whose mixture of topicality, genre writing, and myth puts his work in this category, at the pop end of the spectrum. See especially *The Manchurian Candidate*

(1959), the brilliant film version by John Frankenheimer (1962), and the assassination novel *Winter Kills* (1974). Leo Braudy reviewed the latter volume in the *New York Times Book Review* (April 14, 1974).

Mark Shechner's essay on Roth appeared in *Partisan Review* (no. 3, 1974); a longer version will form part of a book on Jewish writers and intellectuals. I have discussed Roth's career in some detail in a review of *My Life as a Man* in the *New York Times Book Review* (June 2, 1974). Richard Locke has done the same for Updike in a review of *Rabbit Redux*, *New York Times Book Review* (November 14, 1971).

On Vonnegut see *The Vonnegut Statement*, ed. Jerome Klinkowitz and John Somer (New York: Dell, 1973). Dell has also published a "critical edition," with useful additional materials, of Joseph Heller's *Catch-22*, ed. Robert M. Scotto (New York, 1973). In the case of Pynchon, a cottage industry of exegetical criticism is gathering strength, but I would single out Richard Poirier's succinct pages in *The Performing Self* (New York: Oxford University Press, 1971), Richard Locke's review of *Gravity's Rainbow* in the *New York Times Book Review* (March 11, 1973), and Alfred Kazin's appreciation of *The Crying of Lot 49* in *Bright Book of Life* (Boston: Little, Brown, 1973).

Arthur M. Schlesinger, Jr.'s, *A Thousand Days* (Boston: Houghton Mifflin, 1965) and David Halberstam's *The Best and the Brightest* (New York: Random House, 1972) offer particularly readable accounts of the political atmosphere of the Kennedy years.

Chapter 5

Tom Wolfe's other books, besides *The New Journalism*, coedited by E. W. Johnson (New York: Harper & Row, 1973), include *The Kandy-Kolored Tangerine-Flake Streamline Baby* (1965), *The Pump House Gang* (1968), *The Electric Kool-Aid Acid Test* (1968), *Radical Chic & Mau-Mauing the Flak Catchers* (1970), and *The Painted Word* (1975). Alan Trachtenberg's incisive critique of Wolfe's anthology and his writing came out in *Partisan Review* (no. 2, 1974); William Phillips dismantled his view of modern painting in the same journal (no. 2, 1975).

Hunter Thompson's books include *Hell's Angels* (1967), *Fear and Loathing in Las Vegas* (1971), and *Fear and Loathing on the Campaign Trail '72* (1973). Rex Reed's naughty interviews were first collected in *Do You Sleep in the Nude?* (New York: New American Library, 1968). Don McNeill's journalism was brought together posthumously in *Moving Through Here* (New York: Knopf, 1970).

Sources and Suggestions for Further Reading

Two remarkable books that straddled the line between autobiographies and first novels were Frank Conroy's *Stop-Time* (New York: Viking, 1967) and Frederick Exley's *A Fan's Notes* (New York: Harper & Row, 1968), the latter subtitled "a fictional memoir." See also Exley's wonderfully comic, knockabout *Pages from a Cold Island* (New York: Random House, 1975), a book trying hard to get itself written, about a life trying to get itself lived; it shows that Mailer's influence need not lead to crude imitation.

Mailer's four collections of essays are *Advertisements for Myself* (1959), *The Presidential Papers* (1963), *Cannibals and Christians* (1966), and *Existential Errands* (1972). His full-length non-fiction works after *The Armies of the Night* and *Miami and the Siege of Chicago* (1968) were *Of a Fire on the Moon* (1971), *The Prisoner of Sex* (1971), *St. George and the Godfather* (1972), *Marilyn* (1973), and *The Fight* (1975). An enormous amount has been written about Mailer, some of the best collected in *Norman Mailer: A Collection of Critical Essays*, ed. Leo Braudy (Englewood Cliffs, N.J.: Prentice-Hall, 1972). See also Richard Poirier's *The Performing Self* (New York: Oxford University Press, 1971) and his *Norman Mailer* (New York: Viking, 1972), Robert Langbaum's *The Modern Spirit* (New York: Oxford University Press, 1970), Kate Millett's attack in *Sexual Politics* (Garden City, N.Y.: Doubleday, 1970), Richard Gilman's long study in *The Confusion of Realms* (New York: Random House, 1969), and my own review of *Of a Fire on the Moon*, *New York Times Book Review* (January 10, 1971).

On the press see, among other things, Ruth Adler's collection of behind-the-scenes articles by *Times*men, *The Working Press* (New York: Putnam's, 1966), Timothy Crouse's account of the press coverage of the 1972 presidential campaign, *The Boys in the Bus* (New York: Random House, 1973), and Gay Talese's inside look at the *New York Times* in *The Kingdom and the Power* (New York: World, 1969).

Chapter 6

Two handy anthologies of black writing were *Dark Symphony*, ed. James A. Emanuel and Theodore L. Gross (New York: Free Press, 1968) and *Black Literature in America*, ed. Houston A. Baker, Jr. (New York: McGraw-Hill, 1971). Richard Gilman's two essays were reprinted in *The Confusion of Realms* (New York: Random House, 1969). Harold Cruse wrote *The Crisis of the Negro Intellectual* and *Rebellion or Revolution?* (New York: Morrow, 1967, 1968). Irving Howe's "Black Boys and Native Sons," his defense of Richard Wright against his literary sons Baldwin and Ellison, has been reprinted most recently in *Decline of the New* (New York: Horizon,

Sources and Suggestions for Further Reading

1970). Ralph Ellison's superbly eloquent reply, along with his other essays and interviews, including his own account of Richard Wright, can be found in *Shadow and Act* (New York: Random House, 1964). James Baldwin's essays on Wright appear in *Notes of a Native Son* (1955) and *Nobody Knows My Name* (1961), his two powerful early collections. Robert A. Bone has surveyed the field in *The Negro Novel in America*, rev. ed. (New Haven, Conn.: Yale University Press, 1965).

Constance Webb has written a biography, *Richard Wright* (New York: Putnam's, 1968), while the magazine *New Letters* devoted a special issue (Winter 1971) to his life and work, later reprinted as *Richard Wright: Impressions and Perspectives*, ed. David Ray and Robert M. Farnsworth (Ann Arbor: University of Michigan Press, 1973). A major biography is Michel Fabre's *The Unfinished Quest of Richard Wright* (New York: Morrow, 1973). Edward Margolies published two critical studies, *Native Sons* (Philadelphia: Lippincott, 1968), on the whole range of twentieth-century black writers, and *The Art of Richard Wright* (Carbondale: Southern Illinois University Press, 1969). Other studies include Dan McCall's *The Example of Richard Wright* (New York: Harcourt Brace, 1969) and Kenneth Kinnamon's *The Emergence of Richard Wright* (Urbana: University of Illinois Press, 1972).

F. W. Dupee's review of Baldwin's *The Fire Next Time* was reprinted in *The King of the Cats* (New York: Farrar, Straus, 1965). Paul Goodman's negative review of *Another Country* appeared in the *New York Times Book Review* (June 24, 1962), while Norman Podhoretz's defense of the same novel can be found in *Doings and Undoings* (New York: Farrar, Straus, 1964). Calvin Hernton's essay "Blood of the Lamb: The Ordeal of James Baldwin" appeared in *Amistad* 1 (New York: Vintage, 1970); Eldridge Cleaver's attack, "Notes on a Native Son," can be found in *Soul on Ice* (New York: Dell, 1968). Cleaver's much less interesting later work was collected in *Post-Prison Writings and Speeches* (New York: Random House, 1969). George Jackson's book of prison letters, *Soledad Brother* (New York: Bantam, 1970), was very much in the vein of *Soul on Ice*. Larry Neal's essay "The Black Arts Movement" can be found in the black theater issue of *tdr: The Drama Review* (Summer 1968). Cecil Brown's essay on singer James Brown appeared in *Black Review* 1 (New York: Morrow, 1971). Ralph Ellison's comments on recent black writers can be found on the back cover of McPherson's *Hue and Cry* (New York: Fawcett, 1970).

Among general works, Louis E. Lomax chronicled the early phases of the civil rights movement in *The Negro Revolt* (New York: Signet, 1963). Nat Hentoff wrote *The New Equality* (1964; New York: Viking, 1969). Calvin Hernton examined *Sex and Racism in America* (Garden City N.Y.: Double-

Sources and Suggestions for Further Reading

day, 1965). Richard Kluger has documented the desegregation conflicts in *Simple Justice* (New York: Knopf, 1976).

Chapter 7

The best ongoing rock criticism, some of it quite sharp, appeared in periodicals associated with the youth culture of the sixties, such as *Rolling Stone, Creem, Crawdaddy,* and the *Village Voice.* A great deal of material from *Rolling Stone,* including a lot of junk, has been collected in volumes like *The Rolling Stone Record Review* (New York: Pocket Books, 1971), *The Rolling Stone Interviews* (New York: Paperback Library, 1971), and *The Age of Paranoia* (New York: Pocket Books, 1972). David A. De Turk and A. Poulin, Jr., edited a first-rate anthology on the earlier period, *The American Folk Scene* (New York: Dell, 1967). My own understanding of rock was influenced by a regular reading of Richard Goldstein's reviews in the *Voice* in the mid-sixties. Some of them were collected in a rather scrappy volume, *Goldstein's Greatest Hits* (Englewood Cliffs, N.J.: Prentice-Hall, 1970), including his unique negative review of *Sgt. Pepper,* but not including my favorite piece, "Baez Meets the Philharmonic," *Village Voice* (October 26, 1967), from which I quote in this chapter. Robert Christgau collected his reviews in *Any Old Way You Choose It* (New York: Penguin, 1973), as did Jon Landau in *It's Too Late to Stop Now* (New York: Simon and Schuster, 1974). I quote from Christgau's reprinted review of Dylan's *Tarantula* and from Paul Cowan's review of Dylan's *Blood on the Tracks, Village Voice* (February 3, 1975).

I found some of the more serious biographies of rock figures useful for pinning down details and recreating the ambiance, especially Hunter Davies' *The Beatles* (New York: Dell, 1969) and Anthony Scaduto's *Bob Dylan* (New York: Signet, 1973). Jonathan Eisen edited a good collection of articles, including the piece from the *New Left Review,* under the title of *The Age of Rock* (New York: Vintage, 1969), while musicologist Wilfred Mellers wrote a critical study of the Beatles, *Twilight of the Gods* (New York: Viking, 1974). Indispensable transcriptions of song lyrics include *The Beatles Illustrated Lyrics,* ed. Alan Aldridge (New York: Delacorte, 1969, 1971), Bob Dylan's *Writings and Drawings* (New York: Knopf, 1973), and, with some music, *The Rolling Stones,* ed. David Dalton (New York: Amsco, 1972).

Too much rock criticism provides mere consumer guidance, fan-mag gossip, or maniacally minute and irrelevant exegesis; not enough of it shows much awareness of the other arts or takes in the broader cultural setting. No-

289

Sources and Suggestions for Further Reading

table exceptions are Marshall Berman's "Sympathy for the Devil," *American Review* 19 (New York: Bantam, 1974), which gives a moving and complex account of how the sixties ended, and Richard Poirier's discussion of the Beatles in *The Performing Self* (New York: Oxford University Press, 1971). On the issue of personal authenticity see Berman's *The Politics of Authenticity* (New York: Atheneum, 1970) and Lionel Trilling's *Sincerity and Authenticity* (Cambridge, Mass.: Harvard University Press, 1972).

The fifties' attack on popular culture can be sampled in *Mass Culture,* ed. Bernard Rosenberg and David White (Glencoe, Ill. Free Press, 1957). Harold Rosenberg's purist review of this volume can be found in *The Tradition of the New* (New York: Horizon, 1959). Sociologist Herbert Gans attacks the fifties line from a pluralist perspective in *Popular Culture and High Culture* (New York: Basic Books, 1974). What we still need is a genuinely critical consideration of the artifacts of popular culture and the issues they raise. The critical tradition has defaulted entirely in the face of this immense and diverse body of work. Between mindless celebration and blind denunciation falls the shadow.

Chapter 8

On modernism see Irving Howe's anthology *Literary Modernism* (New York: Fawcett, 1967), while Robert Alter has studied the self-conscious novel in *Partial Magic* (Berkeley: University of California Press, 1975). Erich Auerbach traces the history of realism and mimetic representation in writing since Homer and the Bible in *Mimesis* (Princeton, N.J.: Princeton University Press, 1953). Recent attacks on mimesis and representationalism can be found in Alain Robbe-Grillet's *For a New Novel* (New York: Grove, 1965), Susan Sontag's *Against Interpretation* (New York: Farrar, Straus, 1966), William H. Gass's *Fiction and the Figures of Life* (New York: Knopf, 1970), and Richard Gilman's *The Confusion of Realms* (New York: Random House, 1969). See also John Barth's essay "The Literature of Exhaustion," reprinted in Marcus Klein's anthology *The American Novel Since World War II* (New York: Fawcett, 1969), Philip Stevick's keen analysis in *TriQuarterly* 26 (Winter 1973), and Donald Barthelme's rare early essay "After Joyce," *Location* 1 (Summer 1964). The contrary viewpoints which I quote come from Philip Rahv's "Notes on the Decline of Naturalism," *Image and Idea* (New York: New Directions, 1957) and Mary McCarthy's contribution to a symposium on cultural conservatism, *Partisan Review* (Summer 1972). In the same number see also Richard Gilman's long introductory essay, "The Idea of the Avant-Garde," and my own discussion of the intellectual backlash against the sixties.

Sources and Suggestions for Further Reading

Jorge Luis Borges' work first appeared in this country in *Ficciones* (New York: Grove Press, 1962) and *Labyrinths* (New York: New Directions, 1962). The influence has been enormous. Donald Barthelme's work has been widely discussed in recent years. An important early statement, whose viewpoint differs from my own, was Richard Gilman's review of *Snow White*, reprinted in *The Confusion of Realms*. An interview with Barthelme can be found in Joe David Bellamy's *The New Fiction* (Urbana: University of Illinois Press, 1974).

Robert Coover's stories were collected in *Pricksongs & Descants* (New York: Dutton, 1969), John Barth's in *Lost in the Funhouse* (Garden City, N.J.: Doubleday, 1968), Barth's novellas in *Chimera* (New York: Random House, 1972), Gass's stories in *In the Heart of the Heart of the Country* (New York: Harper & Row, 1968), and Leonard Michaels' stories in *Going Places* and *I Would Have Saved Them If I Could* (New York: Farrar, Straus, 1969, 1975). Anthologies of innovative fiction include Philip Stevick's *Anti-Story* (New York: Free Press, 1971), Joe David Bellamy's *Superfiction* (New York: Vintage, 1975), and the Fiction Collective's *Statements* (New York: Braziller, 1975).

Chapter 9

This more subjective chapter really has few specific sources, but I can suggest some additional reading. My two examples of the more subjective turn of literary and historical scholarship after the sixties were Daniel Hoffman's *Poe Poe Poe Poe Poe Poe Poe* (Garden City, N.Y.: Doubleday, 1972) and Martin Duberman's *Black Mountain: An Exploration in Community* (New York: Dutton, 1972). One could also cite the rise of interviewing techniques, beginning with the work of Oscar Lewis and Studs Terkel, which brings cinéma vérité into social science.

A broad overview of the Columbia curriculum can be found in Daniel Bell's *The Reforming of General Education* (Garden City, N.Y.: Doubleday Anchor, 1968), first commissioned as an internal investigation and report, as was the Cox Commission report on the 1968 uprising, *Crisis at Columbia* (New York: Vintage, 1968). Excellent day-to-day coverage of the crisis can be found in the files of the *Columbia Daily Spectator*, some of whose staff also put out *Up Against the Ivy Wall* (New York: Atheneum, 1969), a postmortem account. Stephen Donadio conducted seven interviews with representative figures, including Lionel Trilling, for *Partisan Review* (Summer 1968), and wrote his own neutral account in *Commentary* (September 1968). F. W. Dupee wrote an almost novelistic evocation of the first

Sources and Suggestions for Further Reading

phase of the upheaval for the *New York Review of Books* (September 26, 1968); it was reprinted in *The Oxford Reader*, ed. Frank Kermode and Richard Poirier (New York: Oxford University Press, 1971). "The Appeal from the Sorbonne," along with other documents of student uprisings, can be found in *The New Left Reader*, ed. Carl Oglesby (New York: Grove, 1969). Harold Jacobs edited *Weatherman* (Palo Alto, Calif.: Ramparts Press, 1970).

Three keen early critiques of Lionel Trilling's work, all from the fifties, are R. P. Blackmur's "The Politics of Human Power" in *The Lion and the Honeycomb* (London: Methuen, 1956), Delmore Schwartz's "The Duchess' Red Shoes" in *Selected Essays of Delmore Schwartz*, eds. Donald A. Dike and David H. Zucker (Chicago: University of Chicago Press, 1970), and Joseph Frank's "Lionel Trilling and the Conservative Imagination" in *The Widening Gyre* (Bloomington: Indiana University Press, 1968). Dan Jacobson wrote an exceptionally thoughtful review of *Beyond Culture* for *Commentary* (March 1966), while Geoffrey Hartman's comments on the later Trilling can be found in *The Fate of Reading and Other Essays* (Chicago: University of Chicago Press, 1975). Two brilliant obituary assessments were by Steven Marcus in the *New York Times Book Review* (February 8, 1976) and Irving Howe in *The New Republic* (March 13, 1976).

ACKNOWLEDGMENTS

One of the pleasures of writing about a contemporary subject is that everyone you know joins you at moments in thinking it through. A secondary pleasure comes now in acknowledging a few of the more tangible contributions. My friend and publisher Erwin Glikes first suggested that I write this book and provoked me time and again to reformulate it in my mind. His enthusiasm and editorial insight were invaluable. Marshall Berman's involvement and fascination with the sixties paralleled mine; our innumerable conversations were a continuous resource and challenge to me. Richard Locke gave me the benefit of his matchless editorial tact, friendly counsel, and an exacting sense of contemporary writing. Robert and Dolores Greenberg encouraged and supported me throughout and reacted most helpfully to my treatment of the cold war period. My colleagues at *Partisan Review,* especially William Phillips, opened the pages of the magazine to viewpoints they didn't always share; our lively discussions galvanized my thinking about contemporary culture. For additional help and encouragement of the most diverse kinds I'd like to single out Jon and Georgia Baumbach, Carole Berman, Peter Biskind, Georges Borchardt, Leo and Dorothy Braudy, Rachel and Shale Brownstein, Richard Gilman, Richard Poirier, Arnold Richards, Harold Schechter, Robert Towers, Carol Vance, Mary Welch, Erik Wensberg, and Paul Zweig.

A fellowship from the John Simon Guggenheim Memorial Foundation enabled me to take a leave from teaching in 1973–74 to devote full time to this book. The work was also supported by summer stipends from the National Endowment for the Humanities and the Research Foundation of the City University of New York, which also provided a grant for the preparation of the manuscript.

Finally, I'm grateful to Jeremy and Rachel Dickstein for learning to share my attention with the sixties without coming to hate the sight of their father reading a book. Above all, I'd like to thank my wife Lore for scanning these pages with a keen editorial eye, a contentious and skeptical mind, and a warm, supportive spirit. Without her constant encouragement the book might never have been written.

INDEX

NOTE: Individual works discussed in substantive detail are indexed separately. Books and names in the bibliography are included only if mentioned in the text or footnotes, with the exception of a few additional primary sources.

Index

Index

Index

FOR THE BEST IN PAPERBACKS, LOOK FOR THE

In every corner of the world, on every subject under the sun, Penguin represents quality and variety—the very best in publishing today.

For complete information about books available from Penguin—including Pelicans, Puffins, Peregrines, and Penguin Classics—and how to order them, write to us at the appropriate address below. Please note that for copyright reasons the selection of books varies from country to country.

In the United Kingdom: For a complete list of books available from Penguin in the U.K., please write to *Dept E.P., Penguin Books Ltd, Harmondsworth, Middlesex, UB7 0DA*.

In the United States: For a complete list of books available from Penguin in the U.S., please write to *Dept BA, Penguin*, Box 120, Bergenfield, New Jersey 07621-0120.

In Canada: For a complete list of books available from Penguin in Canada, please write to *Penguin Books Ltd, 2801 John Street, Markham, Ontario L3R 1B4*.

In Australia: For a complete list of books available from Penguin in Australia, please write to the *Marketing Department, Penguin Books Ltd, P.O. Box 257, Ringwood, Victoria 3134*.

In New Zealand: For a complete list of books available from Penguin in New Zealand, please write to the *Marketing Department, Penguin Books (NZ) Ltd, Private Bag, Takapuna, Auckland 9*.

In India: For a complete list of books available from Penguin, please write to *Penguin Overseas Ltd, 706 Eros Apartments, 56 Nehru Place, New Delhi, 110019*.

In Holland: For a complete list of books available from Penguin in Holland, please write to *Penguin Books Nederland B.V., Postbus 195, NL-1380AD Weesp, Netherlands*.

In Germany: For a complete list of books available from Penguin, please write to *Penguin Books Ltd, Friedrichstrasse 10-12, D-6000 Frankfurt Main 1, Federal Republic of Germany*.

In Spain: For a complete list of books available from Penguin in Spain, please write to *Longman, Penguin España, Calle San Nicolas 15, E-28013 Madrid, Spain*.

In Japan: For a complete list of books available from Penguin in Japan, please write to *Longman Penguin Japan Co Ltd, Yamaguchi Building, 2-12-9 Kanda Jimbocho, Chiyoda-Ku, Tokyo 101, Japan*.

FOR THE BEST IN HISTORY, LOOK FOR THE

☐ **THE FACE OF BATTLE**
John Keegan

In this study of three battles from three different centuries, John Keegan examines war from the fronts—conveying its reality for the participants at the "point of maximum danger."

366 pages   *ISBN: 0-14-004897-9*   **$6.95**

☐ **VIETNAM: A HISTORY**
Stanley Karnow

Stanley Karnow's monumental narrative—the first complete account of the Vietnam War—puts events and decisions of the day into sharp, clear focus. "This is history writing at its best."—*Chicago Sun-Times*

752 pages   *ISBN: 0-14-007324-8*   **$12.95**

☐ **MIRACLE AT MIDWAY**
Gordon W. Prange
with Donald M. Goldstein and Katherine V. Dillon

The best-selling sequel to *At Dawn We Slept* recounts the battles at Midway Island—events which marked the beginning of the end of the war in the Pacific.

470 pages   *ISBN: 0-14-006814-7*   **$10.95**

☐ **THE MASK OF COMMAND**
John Keegan

This provocative view of leadership examines the meaning of military heroism through four prototypes from history—Alexander the Great, Wellington, Grant, and Hitler—and proposes a fifth type of "post-heroic" leader for the nuclear age.

368 pages   *ISBN: 0-14-011406-8*   **$7.95**

☐ **THE SECOND OLDEST PROFESSION**
Spies and Spying in the Twentieth Century
Phillip Knightley

In this fascinating history and critique of espionage, Phillip Knightley explores the actions and missions of such noted spies as Mata Hari and Kim Philby, and organizations such as the CIA and the KGB.

436 pages   *ISBN: 0-14-010655-3*   **$7.95**

☐ **THE STORY OF ENGLISH**
Robert McCrum, William Cran, and Robert MacNeil

"Rarely has the English language been scanned so brightly and broadly in a single volume," writes the *San Francisco Chronicle* about this journey across time and space that explores the evolution of English from Anglo-Saxon Britain to Reagan's America.

384 pages   *ISBN: 0-14-009435-0*   **$12.95**

FOR THE BEST LITERATURE, LOOK FOR THE

☐ **A SPORT OF NATURE**
Nadine Gordimer

Hillela, Nadine Gordimer's "sport of nature," is seductive and intuitively gifted at life. Casting herself adrift from her family at seventeen, she lives among political exiles on an East African beach, marries a black revolutionary, and ultimately plays a heroic role in the overthrow of apartheid.

354 pages   ISBN: 0-14-008470-3   **$7.95**

☐ **THE COUNTERLIFE**
Philip Roth

By far Philip Roth's most radical work of fiction, *The Counterlife* is a book of conflicting perspectives and points of view about people living out dreams of renewal and escape. Illuminating these lives is the skeptical, enveloping intelligence of the novelist Nathan Zuckerman, who calculates the price and examines the results of his characters' struggles for a change of personal fortune.

372 pages   ISBN: 0-14-009769-4   **$4.95**

☐ **THE MONKEY'S WRENCH**
Primo Levi

Through the mesmerizing tales told by two characters—one, a construction worker/philosopher who has built towers and bridges in India and Alaska; the other, a writer/chemist, rigger of words and molecules—Primo Levi celebrates the joys of work and the art of storytelling.

174 pages   ISBN: 0-14-010357-0   **$6.95**

☐ **IRONWEED**
William Kennedy

"Riding up the winding road of Saint Agnes Cemetery in the back of the rattling old truck, Francis Phelan became aware that the dead, even more than the living, settled down in neighborhoods." So begins William Kennedy's Pulitzer-Prize winning novel about an ex-ballplayer, part-time gravedigger, and full-time drunk, whose return to the haunts of his youth arouses the ghosts of his past and present.

228 pages   ISBN: 0-14-007020-6   **$6.95**

☐ **THE COMEDIANS**
Graham Greene

Set in Haiti under Duvalier's dictatorship, *The Comedians* is a story about the committed and the uncommitted. Actors with no control over their destiny, they play their parts in the foreground; experience love affairs rather than love; have enthusiasms but not faith; and if they die, they die like Mr. Jones, by accident.

288 pages   ISBN: 0-14-002766-1   **$4.95**